Withdrawn

ALSO BY MAX EGREMONT

SOME
DESPERATE
GLORY

SOME DESPERATE GLORY

The First World War the Poets Knew

MAX EGREMONT

Farrar, Straus and Giroux
New York

Farrar, Straus and Giroux
18 West 18th Street, New York 10011

Owing to limitations of space, illustration credits can be found on page 337.

Library of Congress Control Number: 2014937209
ISBN: 978-0-374-28032-1

Farrar, Straus and Giroux books may be purchased for educational, business,
or promotional use. For information on bulk purchases, please contact the
Macmillan Corporate and Premium Sales Department at 1-800-221-7945,
extension 5442, or write to specialmarkets@macmillan.com.

www.fsgbooks.com
www.twitter.com/fsgbooks • www.facebook.com/fsgbooks

1   3   5   7   9   10   8   6   4   2

For Simon Head

Contents

Preface

We know the war through their poetry. Siegfried Sassoon's scathing satires; Wilfred Owen's compassion; Edmund Blunden's gentle but shocking lyricism; Julian Grenfell's joy in battle; Rupert Brooke's surge of patriotism; Isaac Rosenberg's mystical vision: all these have shaped how we see the western front. Then there's the tragic sacrifice: Brooke and Grenfell dead in their twenties, Charles Sorley killed when hardly out of his teens, Edward Thomas older but not yet three years into his time as a poet, Robert Nichols breaking down during the battle of Loos, Owen and Rosenberg victims of the war's last year. All this makes for a powerful myth in which a poet's imagined life can be as moving as his poems.

The poets of the First World War have a memorial in Westminster Abbey, recognizing their place in Britain's last century as a world power. But some historians believe that much of the best-known poetry of the war is defeatist, symbolizing loss of will, even decline – that it misses the spirit that led to victory. The poets have been accused of contributing to a climate of appeasement that led to a second world war. Critics have said that their work is too dominated by its subject, leading to a kind of lyrical journalism.

What remains true is that they were made by the war and then made a lasting vision of it. Their lives reflect its emotion and its history; their work shows how it was, for them, to be there. They also show some of the hopes and disappointments of early twentieth-century Britain.

In this book, I have chosen eleven poets who fought. I have set their poems in the year that they were written. Rupert Brooke and

Charles Sorley are there strongly at the start of the war; Sassoon enters after his first experience of the trenches at the end of 1915; Isaac Rosenberg's war also starts in late 1915; Edward Thomas writes from England, not reaching the front until some two and a half months before his death in 1917; Wilfred Owen isn't represented until the war's last two years; Ivor Gurney and Edmund Blunden have many poems in the Aftermath chapter, a reflection of how long their war lasted. Some poets feature less: Julian Grenfell because he wrote only one memorable war poem; Robert Nichols through his erratic quality, although I admire some of his work and wanted to include a poet thought of at the time as a new Byron.

I began writing about the first two decades of the twentieth century some forty years ago. The First World War featured in my books about the soldier and writer Sir Edward Spears and about the politician Arthur Balfour, and particularly in my biography of Siegfried Sassoon. In the 1980s and 1990s I wrote novels set in contemporary Britain, but the characters felt the two wars – the First and the Second – strongly in their lives, either in their own memories or in their country's idea of itself. Having also written about Germany, I believe that for Britain – especially for quite prosperous Britons (which many of the war poets were) – there was something uniquely shocking in the reality of the First War. For almost a century, most British lives had been more sheltered from threat and conflict than their European counterparts, even if the nation was becoming less confident as the twentieth century began.

Britain's recent wars were part of my childhood during the 1950s and 1960s. The First World War memorials at my schools and at Oxford astonished me with their quantity of names. I leafed through old bound copies of the wartime *Illustrated London News* that we had at home, awed by the many photographs of officers who'd been killed (other ranks didn't feature) and drawings of artists' ideas of the Somme or Ypres.

Both my grandfathers had fought: one in the Royal Navy, the other as a young officer in France and Belgium. To them it had been the Kaiser's War; they didn't speak much about it, although the name showed whom they blamed. It was the poets who evoked the war most vividly for me when, as a schoolboy, I first read them. They gave dramatic and clear shape, and emotion, to the change from enthusiasm to pitiful weariness – from Brooke to Sassoon and Owen: a reflection of how an adolescent might see the arc of life.

Later I learned that Brooke's enthusiasm was fading as he sailed towards the Dardanelles, that Owen's last letters to his mother from the front said that there was no place where he would rather be. Trying to fathom their feelings and experiences has become one of my obsessions as I searched for an intimate glimpse of what had been perhaps the most significant and far-reaching European event of the twentieth century.

The poets in this book range from the aristocratic Julian Grenfell to Isaac Rosenberg, the son of a poor Jewish pedlar, and Ivor Gurney, whose father was a tailor. Most of them were uneasy in the pre-war world. Many were formed by those powerful institutions, the late-Victorian public schools (or, more accurately, private schools). Some saw war as a rescue.

Those who survived couldn't leave the war. Robert Graves wrote a brilliant memoir of it, *Goodbye to All That*, and then left England, as if to shake off the past, disowning his war poems. Yet the trenches stayed in his dreams until he died in his eighties. Ivor Gurney and Edmund Blunden wrote some of their best war poems after 1918. Neither Robert Nichols nor Siegfried Sassoon again found poetry strong enough to match what they'd written about the western front.

Other poets wrote about the war – Thomas Hardy, W. B. Yeats, Wilfred Gibson, Laurence Binyon – yet saw no fighting. Through these eleven, you can see the war's course through their writing and their lives. All were warriors.

PRELUDE

AT LEAST ONE POET had been looking forward to war. In the summer of 1913, Julian Grenfell was a twenty-five-year-old army officer returning to his regiment in South Africa after some months of home leave. Grenfell had the best that Edwardian Britain could offer. He'd joined the Royal Dragoons, a cavalry regiment, in 1910, after Balliol College, Oxford, where he had gone from Eton. He had glamour; clever, strong and handsome, he was a hard-playing sportsman. But there was also violence; he boxed ferociously, he chased a Jewish millionaire undergraduate round the quad with a stock whip and beat up a cab driver who overcharged him. The Balliol authorities, perhaps in awe of his aristocratic status, brushed off complaints from other students about his rowdiness.

Yet Julian Grenfell was no mindless hearty. His mother, Lady Desborough, was a renowned hostess; her children grew up with cabinet ministers, writers and generals. At Balliol, he read Greats, or classics and philosophy; he drew and wrote essays challenging the complacency of his parents' world – that of conventionally cultured Edwardian high society. Resentment of the power of this world, and its relentless pressure, drove him to have a nervous breakdown. Apparently trapped by his position and success within it, and its strong, predictable expectations, he thought of suicide. The violence, the loaded shotgun beside him during his convalescence in his parents' country house, betrayed anger and despair. All this was before he became a soldier.

Why had Grenfell joined the Edwardian army? The Boer War, some thirteen years earlier, had demonstrated how stupidly led this army was. Rudyard Kipling might glorify 'Tommy', the long-suffering private soldier, but it was harder to praise the High Command, although Kipling did write a poem about Lord Roberts, the British general who had broken the chain of disasters against the Boers. Julian Grenfell – intelligent and brave – liked the wild country of India and South Africa but told a friend that he 'hated' the army. What he wanted was to break out. But the Grenfells were so glorified, so sated, that it was hard to know what might be better. Only a complete upheaval – exile, collapse, even death – could bring it all down and give an alternative.

A year later, in June 1914, a young Jewish man also arrived in South Africa. Isaac Rosenberg, like Julian Grenfell, painted and wrote poetry. But Rosenberg came from an atmosphere of greater intellectual freedom among immigrants in London's Whitechapel. When Grenfell announced that he thought of leaving the army to study art in Paris, his family mocked him; this was not what the eldest son of Lord Desborough did. Rosenberg may have been proud that 'Nobody ever told me what to read, or ever put poetry in my way,' but his father, a Jewish pedlar who had fled Lithuania to escape conscription in the Russian army, was a cultured man. Barnett Rosenberg had trained for the rabbinate and wrote poetry. Isaac's parents were both pacifists.

They were also very poor. At the age of fourteen, Isaac was apprenticed to an engraver, which he hated. He went to evening classes at Birkbeck College, wrote verses influenced by Swinburne, Rossetti and Francis Thompson, and looked back to Keats, Shelley and an earlier engraver and poet, William Blake. In 1911, rich Jewish patrons paid for him to study at the Slade School of Fine Art alongside the artists David Bomberg and Christopher Nevinson. Yiddish had been Isaac Rosenberg's first language; as late as 1913, wanting to enter for an art prize while at the Slade, he was unsure if he was a British subject. Like Julian Grenfell, he felt trapped by what he called 'the fiendish persistence of the coil of circumstance'. Yet he thought, 'it is the same with all people no matter what the condition'.

Grenfell and Rosenberg grew up in an increasingly anxious Britain. The country still had the empire but faced civil unrest at home and competition abroad. Hysteria could burst out, as when, in 1900, the relief of Mafeking – where the Boers had besieged a British garrison for months – set off wild celebrations, at which the young Edward Thomas caught a venereal infection. The disease blighted his final exams at Oxford, perhaps making him miss the first-class degree and fellowship of his college that would have given enough financial security for him to escape grinding work as a hack writer.

Britain wasn't a static society. There was much movement and desire for change during the decade before 1914, although this was hard to see from the fortress of Julian Grenfell's background. Virginia Woolf believed that the world changed in 1910, because of French post-impressionist art and Viennese psychoanalysis. In 1913, Siegfried Sassoon went night after night, usually alone, to the Russian ballet, watched Richard Strauss conducting the *Legend of Joseph* or heard Schoenberg's *Verklärte Nacht*, feeling mystified and overcome by 'that yearning exotic music' and its sense of 'the unknown want' that in Sassoon's case was 'deep and passionate love'. He and Robert Graves wrote admiringly to Edward Carpenter, upper-class rebel and pioneer of homosexual freedom; Wilfred Owen broke down before the demands of evangelical Christianity; Rupert Brooke joined the Fabians; Ivor Gurney fell into depression; Isaac Rosenberg met revolutionaries; Charles Sorley wanted to work with the poor; Grenfell and Edward Thomas yearned for death.

They would all be part of Britain's Greatest War. More than twice as many British were killed in the First World War as in the Second. From 1914 until 1918 British forces were essential to the Allies' success whereas, after 1942, most of the fighting against Germany and Japan was done by the Russians or the Americans.

The western front in particular came as shock to a people that hadn't been involved in a war on the European continent since the time of Napoleon. The country had never known conscription, when young men were forced to fight. The war damaged Britain, perhaps fatally, through massive financial indebtedness; and there began to be stirrings in the empire, in India and among what were called the colonies of white settlement such as Australia, after battle-field losses in the British cause during incompetently planned campaigns. The old idea of imperial Britain, safe from European involvement, had gone. Britain, still a great power, seemed more vulnerable – a drifting and declining force.

The war ate deep into the nation's sense of itself; every family was affected through death or wounding. Such was the war's extent that the break with an earlier peace became a powerful myth, of shattered calm or beauty, of broken illusion. Its relentless course, the reason why the heirs of western civilization began it, still seems a mystery. Could it really be that the great nations of Europe had let themselves drift into such chaos?

War was not generally expected until a few days before it began. The European crisis was acted out among politicians and diplomats, away from the people. A typical response was that of H. G. Wells's fictional literary man, the well-informed Mr Britling from the novel *Mr Britling Sees It Through*, who sat in the garden of his country house imagining that yet another flare-up in the Balkans must soon fade.

Hadn't war held off for forty years? 'It may hold off forever,' Mr Britling thought, in the early summer of 1914. He admitted that if Germany attacked France through Belgium, Britain would have to go to war ('of course we should fight') because of treaty obliga-tions. But the Germans knew this and 'they aren't altogether idiots'. 'Why should Germany attack France? ... It's just a dream of their military journalists ...' The impasse over Ireland, where the Ulster Protestants in the north would not countenance the British govern-ment's plans for Irish Home Rule, seemed much more serious. Not until 29 July and the bank holiday weekend did things change.

News of the German ultimatum to Belgium came on 3 August. What had brought about this switch from years of British aloofness? Britain had watched while Bismarck humiliated Austria and France and created the German empire. There'd been trouble in the Balkans for years, among the peripheral lands of the declining Ottoman and Habsburg empires, places that to most Britons were as fantastical as the late-Victorian best-selling novel *The Prisoner of Zenda*. Crises provoked by assassinations, even small wars, had been resolved peacefully before, or at least with the bloodshed of others. Surely this time would be no different.

To protect her imperial position and to preserve the balance of power in Europe had been Britain's aim; Lord Salisbury, Prime Minister at the end of Queen Victoria's reign, tried to ensure this while staying free of continental entanglements. But the unification of Germany, after Prussia's victory over France in 1870, had begun the disruption by creating a strong, neurotic, assertive presence at the centre of Europe. A new economic, military and would-be imperial power surged ahead of France and challenged Britain. Germany felt vulnerable, threatened by encirclement, fearful of the French desire for revenge and of the potential of a vast and mysterious Russia.

The British ventured tentatively into foreign alliances as the twentieth century began. A treaty was signed with Japan in 1902; there were understandings – or ententes – with France in 1904 and with Russia in 1907. Military and naval talks – unofficial, not known even to most of the cabinet – began with France, senior British officers cycling across Flanders and Picardy to assess possible battle-fields. The concern about Germany was fuelled by its Emperor William II's aggressive speeches, by his foolhardy posturing and by German naval expansion. As early as the 1890s, novelists were imagining a German invasion. The German army, buttressed by conscription, had been building up for years, in an atmosphere of brash nationalism, dwarfing the small British all-volunteer force designed principally for colonial wars; now the Royal Navy, seen as

Britain's ultimate protection, was threatened perhaps with future parity with Germany, even with eclipse.

Britain began to seem weak, old-fashioned, against this new, rich and fascinating giant. In E. M. Forster's *The Longest Journey* (published in 1907) an elderly woman questions a Cambridge undergraduate who'd been to Germany. Was the country's scholarship overestimated? Had it impressed him? 'Were we so totally unfitted to repel invasion?'

A campaign in favour of conscription was launched, under Lord Roberts, the hero of Kipling and of the Boer War. To the Liberal government, ideologically opposed to militarism or to state intervention, this seemed wrong and, at a time of high spending on the new welfare state, too expensive. In 1911 and 1912, senior British diplomats at the Foreign Office wanted an open alliance with Russia and France. It was thought, however, that neither the public nor Liberal opinion would stand for this, particularly if it involved Tsarist Russia, the great autocracy and oppressor of her own and subject peoples such as the Poles.

In Germany, there was doubt that Britain would fight for Belgium or join France and Russia in a war. In August 1913, the British Foreign Secretary Sir Edward Grey had, with German cooperation, mediated successfully between Austria and Russia and Turkey at a London conference on the Balkans. As late as July 1914, as Serbia was rejecting Austria's demands following the assassination at Sarajevo of the Archduke Franz Ferdinand, heir to the Habsburg throne, Asquith's cabinet was confident that Britain could keep out of any conflict, even if Germany, Austria's ally, sent troops through southern Belgium into northern France. But the ministers of the old world proved unable to force or to guide Serbia and Austria – and their allies – back to peace. So the generals – men like Siegfried Sassoon's 'cheery old card' who 'did for' the men by 'his plan of attack' – went to war as a result of political and diplomatic failure. Britain's small, poorly equipped army had been given to its commanders by the politicians.

On 2 August the Germans demanded clear passage through the whole of Belgium to enable them to attack France. The King of the Belgians refused the demand and asked for British support, under the treaty that guaranteed his country's neutrality.

It fell to the Foreign Secretary Sir Edward Grey to guide Britain's declaration of war through parliament. He feared that elements of his own Liberal party would be against the war, although he knew he could count on the support of the Conservative Opposition. On 30 July the Liberal paper the *Manchester Guardian* had opposed the idea that Britain should guarantee 'the peace of Europe'; the parliamentary Liberal party also resolved against being 'dragged into conflict'. But once Belgium – poor little Belgium – had been invaded by the bully Germany the cause became almost a liberal one, of maintaining treaty obligations and international order.

Sir Edward was thought to be the steadiest of hands, not at all showy, personifying a serene Britain that was the opposite of the bumptious German Reich. The reality was rather different. In fact the country was in the grip of a series of strikes; women demanding the vote were resorting to violence; there was open rebellion against British rule in Ireland; and a new artistic modernism arriving from Europe had moved even the young, fox-hunting Siegfried Sassoon. The Foreign Secretary's passions, however, were fly-fishing and watching birds. He was a countryman who loved his cottage garden on the banks of the River Test and could quote endlessly from Wordsworth – a man whose refusal to be bamboozled by foreigners was shown by his inability to speak any of their languages.

The Conservatives liked Grey who, although a Liberal, had imperialist sympathies that had been shown in his support for the Boer War. On becoming Foreign Secretary in 1905, he mostly continued with the policies of the previous Conservative government but became more involved in Europe, agreeing to unofficial staff talks with the French. Grey should feature alongside bungling generals in the questions asked by poets and very many others. Had there been enough preparations for the war? Could it have been avoided? Was the country incapable of sensing a new world?

Victorian complacencies and confidence may have been fading, but Britain was still proudly set apart from the continent as head of the greatest empire in history. It was to India with its military life of pig sticking and retinues of servants that Julian Grenfell went as a young army officer, to get away from his parents' world of slippery brightness, what his mother called 'the gospel of joy'; then he went to South Africa.

Both countries formed part of the pre-1914 army's duties as an imperial police force. In South Africa, he found his work – facing down strikes in the mines of what he told his mother was 'this utterly abominable country' – disappointing. It showed 'the utter beastliness of both sides – the Jews at the Rand Club who loaf about and drink all day, and the Dutch and Dagos who curse and shoot in the streets'. Grenfell sought relief in challenging all comers at army boxing matches. He dreamed of farming in remote Kenya.

Britain had begun to seem ugly and constricted. E. M. Forster's early novels – particularly *Howards End* and *The Longest Journey* – show a regret for the suburbanization of the country near London and the vulgar commercialization of English life. Near the end of *The Longest Journey* the suburbs of Salisbury – 'ugly cataracts of brick' – are condemned as neglecting 'the poise of the earth ... They are the modern spirit.' Forster admits that 'the country is not paradise ... But there is room in it and leisure.' Towns seem 'excrescences, grey fluxions, where men, hurrying to find one another, have lost themselves'.

Howards End pits the cultured, sensitive, liberal and brave Schlegel sisters against the crude, materialistic Wilcoxes. Forster admits that it is the Wilcoxes who make things happen, even if they have no poetry, no sense of the past. Who owns England, the novel asks, the people who are narrowly practical or those with imagination? The Schlegels are half German, with the German concern for *Kultur* and the spirit. In London restaurants there's talk of how the

German Emperor wants war. The sisters' father had left the new Germany after 1871 because he hated its vulgarity, power hunger and materialism. To the Schlegels, the British equivalent of this is jingoistic imperialism, the religion of the empire.

The Schlegels get the better of the Wilcoxes. But worrying questions are asked. Is the country – the fields and woods of Hertfordshire, near Howards End, that are encroached on by London – now irrelevant? Can't countrymen, who work the fields, still be England's hope? Are the English reduced to being comrades, not warriors or lovers, scorned by visiting Germans for their dreary music or inability to engage in intellectual discussion? Where is the greatness? Even old London is being pulled down, sacrificed to developers' greed.

H. G. Wells showed similar disdain for pre-1914 England. Wells's character Mr Britling is a successful writer who lives in a comfortable country house in Essex yet senses complacency and frivolity, an intellectual laziness. *Mr Britling Sees It Through* describes a drifting place, beset by unaddressed problems such as a rebellious Ireland and uncompetitive industry, a soft country of gentrified farm buildings and a political philosophy of wait and see, a slack but lucky country where too many intelligent people passed 'indolent days leaving everything to someone else'. To a German visitor, it's pleasant but not serious, an informal, quite chaotic place where people are kind but not polite. The whispers of change – from Ireland, from the empire, from Germany, 'intimations of the future' – were there to be heard, while the British, like 'everlasting children in an everlasting nursery', played on.

Even in the Whitechapel of Isaac Rosenberg's childhood, there were dreams of the past – of the lost vast spaces of the Russian Jewish pale of settlement. London's East End was far from any quaint notion of English country life, but Isaac's mother made gardens at their various homes. Rosenberg wanted to move from the city to the country if he survived the war. Many in Whitechapel had an ultimate yearning – that of a new life in the United States, seen as the golden land.

Isaac Rosenberg had an outsider's oblique vision. He met the artists David Bomberg and Mark Gertler at the Slade and resembled them in his bold use of colour but held back from their experimental art in favour of traditional representation of people and nature. Introspective, unable to afford models, Rosenberg went in for self-portraits, for conventional landscapes, partly because these were more likely to sell. Unlike Bomberg, he painted nature rather than the city.

In November 1913 he found himself in different company when Mark Gertler introduced him to the civil servant, art collector and friend of writers Edward Marsh. They met at the Café Royal, once the haunt of Oscar Wilde and London's *fin de siècle* decadents, still a place where Isaac could also meet Yeats and Ezra Pound. The sociable 'Eddie' Marsh featured in many poets' lives; the boy from Whitechapel, some of whose friends were Marxists, was now within reach of Rupert Brooke and Siegfried Sassoon (Sassoon's rich Sephardic Jewish Iraqi forebears were quite different to the Lithuanian Ashkenazim Rosenbergs).

Eddie Marsh, a homosexual made impotent by mumps in adolescence, had a chirruping, squeaky voice and could seem afloat on a wash of anecdotes, quotations and social urbanity. Yet even Marsh knew there had to be change, although he thought that this had to be grafted on to the best of the past. 'Nine-tenths of the Tradition may be rubbish,' he wrote, 'but the remaining tenth is priceless, and no one who tries to dispense with it can hope to do anything that is good.' A classical scholar and son of a successful surgeon, he was mocked by Julian Grenfell's Eton and Balliol set. Patrick Shaw-Stewart, a friend of Grenfell, was invited to breakfast by Marsh and jokingly left a cheque under his plate as a tip for the host.

Eddie never introduced Rosenberg, a shy, stammering, awkward man, to Sassoon or to Brooke. But his patronage, using funds granted by the government to the family of the early nineteenth-century assassinated Prime Minister Spencer Perceval (from whom he was descended), ranged quite far. Marsh bought pictures from John and Paul Nash, from Stanley Spencer, Isaac Rosenberg, Mark Gertler and William Roberts. He hung Rosenberg's painting in the spare bedroom of his London flat so that every guest would see it; in 1913, he paid for the publication of Rosenberg's second book of poems; he used his influence to get the poet an emigration permit to visit his sister in South Africa; he found rooms for the young Siegfried Sassoon near his own in Gray's Inn; he read (and didn't particularly like) the early poems of Robert Graves. In August 1914, he persuaded Winston Churchill, the First Lord of the Admiralty whose private secretary he was, to let the untrained Rupert Brooke become an officer in the Royal Naval Division.

Marsh disliked post-impressionist art and wasn't moved by Imagist or modernist writers like T. E. Hulme. The anthology that he edited and published in 1912 – *Georgian Poetry* – was the apotheosis of his influence. Launched at the new Poetry Bookshop near the British Museum, the book included work by D. H. Lawrence, John Masefield and Rupert Brooke as well as limper verses by other poets about landscape or love. Marsh, aided by Brooke, defined the Georgians by choosing poems that were more colloquial in style and more down to earth in subject matter than the lushness and high language of Swinburne or Francis Thompson. Rupert Brooke contributed a poem that included a precise description of being sick at sea.

It was possible to move between different worlds – that of Julian Grenfell's parents (who had Marsh to stay) and that of the Whitechapel Yiddish theatre where Gertler and Rosenberg took him – and to be private secretary to the Liberal cabinet minister Churchill while loving the Fabian socialist Rupert Brooke (who wrote 'I HATE the upper classes'). Ford Madox Ford delighted in a London that was a 'great, easy-going, tolerant, lovable old dressing gown of a place'. At the height of the row over the powers of the hereditary House of Lords in 1911, the party leaders, Asquith and Balfour, had been fellow guests at a fancy-dress ball.

But on the eve of the First World War divisions outside the world of the arts (which in Britain wasn't taken particularly seriously) were hardening; it was difficult to imagine that amiable scene two years later. By 1913 politics had become much more vicious. The 1911 House of Lords crisis seemed good-natured compared to the strikes, the violence and suicides of suffragettes and the threat of armed rebellion if Home Rule for Ireland was forced upon Ulster.

Britain had once been the most modern country, a pioneer of democracy. Now it had the most restrictive franchise in western Europe. There was also, in the English public schools, a system of education for the rich that was confident, rigid and circumscribed. Most of the poets whose work features in this book went to public schools (the exceptions are Isaac Rosenberg, Wilfred Owen and Ivor Gurney) and imbibed the public school creed of patriotic sacrifice, of imperial greatness, of the overwhelming importance of character. Britain was the modern incarnation of ancient Greece and Rome; the classics were still the foundation of school work; the poets thought of ancient heroes as they went to war. The power of these places was immense. Robert Graves kept the welterweight boxing cup he won at Charterhouse brightly polished on his desk in Majorca until the end of his life. Boxing had saved him from the bullies. It had made his nightmares cease.

These schools could be grim. In *The Longest Journey*, E. M. Forster, once a day boy at Tonbridge, describes the horrors of 'Sawston': how what had been a free grammar school for locals had over the years turned into an expensive philistine monstrosity whose credo was 'patriotism for the school' and 'patriotism for the country'. At Sawston, the sight of the original Jacobean part of the chapel makes a visitor rejoice that his country is 'great, noble and old' – so much so that he exclaims, 'Thank God I'm English,' before adding, 'We've been nearly as great as the Greeks, I do believe. Greater, I'm sure, than the Italians, though they do get closer to beauty. Greater than the French, though we do take all their ideas. I can't help thinking that England is immense.' Even this is not enough for his schoolmaster guide who worries that it is too rational, for 'genuine patriotism comes only from the heart'. The spirit of Sawston is said to derive from a quotation from Aristophanes about bodily perfection and placidity of mind: 'perhaps the most glorious invitation to the brainless life that has ever been given'.

The buildings and atmosphere of these schools were overpowering. Gradually during the nineteenth century they had changed. Marlborough – where Charles Sorley and Siegfried Sassoon were educated – had been founded in 1843, with a weak headmaster, brutal staff and appalling conditions that set off a mass rebellion in 1851. A new head adopted the methods of Thomas Arnold, Rugby's legendary headmaster, appointing a responsible Sixth Form and younger masters and promoting games as well as work so that, according to the school historian, 'a civilized out-of-door life in the form of cricket, football and wholesome sport took the place of poaching, rat-hunting and poultry-stealing'. Mid-Victorian gothic architecture, soaring chapels and stained-glass windows with martial boyish saints vanquishing forces of darkness showed a revival of romantic chivalry. Marlborough chapel, built in 1886, has memorial windows to the dead of the South African and Crimean wars and glass by the Pre-Raphaelites Edward Burne-Jones and William Morris.

All this affected even those who had escaped it; Wilfred Owen, after weeks of treatment for shell shock at Craiglockhart sanatorium with Siegfried Sassoon (an old Marlburian), wrote to his mother in February 1918 about a novel he was reading, *The Hill* by Horace Vachell, set in Harrow School: 'a tale of Harrow and the hills on which I never lay, nor shall lie: heights of thought, heights of friendship, heights of riches, heights of jinks. Lovely and melancholy reading it is for me.' In August, during Owen's last hours before embarkation for the western front, when he had less than three months to live, what moved him was a vision of 'the best piece of Nation left in England': a homoerotic swim in the Channel with 'a Harrow boy, of superb intellect and refinement, intellect because he detests war more than Germans, and refinement because of the way he spoke of my going away; and the way he spoke of the Sun; and of the Sea, and the Air: and everything. In fact the way he spoke ...'

The public-school accent gave immediate identification. Some fifteen years later, when his dead friend, his 'little Wilfred', was reaching new heights of admiration, Siegfried Sassoon, perhaps out of jealousy, said that Owen's Shropshire accent had made him 'an embarrassment'.

Charles Sorley was the son of a Cambridge professor of moral philosophy. While a boy at Marlborough, Sorley rebelled, giving a paper to the school's Literary Society about John Masefield's collo-quial poetry, saying that it was 'the lower classes' – because 'they did not live in our narrow painted groove' – who know 'what life is'. He thought of becoming an instructor at a working man's college and wanted to escape the relentless classics. He feared he might get too conceited when his achievements at work and games raised him to the top of the school. Memories of his time as captain of his house later repelled him.

If you were a success, the public-school experience was intoxi-cating. Sorley found that Marlborough constantly came back to him while he was studying in Germany before Oxford. When during his schooldays Sorley had cut chapel to walk on the Wiltshire Downs, the master on duty that day had refused to penalize him although Sorley had argued strongly that he should be punished. He liked to think that walks like these unrolled a better land, the landmarks poetic – Liddington, the Vale of the White Horse, the Kennet valley, towards Coate, where Richard Jefferies, the Victorian writer on nature and rural life, had grown up, ten miles from Marlborough, a good place to stop for an hour to read Jefferies's *Wild Life in a Southern County*, with its description of Liddington Castle, site of a Roman camp. But friendships made at school were irreplaceable, even though Sorley had begged his father to take him away. In fact Marlborough had given him 'five years that could not have been more enjoyable'. This seemed a mystery: 'I wonder why.' Could it have been because 'human nature flourished better in a poisonous atmosphere'?

The German student fraternities – often drunken, aggressive and anti-Semitic – seemed worse. But towards the end of his time in Germany, Charles Sorley wanted to stay on, perhaps go to university in Berlin. He felt he was in a serious country. He liked many Germans that he met, particularly German Jews. He admired their unashamed patriotism and intellectual curiosity, contrasting these with English puritanism, prurience, frivolity and hypocrisy: 'England is seen at its worst when it has to deal with men like Wilde. In Germany Wilde and Byron are appreciated as authors: in England they still go pecking about their love affairs ...'

Charles Sorley wrote poetry at school, inspired by the Downs. When Marsh's first Georgian anthology came out in 1912, Sorley showed only mild enthusiasm, liking Lascelles Abercrombie, Walter de la Mare, G. K. Chesterton and Wilfred Gibson ('the poet of the tramp and the vagabond') whose simple language was typical of the group. Already he'd glimpsed Brooke, the most glamorous Georgian, shirtless at Cambridge. This was during Brooke's 'neo-pagan' phase of naked swimming, sleeping in fields, tumbling with girls from the liberal school of Bedales and tossing back his longish hair. To Sorley, Brooke seemed 'undoubtedly a poet', if a slight one. Socialism seemed right to them both. Brooke read reports on poor-law reform and spoke at Fabian meetings.

It was the Victorians that these two brilliant young men wanted to escape. Unlike Sorley, Brooke admired Robert Browning, but the stately laureate Tennyson was too much for them both, Sorley declaring in 1913, while still at Marlborough, that 'all through the closing years of the last century there has been a grand but silent revolution against the essential falseness and shallowness of the mid-Victorian court poets'. Pre-industrial England – a landscape of imagined freedom – moved Sorley, as it did Brooke and Edward Thomas. Sorley and Thomas approached it through Richard Jefferies. Escaping from Marlborough, the school and the town, Sorley climbed up to the Downs; some years earlier, on his first day as a Marlborough boy, Siegfried Sassoon had fled there, also on his own; Wilfred Owen had looked upon Broxton Hill in Cheshire as a place of mysterious possibility. For Edward Thomas a ghost could come at such moments, an uneasy but vital part of him, an alter ego hinting at dark truth.

Such places of beauty and history were, for Charles Sorley, for Edward Thomas, for Siegfried Sassoon and for Edmund Blunden, what England meant – more than the empire or military glory or past victories. Wilfred Owen wrote: 'Even the weeks at Broxton, by the Hill / Where I first felt my boyhood fill / With uncontain-able movements; there was born / My poethood ...' For Sorley, patriotism didn't become impressive until he saw some soldiers in Germany returning from a field day, singing as they marched – 'the roar could be heard for miles ... Then I understood what a glorious country it is: and who would win if war came.' He told his old master at Marlborough how 'I felt that perhaps I could die for Deutschland – and I have never had an inkling of that feeling for England, and never shall ... It's the first time I have had the faintest idea of what patriotism meant.'

Any homesickness was for those long walks: 'it is chiefly the Downs I regret'. The German 'simple day system' of education seemed better than an English boarding school. At Marlborough there had been too much competition over trivial matters and the confusion of 'strength of character with petty self-assertion'. Yet Sorley slipped back, admitting that 'there is something in Marlbor-ough that I would not have missed for worlds ...' From Germany, he asked his parents for *The Life in the Fields* by Richard Jefferies; 'in the midst of my setting up and smashing of deities – Masefield, Hardy, Goethe – I always fall back on Richard Jefferies'.

In Germany he stayed with a family in Schwerin, had language lessons and then moved on to the university of Jena. The friendliness of the people, the much greater interest in art and poetry, the unashamed intellectualism, overwhelmed him; only gradually did the heavy bourgeois domestic life, the sultry weather, the boastful and drunken student corps and the shrill celebration of the French defeat of 1870 dull his enthusiasm. The Jews were the liveliest people; every Prussian could seem 'a bigot and a braggart'. Germans wanted to know what England would do. Hadn't King Edward VII 'spent his life in attempting to bring about a German war'? During the Ulster crisis, when British officers threatened mutiny if Irish Home Rule was imposed, Germans thought it 'inconceivable that the army should refuse to obey its government'.

Austria's ultimatum to Serbia that followed the Archduke Franz Ferdinand's assassination exposed a combustible alignment of great powers, with Russia on the Serbian side and Germany with the Austro-Hungarian Empire. By 26 July 1914, the Jena students were shouting 'Down with the Serbs', a new edition of the newspapers came every half-hour 'with wilder rumours' so that Sorley could 'almost hear the firing in Belgrade'. He wrote, 'It seems that Russia must settle the question of a continental war, or no.' A few days later he was put in a German jail, then let out to go back to a Britain that had joined the fight. Aged only nineteen, he volunteered for the army.

Why was Charles Sorley suddenly prepared to die for his country? The outbreak of war caused even those who had rebelled at their schools to snap to attention. Robert Graves came from an exceptionally cultivated family: his literary father was a schools inspector who collected and wrote ballads and Irish folk tales; his German mother descended from the historian Ranke. Winning a scholarship to Charterhouse, the puritanical young Graves had at first loathed the school with its bullying, rampant sexuality and contempt for learning; then a reforming Head and young masters like the mountaineer George Mallory made it better, helped by the writing of poetry, a crush on another boy and the discovery that he had enough boxing skill to defend himself.

Robert Graves had also been to Germany, for holidays with his mother's German family in Bavaria. Here the prim young Graves wandered joyfully around the family estate, but, outside it, found riotous beer gardens, thick clouds of cigar smoke and glutinous eating; his fears of hell, instilled by his mother, were inflamed by the 'wayside crucifixes with the realistic blood and wounds, and the *ex-voto* pictures, like sign-boards, of naked souls in purgatory, grinning with anguish in the middle of high red and yellow flames'. Family trips to France, Germany, Brussels and Switzerland made Graves's childhood cosmopolitan – a contrast to Siegfried Sassoon's fox-hunting, Edward Thomas's long English walks, Edmund Blunden's Kent villages and Ivor Gurney's Cotswolds. His British landscape was the bare land and mountains of north Wales where the family had a holiday home.

Graves had been a rebel. He resigned from the Officer Training Corps and spoke up for pacifism in debates. Yet when war broke out he joined up, at scarcely nineteen, incensed by the German invasion of poor little Belgium and reports of atrocities that resembled the bullying that he'd known at Charterhouse.

Robert Nichols had also apparently not conformed to the contemporary idea of an enthusiastic patriot. The son of an atheist, from a family of successful printers, Nichols had a prosperous but awkward childhood, divided between London and a country house in Essex, with a cold father and a mother who could show a startling love, but suffered a series of nervous breakdowns. Brought up to have no belief, he became fascinated by religion although never an adherent to any one faith. The nervous Nichols – who'd inherited the family mental instability in the form of insomnia and manic depression – was unhappy at school, especially at 'hellish' Winchester from which he was sacked for going up to London during term time. At Oxford he became a blood, throwing mangel-wurzels and dead pheasants at the visiting Chancellor of the Exchequer Lloyd George and getting sent down for failing exams.

Already, however, there was a fanatical dedication to writing poetry, encouraged by a friendship with the composer Philip Heseltine who introduced him to D. H. Lawrence. The verses poured forth from Nichols – about fauns, the Virgin Mary and love, often in bits of projected poetic dramas. Over all this is the sense of a search for a great subject, worthy of so much effort and time. Might his country – and its cause in August 1914 – give new fire to his life? Nichols enlisted in September, aged twenty-one. He felt that he should stand up for England and 'all she stood for', even if she was wrong.

It was Rupert Brooke, a Fabian socialist and friend of the Bloomsbury Group, who became the war's first famous poet. Brooke saw war as a joyous simplification of his and his country's destiny. It was as if he had come back to his childhood. Britain in 1914 was for the status quo. She was aiding France and Belgium which had been invaded by Germany, the disruptive new usurper and challenge to the empire. This was a war to defend the old world.

Rupert Brooke was even born in a public school, growing up at Rugby (where his father was a housemaster) in an atmosphere of Puritanism and success worship. His mother, descended from a Cromwellian fanatic, was the centre of the family; it was said that Mr Brooke was sent out at night to pick up horse manure from the roads for her roses. At Rugby her adored Rupert became head of house and captain of the house rugby team, and won the poetry prize and a sonnet competition in the *Westminster Gazette*. In 1905, while ill at home, he announced, 'I have read the whole of the Elizabethan Dramatists through in 3 days.' The young Brooke admired Wilde and Housman, had adolescent homosexual passions, became a classical scholar at King's, Cambridge (where his uncle was Dean) and a member of the exclusive intellectual society the Apostles, moving in a proudly superior clique, keen – as his correspondence shows – to exclude others.

At Cambridge Brooke was ostensibly a rebel against the old world of Tennyson and duty, of religion and sexual repression. After losing his virginity to a man at the age of twenty-one, he wrote clinically of the love-making to James Strachey, Lytton Strachey's brother; the description must have driven James, who loved Brooke, to a frenzy of frustration. Behind it there may have been an urge to torture, or at least to tease. Rupert Brooke seems to have taken up socialism while at Rugby, partly to shock what he saw as the place's complacency and philistinism.

But there was always the pull of public-school values, of his strong conventional mother, and also the effortless power of his looks. Edward Marsh, after seeing him in 1906 at Cambridge as the herald in a production of *Eumenides*, fell in love. Even the sceptical Leonard Woolf, on meeting Brooke for the first time, thought, 'That is exactly what Adonis must have looked like in the eyes of Aphrodite.' Brooke could be a wonderful companion – witty, clever, teasing, well-read, sympathetic. His taste was wide; it was he who had suggested to Marsh that Ezra Pound should be asked to contribute to *Georgian Poetry*. Friends, however, were surprised later when his letters were published by how different their Rupert could be when he was with others, how quickly he could switch moods.

Rupert Brooke hated getting old. To be twenty in 1907 had filled him 'with a hysterical despair to think of fifty dull years more. I hate myself and everyone ... What I chiefly loathe and try to escape is not Cambridge nor Rugby nor London, but – Rupert Brooke.' In 1909, he moved to digs in Grantchester, a village near Cambridge, his enthusiasm for Swinburne weakening in favour of John Donne as he embraced a revolt against materialism and hypocrisy. This 'neo-paganism' involved camping, diving into ponds and rivers (Brooke's party trick was to surface with an erection, impressing Virginia Woolf), wandering barefoot or naked. Yet such a life was by no means idyllic; he found himself caught up in the jealousy and cattiness of a small, self-conscious and arrogant circle. Increasingly narcissistic and self-centred, he became petulant if challenged, especially by another man.

In 1910, Edward Thomas, a respected critic and writer of prose, not yet a poet, stayed with Brooke at Grantchester. Later that year Brooke was with Thomas at Steep, at the Thomas's cottage. Mrs Thomas was away, leaving the two writers together. Edward Thomas noticed how Brooke moved quickly between 'a Shelleyan eagerness and a Shelleyan despair': also that the man resembled his poetry with his fair hair, laughter, easy 'indolent' talk that suggested he could admire 'as much as he was admired'. Thomas, weighed down by self-pity, self-loathing (particularly over his treatment of his family) and financial worry, was ostensibly very different from his brilliant guest.

Like Sorley and Graves, Rupert Brooke went to Germany. He stayed in Munich, wanting to learn German to help him get a fellowship at King's. Brooke thought at first that the Germans were 'a kind people', then decided, with swooping superficiality, that he was in favour of a larger Royal Navy as 'German culture must never, never prevail. The Germans are nice and well-meaning and they try; but they are soft ... The only good things (outside music perhaps) are the writing of Jews who live in Vienna ...' Italy appealed to him more. 'I renounce England,' he wrote from Florence.

Sidgwick and Jackson published Brooke's poems in December 1911. This coincided with the poet's collapse, when a love affair with Ka Cox seemed to end before flaring up again. Through the maelstrom he wrote, while in temporary exile in Berlin, 'The Old Vicarage at Grantchester', as if taking comfort from a nostalgic, witty yearning for an ideal England. He was in London for the launch of *Georgian Poetry*, which he had brought about with Marsh and Wilfred Gibson, and the exhibition of post-impressionist paintings. As if to show her that he too could shock, Brooke wrote to Virginia Woolf during his breakdown, describing an assault on a choirboy by two older youths in the church vestry, when the boy's cries were drowned 'by the organ pealing' and the result so severe that 'he has been in bed ever since with a rupture'.

Success rolled on. Having become a Fellow of King's and had 'The Old Vicarage' named the best poem of the year, Brooke was sent in May 1913 by the *Westminster Gazette* to write about his impressions of the United States. By October he'd left America for the South Seas, to what was to be perhaps the easiest time of his life and a love-affair with a Tahitian woman that inspired the tender poem 'Tiare Tahiti'. His thoughts on England showed confusion, anti-Semitism and harshness towards women. The problem was, Brooke thought, that it was hard to believe in a place still 'under that irresponsible and ignorant plutocracy', with London full of 'lean and vicious people, dirty hermaphrodites and eunuchs, moral vagabonds, pitiable scum ...' By June 1914 he was back. Rupert Brooke's last summer was a packed season, under Marsh's sway.

During the final months of peace, he went down to Dymock, to visit the poets who gathered round this village on the border of Herefordshire and Gloucestershire. Wilfred Gibson was there, as were Lascelles Abercrombie and John Drinkwater, and the predominant tone was Georgian. To Brooke, Dymock was a paradise where, staying in Gibson's cottage, 'one drinks great mugs of cider, & looks at fields of poppies in the corn'. After 1918, the village and its poets became part of the myth of a lost England. Among those who went there were the American poet Robert Frost and the Englishman Edward Thomas.

Edward Thomas had a sense that 'all was foretold', that man was ultimately helpless, even with his vast destructive power. From a large family, the son of a civil servant who had raised himself from a poor Welsh background, he grew up in south London. Educated at various schools, including briefly the private St Paul's, before winning a scholarship to Oxford, Thomas found life with his parents hard. His domineering father was a late-Victorian and Edwardian success story. Mr Thomas pushed his children and was once furious with his son for faltering when about to win a half-mile race. Mrs

Thomas was loving, but her husband ruled. The failure in the half-mile, and his father's refusal to forgive, was etched into Edward, as would a later incident of what he saw as his cowardice in the woods near Dymock.

A mist over Clapham Common could hint at unexplored wild-ness during his boyhood and there was open country to the south. When Edward Thomas stayed with his father's mother at Swindon, he could reach a wilder landscape, stirring an early romanticism and love of solitude. Always, however, there was pressure. Mr Thomas, in spite of his success, felt thwarted; he had stood unsuccessfully for parliament as a Lloyd George Liberal and his debating skills were restricted to advocating positivism in south London. He became jingoistic and shrill.

Edward married early; this brought escape, but the marriage had been forced upon him. Helen Noble was the daughter of a literary critic who had encouraged Edward's first writings about landscape and walking. While Edward was still at Oxford, Helen told him she was pregnant; Mr Thomas disapproved of the marriage and of his son's wish to be a writer rather than a civil servant. How would they provide for their children?

It was a good question. Edward's failure to get a First barred him from the security of an Oxford academic post. He set out as a writer, desperately seeking work, and the struggle darkened his depression and self-pity. Domestic life was hard, not made easier by platonic liaisons, one with the writer Eleanor Farjeon. But by 1914 Thomas was earning £400 a year from reviewing and writing – the equivalent today of some £30,000 to £40,000 – and had become an influential critic, particularly of poetry. The desired life, however, with his family or having the time to appreciate beauty, to write what he wanted, became impossible. 'I was born to be a ghost,' he wrote.

The Thomases lived in Kent and Hampshire. Edward came to know the south of England, although he still thought himself Welsh. He liked small country churches rather than cathedrals, folk songs rather than oratorios and took Richard Jefferies to his heart. Like Sassoon, Blunden and Gurney, he saw the rural world romantically, disliking intrusions such as businessmen who bought up hop fields in Kent – and his later poem 'Lob' cherished what might go, as if willing it to survive. On his long walks, he found beauty and escape from a family life, but everything was blighted by his moods and financial uncertainty. Thomas saw a psychoanalyst, but the darkness remained. 'I sat thinking about ways of killing myself,' he wrote. There was one definite suicide attempt.

In 1906 the Thomases moved to the village of Steep, near Petersfield. Near by was the progressive school Bedales, where boys and girls boarded together and where Helen Thomas taught, so their children could be Bedalians at a greatly reduced cost. The house at Steep was on a ridge, buffeted by winds, and he had a breakdown there in September 1911. But work had to go on. Edward Thomas needed to write a stream of books like *The South Country*, *The Heart of England*, *Horae Solitariae* and *Oxford*, his style becoming more natural or Georgian, less influenced by Walter Pater.

A typical journey was that begun on Good Friday 1913, from his parents' house in south London, where he stayed, in uneasy proximity to his father, on visits to the capital to see publishers or editors. Thomas wanted to follow the spring south-west; the account tells of another man met in inns or on the path, symbol of a more elemental self whose strong moods could bring leaden gloom or brilliant joy. This was very different to his father's Edwardian liberal, positivist certainties. Edward Thomas's thoughts of suicide show barely controllable desperation, not faith in progress.

In January 1913, as an important critic, he came to the new Poetry Bookshop, near the British Museum, to a party given to celebrate Marsh's Georgian anthology that had been published at the end of 1912. At the party too was an American, Robert Frost. But Thomas and Frost didn't meet that night.

Edward Thomas reviewed *Georgian Poetry*, teasingly mentioning its feeling for 'the simple and the primitive', as seen in 'children, peasants, savages, early men, animals and Nature in general', which was, he thought, typical of the age. The collection broke with the Victorians and the aesthetic crimson and velvety world of the 1890s. There was romance and nightingales – but they sang along-side Rupert Brooke being sick at sea or D. H. Lawrence's frank sensuality.

W. H. Hudson declared in 1913, 'I believe he has taken the wrong path', that poetry, not prose, was more suitable for Thomas's voice; the same year, however, Thomas published another account of an English journey, *The Icknield Way*, which didn't sell well enough. He considered becoming a teacher in London or leaving England. More robust types looked down on what Ezra Pound called 'a mild fellow with no vinegar in his veins'. Then, in October 1913, he met Robert Frost.

Over the next year and a half, until Frost returned to the United States with his wife and children, the two writers were often together, usually in Dymock. The Frosts were living there in poverty, alongside Abercrombie, Drinkwater and Gibson. To the American, the landscape's dereliction and its often destitute inhabitants were shocking. British farming had suffered from free trade and the huge influx of cheap American and Canadian wheat. Wages had scarcely gone up since 1870, making lives more like the grimmer parts of Hardy's novels than the nostalgic yearning evident in Siegfried Sassoon's memories of the pre-1914 Weald of Kent, in Ivor Gurney's beloved Cotswolds or in Rupert Brooke's 'hearts at peace under an English heaven'.

Robert Frost felt that Thomas should write poetry, of the kind that Frost wrote, where each word – and the sound of each word – conveyed a sense of natural speech. The atmosphere of Dymock and its poets encouraged friendship; the Georgians, although not the outspoken Frost, were soft in their manners and their verses, gentle and polite.

In February 1914 Edward Thomas received a grant from the Royal Literary Fund. By the spring he was staying at Dymock with the Frosts or in rented rooms with his own family or in a cottage taken by Eleanor Farjeon, whose love for Edward was encouraged by Helen as it soothed him. In March, Thomas came to breakfast in Marsh's rooms and it was a failure, the host thinking that the poet was sour, superior and critical of the food. Thomas wrote an admiring review of Frost's collection *North of Boston*, some weeks after the assassination of the Archduke Franz Ferdinand at Sarajevo. They spoke of moving to the United States with their families, to farm together in New England where the Frosts had lived, and failed, before crossing the Atlantic. Edward Thomas was cycling from Steep to Dymock with his son when war was declared.

A new feeling came, stimulated by war, a suspicion of foreigners and the search for spies. The police round Dymock were anxious about a Mr van Doorn who was said to be staying with the weird poets. There were rumours that Frost had been singing German songs. Were Germans so different, or so much worse, than the British whose faults Edward Thomas knew too well? He believed in a version of England. His patriotism was for the land, for what he'd seen or imagined of it and its history.

Since Marlborough and Cambridge (which he'd left without taking a degree), Siegfried Sassoon's life had become a perpetual holiday, a private income letting him do more or less what he wanted. His most successful poem, *The Daffodil Murderer*, a parody of John Masefield, had been praised by Edmund Gosse and Edward Marsh and received some reviews but sold few copies. Convention and timidity had manoeuvred him into a life of fox-hunting, cricket, the writing of sweet, privately printed verse and buried homosexuality.

Through Marsh, Sassoon had met two Georgian poets – W. H. Davies and the 'absolutely delightful' Rupert Brooke, who'd patronized him – but *Georgian Poetry* had none of Sassoon's poems in it. He left London in July 1914, returning to Kent and his mother to wait for the next hunting season. Perhaps he should enlist in the peacetime army and become a cavalry officer; then suddenly war was at hand. The newspapers foretold British involvement, and this must change his life. While playing in a two-day cricket match at Tunbridge Wells, Sassoon saw telegrams arrive at the ground summoning officers to their regiments.

He recalled the absurdly amateurish training he had received in the Officer Training Corps at Marlborough and thought how near Kent, his home, was to the coast and the Continent. Could it all soon be burned and plundered? Was a new barbarism imminent? The enemy was the Germany of the Kaiser and his generals, not that of Schumann and Richard Strauss, whom he'd seen at Drury Lane. Soon the newspapers were reporting crimes of inhumanity previously unimaginable to a secluded British gentleman. Sassoon had no doubt that he wanted to defend the Weald from this. He enlisted in the army as soon as he could.

Robert Graves saw an opportunity. Graves had been dreading going to Oxford in October; the new war would at least delay that. At Harlech, on holiday with his family, he decided to enlist. He wrote a poem promising revenge for the enemy's burning of Louvain in Belgium in late August.

Another survivor left no record of how he spent that summer. Ivor Gurney never wrote an autobiography, perhaps because he wished to write new poetry and music or because his last years were too tormented by madness.

Gurney was, like Edward Thomas, born a town boy, growing up in Gloucester, the son of a tailor and a powerful mother. Like Isaac Rosenberg, he passed the war as a private soldier; like Rosenberg, he had two arts, in his case music and poetry; like Rosenberg, he was helped by the influence of others; unlike Rosenberg (but like Blunden), his best work came after the war.

Gurney's musical gifts were encouraged at Gloucester Cathedral's choir school. The cathedral organist Dr Herbert Brewer gave him a good grounding but may have sensed the contempt the boy felt for Brewer's own dull compositions as the organist never mentions Gurney, by then a published poet and composer, in his memoirs. After 1911, when he arrived at the Royal College of Music, Gurney quickly gained a reputation. Marion Scott, a fellow student, noticed 'the look of latent force in him', particularly the eyes, bright behind spectacles, 'of mixed colouring', which 'Erasmus once said was regarded by the English as denoting genius'. She thought this boy 'must be the new composition scholar from Gloucester whom they call Schubert'.

Already suffering from mental illness, perhaps inherited from his mother's unstable family, and brought near to a complete breakdown in 1913, Ivor Gurney found London a trial – but Gloucestershire could heal. A letter describes a spot where the Forest of Dean, the Severn, the Malvern Hills and the Cotswolds could be seen together. 'London is worse than ever to bear after that.' The best hope seemed to be the suffragettes: 'let us hope that the Militants will blow it up soon'.

In July and August 1914, Gurney was probably on holiday in the place that he loved, the country near the medieval city of Gloucester. Dymock was not far away and the poets there fascinated Gurney when a friend spoke of them. He may have gone to readings at the Poetry Bookshop in London, but was too shy to introduce himself to anyone, certainly not to Edward Marsh, who helped him later.

Like Sassoon and Thomas, Gurney fashioned a country of his own that could make even the trenches bearable.

> God, that I might see
> Framilode once again!
> Redmarley, all renewed,
> Clear shining after rain ...

In 1913 came the mental collapse and, a year later, a whimsical poem in the style of Hilaire Belloc, before the war, and memories of war, released true poetry. Gurney tried to enlist early on – as Brooke, Graves and Sassoon did – but was turned down because of bad eyesight. He wished to do what he thought of as his duty, to Gloucestershire rather than to England. Ivor Gurney hoped also that the army might restore the balance of his mind.

Isaac Rosenberg and Ivor Gurney were free of the English public-school world, whereas Edmund Blunden stayed loyal to it all his life.

The son of schoolteachers, Blunden grew up in a village in Kent that perpetually glowed in his memory. He can seem a typical Georgian, with his love of cricket, rural life and villages – and he featured in Marsh's later anthologies. But Siegfried Sassoon was right when he told him, 'Your best poems have a spontaneity which is priceless,' reaching beyond the Georgian movement's more genteel side. Blunden did, however, write often about his childhood, prompting doubts as to whether the sun had really been so golden or the convolvulus so white and miraculous before 1914. He had a passion for country lore, for Kent and Sussex dialect words learned originally during the 'golden security' of King Edward's reign. Leaving this village world to board at Christ's Hospital school was painful; 'farewell the bread-and-butter pudding and toasted cheese round Cleave's fume-emitting stove, farewell the hours as volunteer teacher in my mother's school, farewell the solos in St Peter and St Paul, and those midnights on the frozen ponds in naked hop-gardens under bobbetty-topped pollards and tingling stars!' Edmund Blunden used such memories constantly, sometimes as a contrast with what came later, as in the post-war poem 'The Midnight Skaters' where ponds become possible graves as potential victims dance on their frozen surface, chancing death as in the trenches.

Christ's Hospital changed Blunden's life. 'C.H. was never out of Edmund's mind,' a contemporary wrote later, 'or if it was, the slightest reminder, a name, an allusion, would bring it back.' For Blunden, it was a school of poets and writers – of Charles Lamb, Samuel Taylor Coleridge, Leigh Hunt, George Dyer, Edmund Campion and William Camden – and he read all these and could quote from them.

Christ's Hospital was quite different from Grenfell's Eton, Brooke's Rugby, Graves's Charterhouse or Sassoon's and Sorley's Marlborough. Boys paid much reduced fees, often no fees at all, for the requirement to be of 'honest origin and poverty' banished social exclusivity. Leigh Hunt wrote of his time there in the eighteenth century that a boy had 'no sort of feeling of the difference of one another's rank out of doors. The cleverest boy was the noblest, let his father be who he might.' The uniform – a long blue coat and yellow stockings, resembling a partly disrobed clergyman – marked its difference, as did the names of the classes and categories of pupil (Little Erasmus and Great Erasmus, Deputy Grecians and Grecians) and its nickname of 'Housey'.

Edmund Blunden excelled there. He loved the cricket, played fives and rugby, learned calligraphy, spent hours in the school library and had his first published poem printed in the school magazine. When he left Christ's Hospital, he had already published two small books of privately printed verse: one of translations from the French, the other charming, old-fashioned poems about nature.

In July 1914 he was in the school's compulsory Officer Training Corps, impressed by the 'deep gentleness' of Field Marshal Sir John French, who a month later would be the commander of the British Expeditionary Force, when French inspected them. Later Blunden saw the Corps as contributing to the 'old lie' of desirable sacrifice, of war as a chivalric contest rather than random killing. In 1914, however, it seemed fun, except when a master said, 'it looks as though within a month the whole of Europe will be at war'. Blunden stayed at the school for another year, becoming head boy and winning an Oxford scholarship, the crown of his Bluecoat years.

Wilfred Owen also waited to join up. When war broke out in August 1914, he was in France and looked on the fate of his countrymen with a certain detachment. 'I feel my own life all the more precious and more dear in the presence of this deflowering of Europe,' Owen told his mother. 'While it is true that the guns will effect a little useful weeding, I am furious with chagrin to think that the Minds which were to have excelled the civilisation of ten thousand years are being annihilated – and bodies, the product of aeons of Natural Selection, melted down to pay for political statues.' There was no conscription in Britain. 'I regret the mortality of the English regulars less than that of the French, Belgian, or even Russian or German armies: because the former are all Tommy Atkins, poor fellows, while the continental armies are inclusive of the finest brains and temperaments of the land.'

Wilfred Owen had come to France in September 1913. First he taught in a language school in Bordeaux, then as a tutor to the Léger family. Madame Léger had been his pupil in the language school, her husband was a teacher of elocution, and they invited the young Englishman to join them at their holiday home in the Pyrenees. The Légers introduced Owen to Laurent de Tailhade, the first poet whom he knew well. The photograph of Wilfred with the elderly Frenchman, a follower of Baudelaire and the symbolists, looks like a parody of a disciple with his 'cher mâitre', as the young man looks down at the book he and Tailhade hold together. Laurent Tailhade has a hand on Owen's shoulder; the scene might come from the 1890s, from the crimson world of the decadents. Another photograph has Wilfred in a bow tie, winged collar and dark suit, wearing a wide-brimmed hat, arms protective across his chest, sitting with Madame Léger, listening to a lecture given outdoors by Tailhade. Owen looks dandyish and absorbed; the date is some three weeks after the outbreak of the First World War. Although Tailhade had been a pacifist, at the end of 1914 the elderly poet volunteered for the French army.

All this is far from Owen's beginnings. He was the eldest of three sons of a railway official who lived first near Oswestry in Shropshire, then at Birkenhead, where Wilfred went to school at the Birkenhead Institute, then at Shrewsbury, where he attended Shrewsbury Technical School. There was an evangelical atmosphere, imposed particularly by Owen's strong mother Susan, which must have brought silent conflict as he became aware of his homosexuality.

Each parent thought also of a past that had faded into disappointment. Tom Owen claimed to be descended from a sixteenth-century baron, a sheriff of Merionethshire; Susan, whose father was Mayor of Shrewsbury, had hoped in vain that the Mayor's will would leave her family much better off. Birkenhead, with its slums and docks, was not where they wanted to be. The Owens were respectable. When teaching in Bordeaux, Wilfred said that he was the son of a baronet.

The Church seemed a possible life; Owen read the Bible each day, dressed up as a clergyman, took mock services and went to work as an unpaid assistant to the vicar of Dunsden, a village near Reading, where he failed to win a scholarship to London University. Encouraged by his mother, he'd started to write poetry at an early age. A cousin, Leslie Gunston, was also a poet. Owen showed Gunston his work, much influenced by the romantics, particularly Keats.

Shocked by how little a religious revival at Dunsden was concerned with the village's poverty, Owen left the parish in 1913, failed for a scholarship to Reading University and seemed to be on the edge of a breakdown. His father had already taken him to Brittany on a holiday in 1908 and 1909, to let Wilfred practise his French. So, in September 1913, with his parents' support, Owen went back to France.

In France he found sophistication, freedom and possibly (although there's no evidence) sex. These months were probably the happiest of his life. But a puritan upbringing still made him flinch at strong artistic feeling. 'I love music,' Wilfred Owen wrote to his mother from Bordeaux in May 1914, 'Violin first, Piano next, with such strength that I have to conceal the passion, for fear it be thought weakness ...'

Owen had his first glimpse of war's reality on a visit to a French military hospital in Bordeaux in September 1914. In Bordeaux he was at the centre of French life, for the government had moved there from an endangered Paris. The French army, still dressed in red trousers and bright-blue jackets and capes, had charged across the eastern frontier into Alsace and Lorraine and suffered terrible casualties. The hospital was in a former lycée where he was taken by a doctor friend. A classroom had become an operating theatre, the ink-stained floor now a 'chamber of horrors'. 'German wretches' lay there, treated exactly the same as the French patients. Owen drew some wounded limbs to show his brother Colin what war was like – a crushed shin bone of a leg, a holed knee, a skull penetrated by a bullet, feet covered in dried blood. The young Englishman – still only twenty-one – reported, 'I was not much upset by the morning at the hospital; and this is a striking proof of my health.' As yet he had no plans to return to England.

News of war spread across Britain's empire, Isaac Rosenberg hearing it in Cape Town. Rosenberg's first collection – *Night and Day* – had been privately printed in 1912 by a sympathetic Jewish printer, the poems influenced by Keats, Shelley and Francis Thompson. Blake and Milton were also there in the sense of an implacable God. Although the shy, stammering Rosenberg was a difficult beneficiary, benefactors helped him, including the writer (and later translator of Proust's last volume) Sydney Schiff and a Mrs Cohen, who persisted even after Isaac and she had quarrelled. In Eddie Marsh's spare bedroom, Rosenberg's painting *Sacred Love* – of a girl and a boy in a clearing in a wood – impressed a guest for whom it 'glowed with a strange, dream-like intensity, reminiscent of Blake – a lovely vision'. The work's mysterious scene showed that its creator had a different imagination to that of the other poets who were lining up for the trenches.

Marsh had helped Rosenberg to get to South Africa. He paid for a second privately printed book of poems, to be called *Youth*, which did not come out until 1915. To Marsh, obscurity was a demon and Rosenberg admitted his own lack of traditional technique. He didn't fit easily into the new art scene. Roger Fry's 1910 post-impressionist show and Bomberg's cubism were quite different from his poetic realism. 'I dislike London for the selfishness it instils into one,' he told a friend, 'which is a reason for the peculiar feeling of isolation I believe most people have in London. I hardly know anyone whom I would regret leaving (except, of course, the natural ties of sentiment with one's own people); but whether it is that my nature distrusts people, or is intolerant, or whether my pride or my backwardness cools people, I have always been alone.' Rosenberg thought of going to the United States or Russia, where he had relations. But his sister Minnie had settled in South Africa with her husband so it seemed an easier destination. The Jewish Educational Aid Society paid for the voyage.

In South Africa, Rosenberg may have had an affair with an actress. He found that there was some interest in lectures which he gave on art. But Cape Town's dazzling light and landscape faded for him and a letter to Marsh reveals contempt for the materialism and the whites (he scarcely seems to have considered the Africans) 'clogged up' with 'gold dust, diamond dust, stocks and shares, and heaven knows what other flinty muck. Well, I've made up my mind to clear through all this rubbish.' Soon he was yearning for home, for intelligent appreciation of his poetry, as the poem 'The Exile' shows:

> O! dried up waters of deep hungering love!
> Far, far, the springs that fed you from above,
> And brimmed the wells of happiness
> With new delight.

'Think of me,' he told Eddie Marsh, 'a creature of the most exquisite civilization, planted in this barbarous land.' He begged Marsh to write to him of the English art scene, and above all 'write me of poetry'.

Julian Grenfell, a quite different Englishman in South Africa, had been waiting for battle during years of dreary peacetime soldiering. If war didn't come, he had a plan to stand for parliament in 1915. Grenfell had already been offered St Albans, the constituency containing Panshanger (the country house his mother had recently inherited), but had turned it down.

Grenfell wrote poetry and kept the poems mostly to himself (although he knew Marsh through his parents). A typical one was a celebration of the energy, freedom, speed and courage of his pet greyhound. He read quite widely – Marlowe and Ovid's *Amores* – and told his mother 'how I love the Rupert Brooke poems, who is Rupert B?' At an exhibition of pictures in Johannesburg, he admired William Orpen and John Singer Sargent and loathed Augustus John, who 'must be a raving lunatic – is he dead yet or have his habits toned down? He is the sort of man who might kill himself or turn round and become a religious maniac.'

In July 1914, Grenfell wrote mockingly to his mother about the crisis: 'Isn't it an exciting age, with Ireland and Austria and the Servs and Serbs and Slabs?' He read Sir Edward Grey's 'wonderful speech', which had persuaded parliament to back the war, and welcomed the arrival of this overwhelming cause. How good to see a 'great rally to the Empire', with Irish nationalists, 'Hindus', organized labour 'and the Boers and the South Fiji Islanders all aching to come and throw stones at the Germans'. To Grenfell 'it reinforces one's failing belief in the Old Flag and the Mother Country and the Heavy brigade and the Thin Red Line and all the Imperial Idea, which gets rather shadowy in peace time, don't you think?'

1914

RUPERT BROOKE was in Norfolk at the beginning of August 1914. The night before Britain's ultimatum to Germany ran out, Brooke had a nightmare. The next day he became melodramatic, telling his hosts, the Cornfords, that the best thing for Ka Cox, with whom he was having a fraught affair, would be 'that I should be blown to bits by a shell' for she could then find someone else. Frances Cornford said that only soldiers fought battles: 'Rupert, you won't have to fight.' Brooke answered, 'We shall all have to fight.'

For Robert Nichols, war meant defending 'the general idea of England and what she stood for', even if she were wrong. The possibility of defeat was hideous: 'Germans in England! Germans in Westminster dictating to us. Immense indemnities beside which that of France in '70 would be nothing. An enslaved generation.' He joined the army in September.

Everything seemed much simpler to Siegfried Sassoon. In this new life he might grow up, even if it was in a destroyed Europe. Courage now was 'the only thing that mattered'. He was advised by a hunting friend to keep away from the bone-headed rich in the regular cavalry and, following this advice, on 4 August (the day that Britain declared war on Germany) went to the Drill Hall in Lewes and enlisted as a trooper in the Sussex Yeomanry, a territorial regiment, signing on for four years. He was twenty-seven years old.

Robert Graves joined up in north Wales that week. Charles Sorley applied for a commission on 7 August and some weeks later, still completely untrained, saw his name in the *Gazette* as second lieutenant. He told an old Marlborough friend that 'since getting the commission I have become a terror ... I have succumbed. I am almost convinced that war is right and the tales told of German barbarism are true. I have become non-individual and British ...'

Not everyone was so euphoric. As the war began, Captain James Jack, a regular soldier who'd fought the Boers, observed the 'fine fettle' of his men and the conscientious reporting of reservists for duty. Jack thought them 'splendid fellows' but knew that they hadn't been trained even to march properly. He had a rush of depression: 'one can scarcely believe that five Great Powers – also styled "civilised" – are at war, and that the original spark causing the conflagration arose from the murder of one man and his wife ... It is quite mad as well as dreadful ... I personally loathe the outlook.' Captain Jack believed that it was necessary to fight, not only because of the treaty with an invaded Belgium but also from self-interest. If France were defeated and 'the Prussian war-lords held the ports just across the English Channel', Britain would be left 'friendless as well as despised for abandoning our present obligations'. Jack thought that it was lucky a Liberal government was in power. There would have been much more opposition to the war if the Conservatives had taken Britain in. As it was, only two members of the cabinet resigned.

There was little public hysteria. Few people had an inkling of what was coming, although Sir Edward Grey, the British Foreign Secretary, did have some premonition and prophesied a dimming of civilization. Foreigners noted a strange calm in London, one observing that a rare sign of change was an unarmed policeman placed outside the German embassy.

But the poets took wing. The first war poem appeared in *The Times* on 5 August, 'The Vigil' by Henry Newbolt, whose work had often celebrated manly virtues, courage and fair play. It wasn't spontaneous as Newbolt had written the lines some sixteen years before, but the patriotic surge led to a flood of verse. More than a hundred poems a day arrived at *The Times* offices during August, the paper printing those by (among others) Gosse, Laurence Binyon's 'For the

Fallen' ('They shall not grow old ...'), Kipling, the poet laureate Robert Bridges, and Hardy in September with 'Men Who March Away'. The Liberal politician C. F. G. Masterman, in charge of the new War Propaganda Bureau, encouraged this, perhaps to counter the enemy claim that Germany was fighting for culture against decadent France and philistine Britain. Germany fought back, with what's been estimated at over a million war poems written in August 1914.

That autumn Edmund Gosse, in an essay entitled 'War and Literature', welcomed a war that must make literary experiment and obscurity seem redundant and effete. 'War is the great scavenger of thought,' Gosse declared. 'It is the sovereign disinfectant, and its red stream of blood is the Condy's fluid [a disinfectant] that cleans out the stagnant pools and clotted channels of the intellect ...' Most writers still thought of chivalry, of warrior courage and sacrifice, of pure patriotism. It was left to John Masefield, in his poem 'August 1914', to imagine trenches winding across downland in a rare, prophetic glimpse of the western front.

By 17 August, Siegfried Sassoon was bored of training near Canterbury. 'Heaven knows how long it will last – 18 months some say – but you probably know better than I do!' he wrote to Marsh. He volunteered for service abroad, shocked that only 20 per cent of the Sussex Yeomanry had done the same. There was 'only one gent' in the ranks, a dull man, but Sassoon turned down the Colonel's suggestion that he should be an officer. It seemed 'a lifetime away' from the arts, from the Russian bass Chaliapin whom he'd heard in London. He felt out of touch. 'Are any of the Georgian poets carrying a carbine?'

One was trying hard to get his hands on a weapon. Rupert Brooke turned for help, as he often did, to Marsh at the Admiralty, and Eddie obliged, even though he dreaded his beautiful genius coming under fire. Julian Grenfell wanted to get back from South Africa; Ivor Gurney volunteered but was turned down because of his eyesight. Brooke should have taken heart; if you came from the right background, it was easy to become an officer.

Graves, Nichols and Sorley were commissioned and then sent to be trained. Owen contemplated the war from Bordeaux, watching the government of a beleaguered France. Edward Thomas, in Dymock, was with what the locals thought of as a strange enclave of poets. Edmund Blunden was still at school.

In August, in South Africa, Isaac Rosenberg had no surge of patriotism for the war or for the prospect of fighting. He hoped, however, that the huge change might melt, or purify, the old, iron-structured world.

> O! ancient crimson curse!
> Corrode, consume.
> Give back this universe
> Its pristine bloom.

Training for the front as a second lieutenant in the Suffolk Regiment, Charles Sorley wondered if he should have stayed a private as they had more freedom, although the officers' quarters were very comfortable. The soldiers seemed to be nicer to each other than his fellow pupils at Marlborough had been.

Sorley read some of the poems that flooded into the newspapers. Thomas Hardy's 'Men Who March Away' he thought was too jingoistic, unworthy of the author of *The Dynasts*. His own 'All the Hills and Vales Along', another evocation of marching, was darker, with its sense of an implacable natural world unmoved by the possibly doomed men. This resembled the Hardy that he admired and was quite different from Brooke's reassuring vision, written a few months later, of a foreign field enriched by the English dead.

Bored by training, Sorley affected not to mind who won the war as long as it ended quite soon; in fact 'for the joke of seeing an obviously just cause defeated, I hope Germany will win'. The enemy was much in his thoughts. He recalled the unashamed intellectual interest he had met in Jena, an aspect of Germany's spiritual superiority, even if the Germans had no insight into the minds of those who differed from them. His letters broke into German, to remind himself of the language's beauty. Sorley wanted to write to the family he'd known in Schwerin. His sonnet 'To Germany', about the tragic break-up of his Europe, laments how 'in each other's dearest ways we stand, / And hiss and hate. And the blind fight the blind.'

Robert Graves, who also received an almost instant commission, had stronger enemy links, with members of his mother's family fighting in the German army. Another connection, this time to the secretary of the Harlech Golf Club, got him into the Royal Welsh Fusiliers. At the regimental depot at Wrexham the puritanical young Graves was shocked by the attitude of the troops to girls and bored by the unheroic duty of guarding interned aliens in a camp at Lancaster.

During leave in October, by now itching to be at the front, he went to Charterhouse to see the boy on whom he had a crush. The school's strength came back, Graves writing that it was 'a grand place in spite of its efforts to cut its own throat and pollute its own cistern'. The casualty list began to feature old pupils; he reassured himself that he hadn't joined up for patriotic reasons but agreed, as another old Carthusian said, that 'France is the only place for a gentleman now.' Graves wouldn't be sent there until well into 1915, partly because of his scruffiness.

None of the poets were in the great retreat. The Germans activated the Schlieffen Plan – the strategy for a quick victory by means of an invasion of northern France and capture of Paris, keeping only a small force against Russia in the east until reinforcements could be sent across the continent after the defeat of the French. The French advanced too, into the territories that they'd lost to the Prussians in 1870, a suicidal scramble in red trousers and blue coats, the uniform of their earlier defeat. The result in the north was German soldiers surging so fast through Flanders and Picardy in the August heat that, as in 1940, their chief fear became one of exhaustion. There was a massacre of the French in Alsace and Lorraine. In Flanders, the French and the small British Expeditionary Force fell back.

Paris was saved in September at the battle of the Marne. This first victory for the Allies coincided with the German Chancellor Bethmann-Hollweg's September Programme of German war aims that embraced huge territorial gains, including industrial areas of France and Belgium, colonial conquests in Africa and a German-dominated customs union extending over much of Europe. Such ambition pointed to a long war.

Rupert Brooke, the first of the poets to see action, felt moved by the national mood; 'all these days', he told his love of the moment, the actress Cathleen Nesbitt, 'I have not been so near to tears. There was such tragedy, and such dignity, in the people.' He wasn't going to be fobbed off with six months' training or 'guarding a footbridge in Glamorgan'. Men were fighting in Belgium; 'if Armageddon is on', he told the writer J. C. Squire, 'I suppose one should be there.'

Brooke felt he should have special treatment. 'I wanted to use my intelligence,' he wrote. 'I can't help feeling I've got a brain. I thought there *must* be some organising work that demanded intelligence. But, on investigation, there isn't. At least, not for ages.' A staff appointment simply wouldn't do. So Marsh helped. A new unit, the Royal Naval Division, could have the poet; the brainchild of Winston Churchill, it was a military arm of the navy, rather like the Royal Marines. Marsh had spoken to Churchill, and Brooke and his friend the composer Denis Browne were seen off by Eddie from Charing Cross station on 27 September, for training on the east Kent coast. On 4 October, these virtually untrained men were marching through Dover to cheering crowds before embarking for France.

The First Lord of the Admiralty, determined to stop the Channel ports falling into the hands of the advancing enemy, had reached Antwerp himself on 3 October. Churchill found the Belgians exhausted and dispirited. On 4 October, the day Brooke left Dover, the Belgian Prime Minister, encouraged by Churchill's promise of British and French support, declared that to hold Antwerp was 'for us a national duty of the first order'.

Brooke and others sat waiting at Dunkirk for about eight hours and were told that they were going to Antwerp on a train that would very likely be attacked. The commanding officer declared that even if they survived the train journey their chances in the besieged city were slim. The poet wrote what he called 'last letters', one to Cathleen Nesbitt saying, 'My dear, it did bring home to me how very futile and unfinished life was. I felt so angry. I had to imagine, supposing I was killed ...' Soldiers kept questioning the inexperienced officers and, still mystified but undamaged, they reached Antwerp, to be greeted by cheering Belgians. Among the party, to show its select nature, was one of the Prime Minister's sons, Arthur Asquith. This was probably how Brooke had imagined war, or at least the beginning of war.

Then it changed. The German artillery had destroyed much of the outskirts of the city, and Brooke's brigade marched to an empty château which seemed 'infinitely peaceful and remote', where they stayed the night and came under shellfire. The next day they took up positions, relieving Belgian troops. No French reinforcements had come so it was three British brigades and the Belgians. Brooke noticed the effects of imminent danger; the 'rotten ones' seemed to take it worst, not the 'highly sensitive people', and 'for risks and nerves and fatigue I was all right. That's cheering.' He wondered what would happen if 'shrapnel was bursting on me and knocking the men round me to pieces'.

They worked on the trenches and waited. Direct hits on the station destroyed the detachment's baggage, including some manuscripts of Brooke's, and the château was blasted to bits. The strength of the German artillery wore down the fortifications. It was decided to withdraw the Royal Naval Division. The troops marched through a landscape lit up by burning petrol from a hit refinery and crossed the Scheldt where two German spies caught trying to blow up the bridge were shot. Pathetic refugees from an evacuated Antwerp clogged the roads, in terrified flight from the threat of German atrocities. Brooke was proud that he stayed in the column;

his friend Denis Browne was in agony from blisters, and several men dropped out.

Rupert Brooke had heard that German behaviour in the big cities had been reasonable; perhaps the Belgians need not have fled. He felt, however, that he'd been 'a witness to one of the greatest crimes of history. Has ever a nation been treated like that? And how can such a stain be wiped out?' This was different from how he'd thought war would be: 'half the youth of Europe' transformed 'through pain into nothingness, in the incessant mechanical slaughter of these modern battles'. By far the greatest number of casualties came from artillery fire, a descent of death from above, as if from heaven, with no chance of fighting it.

Brooke would meet this with sentiments from an earlier time, evoking thrill and patriotic duty to a mythical land that must have seemed remote, if beautiful, to most soldiers. First, however, he had to get back to England. They reached troop trains that took them to Ostend and then on 9 October through thick mist into Dover. After arriving in London, Brooke and Arthur Asquith went to the Admiralty, Marsh ushering them in to give a first-hand report to Churchill. Antwerp surrendered to the Germans on the night of 10 October.

Churchill defended the British intervention and the sending of untrained troops, claiming that it had held up the German advance to the Channel ports. But the First Lord was attacked, particularly by the Conservative press that loathed him because of his defection to the Liberals in 1904 and his eloquent support of the radical Budget of 1910. Antwerp damaged Churchill; the episode came to be seen as evidence of his lack of judgement, of his vainglorious impulsiveness: how these led others to suffer and be killed. Prime Minister Asquith, after hearing an account from his son, wrote of 'the wicked folly of it all'. Lloyd George castigated Churchill for behaving 'in a swaggering way', standing for photographers when shells were bursting near by and 'promoting his pals on the field of action'. In fact such was the shortage of British manpower that there had been no fully trained men available and Churchill had tried to keep the recruits out of the battle. The First Lord blamed the collapse on the Belgians and the French for not sending the promised reinforcements.

Brooke had some leave in Rugby with his mother and in London where he called on Harold Monro at the Poetry Bookshop and talked emotionally about what he had seen. Then he went back to camp, in Kent. Here the officers and men detested their commanding officer and a sense of incompetence and anger was darkened by cancelled leave when a German warship was seen off Yarmouth. Brooke's emotions rose, as if to smother possible despair. He told E. J. (Edward) Dent, an anti-war Cambridge friend, about what he was passionately proud of having seen: 'the sight of Belgium, and one or two other things make me realize more keenly than most people in England do – to judge from the papers – what we're in for, and what great sacrifices – active or passive – everyone must make'. To Cathleen Nesbit he wrote that 'the central purpose of my life, the aim and end of it, now, the thing God wants of me, is to get good at beating Germans'.

Rupert Brooke was sent to Portsmouth, then to Blandford where he joined the Hood Battalion as a sub-lieutenant in charge of a platoon. News came of old schoolfriends killed. On Christmas Day he assured an American friend that 'England is remarkable'; especially heartening was the way the 'intellectuals were doing their bit'. The adventure had given him a feeling of strange joy; 'apart from the tragedy – I've never felt happier or better in my life than those days in Belgium'.

He worked on five sonnets inspired by the war, poems that took him back to his boyhood in the huge chapel at Rugby, their patriotic emotion matching the idea that duty meant sacrifice. They were to be finished during leave at Rugby, soon after Christmas, and go back in spirit to the time of his enlistment, justifying the new emotional direction that the war had given to his life. England in these sonnets becomes a religion; one, 'The Soldier', was quoted by the Dean in St Paul's Cathedral, its solemnity quite different from earlier poems like 'Tiare Tahiti' or 'Heaven', a change from Marvel to Tennyson in these new times. Those bathing days at Grantchester come back in 'swimmers into cleanness leaping', but there's no hint of the erection that had impressed Virginia Woolf. Rupert Brooke is on parade. 'Half-men' and 'their dirty songs' had been left behind, with 'all the little emptiness of love' as well, in this 'release' from shame, showing Brooke's strange but lasting self-disgust. The sonnets were his triumph. For a few, they seemed tarnished from the start, unworthy of their Rupert; but to many the sentiments were an uplifting antidote to bad news or dreariness. Later, however, despite their smooth flow, they could sound discordant as the war news became worse.

Another officer reached the Continent some two days after Rupert Brooke. Julian Grenfell, the regular soldier, left Southampton at five o'clock on the morning of 6 October; by the 11th he was telling his mother that he was fifteen miles from the Germans and hoped to reach them the next day. The casualties were heavy among junior officers, but 'It's all the best fun one ever dreamed of – and up to now it has only wanted a few shells and a little noise to supply the necessary element of excitement.'

French and Belgian civilians cheered Grenfell and his men, making him think the locals were 'wonderful'. At first he felt lost in a fog of marching and counter-marching where 'only the Christian virtue of Faith emerges triumphant'. But 'it is all the most wonderful fun; better fun than one can ever imagine. I hope it goes on a nice long time ...' Grenfell was near Ypres. He had shot at the enemy. British cavalry were fighting German patrols but 'none of us know anything'.

The battle of Ypres began in the middle of October, with the Germans determined to recapture the city which they'd held earlier that month. Julian Grenfell's cavalry division was sent as infantry to the sector to the south-west of Ypres, near the Menin Road, and came under fire at close quarters, once suffering what he called 'the white flag dodge' when apparently surrendering Germans lured the British into an ambush. Men were killed alongside him; this wasn't yet trench warfare but still a war of movement, dashing through villages and across fields, fired on by snipers. Grenfell was disappointed when his regiment was taken out of the line.

His letters show that he'd found what he thought he'd always needed: something not only more exciting than boxing or polo but also a worthwhile part of his parents' hopes for him. The noise, Grenfell admitted, was terrible – the shelling and the explosions. Faltering was part of the challenge. 'One's nerves are really absolutely beaten down,' he admitted. 'I can understand why our infantry have to retreat sometimes,' although he'd been brought up to believe that 'the English infantry cannot retreat'. A captured German officer saluted him; 'I've never seen a man look so proud and resolute and smart and confident in his hour of bitterness. He made me feel terribly ashamed.' Grenfell saw it was nonsense to say that the war would end soon. The Germans were far from beaten – which he admired. 'One loves one's fellow man so much more when one is bent on killing him.'

The defence of Ypres held although the German onslaught did terrible damage to what was left of Britain's small professional army. Grenfell, back in the trenches, was given permission to go out on patrol alone. He described to his mother how he had shot several of the enemy at close quarters: one 'laughing and talking' so that 'I saw his teeth glisten against my foresight, and I pulled the trigger very steady.' He crawled back in daylight; half an hour later the Germans advanced slowly and 'we simply mowed them down; it was rather horrible ...'

The stalking expedition became part of his myth, added to by a medal for gallantry, the Distinguished Service Order, and the entry in his game-book, following '105 partridges' at Panshanger in early October: 'November 16th: 1 Pomeranian'; 'November 17th: 2 Pomeranians.' By then, since the battle of the Marne and the deliberate flooding of parts of Belgium from the River Yser and the Bruges canals, the line of trenches snaked in stalemate across from the English Channel through northern and eastern France down to the Swiss border. Antwerp, Ostend and Zeebrugge were occupied by the Germans. Calais and Dunkirk were still free, allowing the passage of troops and supplies from Britain.

Julian Grenfell's letters were printed anonymously in *The Times*, sent to the newspaper by his mother. The editor put an extract from one of them as a headline, to show that pre-war political disputes had ended in a unity of purpose and faith: 'Isn't it luck for me to have been born so as to be just the right age and just in the right place?'

Waiting to go out could be frustrating. But Robert Nichols found these months among the best of his life. Having enlisted in September 1914, he stayed in England for almost a year. He'd been commissioned in the Royal Field Artillery, his weak health making the medical an ordeal which he only just passed. His training took place in Surrey and Hampshire; later he saw this time as 'the happiest I have so far experienced'. His sad home life – his cold father and unstable mother – seemed bleak in contrast with 'the sky over me, beautiful horses, loyal companions in the men, an officer whom I intensely admire as my major, a definite and, in its way, noble creed – for I never thought of killing'. Nichols, however, thought that he would certainly be killed. This sense of death's proximity, and an involvement in an immense cause, inspired him, and other poets, to write with a new energy.

Siegfried Sassoon seemed not to share this excitement. The first months of his war were dull and disappointing. Riding during a break from learning how to dig trenches, he fell and broke his arm which had to be reset and gave pain: the dreary pain of peace. Sassoon, still a trooper in the Sussex Yeomanry, read about the battle of the Marne. By November, he was feeling depressed, latching on to rumours that they would go to France soon after Christmas. From the front, a hunting friend, an artillery officer, wrote about what 'Sig' could expect, that he shouldn't hurry to come out: 'Honestly & bar all rotting – <u>please</u> don't. We are in action now, and have been firing a lot the last 3 days – with considerable success we are told – in support of infantry.' There was time to write poems that were still charmingly Georgian, with titles like 'Today' or 'Storm and Rhapsody', to be collected in 1915 into another thin privately printed volume. Sassoon remembered these later as an escape from the war.

At Dymock in August 1914, a friend of Brooke hadn't yet discovered that he too was a poet. Although Edward Thomas disliked the nationalistic outpourings, in the press and among poets, he thought of enlisting, partly for money but also because of his love for a version of England, the land that he'd walked across rather than the proud imperial nation. Another poet, Ralph Hodgson, accused him of lacking patriotism. In November, while on one of their long walks, Thomas and Robert Frost were confronted by a gamekeeper who accused them of trespassing; the American stood up to the bully, but Thomas cowered, backed down and afterwards felt ashamed of his unmanly response. The shame stayed with him.

The poetry began in December. Some of Edward Thomas's themes resembled Frost's: landscape, the seasons, characters met on those long journeys, then his past life, the flickering of ghostly selves, regrets, echoes of childhood, in language that resembled speech. 'Up in the Wind', in December, was the first one, worked up from a prose piece; and there came a sense of a unique view, as in 'An Old Song II':

> A light divided the swollen clouds
> And lay most perfectly
> Like a straight narrow footbridge bright
> That crossed over the sea to me;
> And no one else in the whole world
> Saw the same sight ...

'The Combe', about a badger – 'that most ancient Briton of English beasts' – that was dug out and fed to the hounds, has a darkness suited to the constant news of death and the dilemma of whether or not to fight.

Harold Monro, to whom Thomas had sent his poems, wrote from the Poetry Bookshop to say he hadn't time to look at them. Robert Frost met some young soldiers in the Poetry Bookshop just before the war's first Christmas, one of whom – Robert Graves – approached him. The country was full of men in uniform. The American wondered if he too should join up; he wasn't an Englishman, yet the voyage home across the Atlantic was becoming unsafe because of German submarines.

Robert Frost's destiny became different to most of the poets he'd met in England before the war. The next year pitched Graves, who hadn't yet seen action, into one of the war's bloodiest early battles. It put Edward Thomas into uniform and took Frost back to New England, among the apple orchards, the poor farmers, the wooden barns and the clapboard houses that made his poetry. Edward Thomas's son Mervyn went with the Frosts to the United States, to escape the war. The American urged his friend Edward to come across as well so that they could farm together. So, at the year's end, the dream of a new life away from a disintegrating Europe was still there.

1914 POEMS

All the Hills and Vales Along

All the hills and vales along
Earth is bursting into song,
And the singers are the chaps
Who are going to die perhaps.
    O sing, marching men,
    Till the valleys ring again.
    Give your gladness to earth's keeping,
    So be glad, when you are sleeping.

Cast away regret and rue,
Think what you are marching to.
Little live, great pass.
Jesus Christ and Barabbas
Were found the same day.
This died, that went his way.
    So sing with joyful breath,
    For why, you are going to death.
    Teeming earth will surely store
    All the gladness that you pour.

Earth that never doubts nor fears,
Earth that knows of death, not tears,
Earth that bore with joyful ease
Hemlock for Socrates,
Earth that blossomed and was glad
'Neath the cross that Christ had,
Shall rejoice and blossom too
When the bullet reaches you.
    Wherefore, men marching
    On the road to death, sing!
    Pour your gladness on earth's head,
    So be merry, so be dead.

From the hills and valleys earth
Shouts back the sound of mirth,
Tramp of feet and lilt of song
Ringing all the road along.
All the music of their going,
Ringing swinging glad song-throwing,
Earth will echo still, when foot
Lies numb and voice mute.
 On, marching men, on
 To the gates of death with song.
 Sow your gladness for earth's reaping,
 So you may be glad, though sleeping.
 Strew your gladness on earth's bed,
 So be merry, so be dead.

CHARLES SORLEY

On Receiving News of the War: Cape Town

Snow is a strange white word.
No ice or frost
Have asked of bud or bird
For Winter's cost.

Yet ice and frost and snow
From earth to sky
This Summer land doth know,
No man knows why.

In all men's hearts it is.
Some spirit old
Hath turned with malign kiss
Our lives to mould.

Red fangs have torn His face.
God's blood is shed.
He mourns from His lone place
His children dead.

O! ancient crimson curse!
Corrode, consume.
Give back this universe
Its pristine bloom.

ISAAC ROSENBERG

Peace

Now, God be thanked Who has matched us with His hour,
And caught our youth, and wakened us from sleeping,
With hand made sure, clear eye, and sharpened power,
To turn, as swimmers into cleanness leaping,
Glad from a world grown old and cold and weary,
Leave the sick hearts that honour could not move,
And half-men, and their dirty songs and dreary,
And all the little emptiness of love!

Oh! we, who have known shame, we have found release there,
Where there's no ill, no grief, but sleep has mending,
Naught broken save this body, lost but breath;
Nothing to shake the laughing heart's long peace there
But only agony, and that has ending;
And the worst friend and enemy is but Death.

RUPERT BROOKE

The Dead

Blow out, you bugles, over the rich Dead!
There's none of these so lonely and poor of old,
But, dying, has made us rarer gifts than gold.
These laid the world away, poured out the red
Sweet wine of youth; gave up the years to be
Of work and joy, and that unhoped serene,
That men call age; and those who would have been,
Their sons, they gave, their immortality.

Blow, bugles, blow! They brought us, for our dearth,
Holiness, lacked so long, and Love, and Pain.
Honour has come back, as a king, to earth,
And paid his subjects with a royal wage;
And Nobleness walks in our ways again;
And we have come into our heritage.

RUPERT BROOKE

To Germany

You are blind like us. Your hurt no man designed,
And no man claimed the conquest of your land.
But gropers both through fields of thought confined
We stumble and we do not understand.
You only saw your future bigly planned,
And we, the tapering paths of our own mind,
And in each other's dearest ways we stand,
And hiss and hate. And the blind fight the blind.

When it is peace, then we may view again
With new-won eyes each other's truer form
And wonder. Grown more loving-kind and warm
We'll grasp firm hands and laugh at the old pain,
When it is peace. But until peace, the storm
The darkness and the thunder and the rain.

CHARLES SORLEY

The Soldier

If I should die, think only this of me:
That there's some corner of a foreign field
That is for ever England. There shall be
In that rich earth a richer dust concealed;
A dust whom England bore, shaped, made aware,
Gave, once, her flowers to love, her ways to roam,
A body of England's, breathing English air,
Washed by the rivers, blest by suns of home.

And think, this heart, all evil shed away,
A pulse in the eternal mind, no less
Gives somewhere back the thoughts by England given;
Her sights and sounds; dreams happy as her day;
And laughter, learnt of friends; and gentleness,
In hearts at peace, under an English heaven.

RUPERT BROOKE

The Combe

The Combe was ever dark, ancient and dark.
Its mouth is stopped with bramble, thorn, and briar;
And no one scrambles over the sliding chalk
By beech and yew and perishing juniper
Down the half precipices of its sides, with roots
And rabbit holes for steps. The sun of Winter,
The moon of Summer, and all the singing birds
Except the missel-thrush that loves juniper,
Are quite shut out. But far more ancient and dark
The Combe looks since they killed the badger there,
Dug him out and gave him to the hounds,
That most ancient Briton of English beasts.

EDWARD THOMAS

1915

ON 25 JANUARY 1915, from Shorncliffe camp, Charles Sorley wrote to an old schoolfriend, 'We don't seem to be winning, do we? It looks like an affair of years.'

The war was going badly for the Allies. The Russians were losing battles in the east. In the west, the Germans still occupied Belgium and much of northern France with its steel plants and coal and iron-ore mines. The British, however, shielded by the Channel, could look away from Flanders. Churchill, still First Lord of the Admiralty, came up with a plan to force the Dardanelles Straits with the aim of eventually taking Constantinople. This, he hoped, would knock Turkey, Germany's ally, out of the war, get supplies to (and wheat from) the hard-pressed Russians and open a way into east and central Europe. The Dardanelles, and Churchill, took Rupert Brooke to war again.

The Antwerp fiasco had shown the Royal Naval Division's lack of training, so Brooke was dispatched to Blandford camp in Dorset, with a gilded group that again included Arthur Asquith, the Prime Minister's son. Brooke sent his war sonnets, which had been finished just after Christmas, to *New Numbers*, the Dymock poets' magazine, where they were welcomed by the editor Wilfred Gibson. Reading the proofs, Brooke thought them 'rough': 'The Soldier' 'good', with 'The Dead' the best.

In February he stayed at 10 Downing Street, where the Prime Minister's daughter Violet ministered to his bad cold. Later that month the Royal Naval Division was inspected by the King and Brooke told the adoring Violet Asquith, 'I've never been quite so happy in my life, I think. Not quite so pervasively happy: like a stream flowing entirely to one end. I suddenly realise that the ambition of my life has been – since I was two – to go on a military expedition against Constantinople.' He and his comrades might fight on the plains of Troy or land on Lesbos and fire shells at Hero's Tower. The Division sailed from Avonmouth on 28 February 1915. By 1 March it had reached the rough waters of the Bay of Biscay.

Ivor Gurney enlisted in February 1915, hoping that the army might jolt him out of his mental confusion. In March, Isaac Rosenberg arrived back in London from South Africa. In the rush of leaving Cape Town, many of his paintings fell into the sea, having been insecurely attached to his luggage. Such a loss was a bad start to his journey towards war.

Rosenberg resumed his old Whitechapel life, with artists and writers, most of whom shunned the war. In May 1915, his pacifism led to a scornful poem about the German sinking of the ocean liner *Lusitania* with the loss of some 1,200 lives; in June the first draft of his verse drama 'Moses' shows how war transforms individual freedom into a kind of slavery. That month he posted copies of his privately printed poems entitled *Youth* (paid for by Marsh) to people whom he thought were influential.

Rosenberg told his new patron Sydney Schiff that the war was less to him than his own struggle to exist. He admitted that his literary technique was clumsy but wondered if he could get some writing about art published. There was now a new way of earning money: 'I am thinking of enlisting if they will have me, though it is against all my principles of justice – though I would be doing the most criminal thing a man can do – I am so sure my mother would not stand the shock that I don't know what to do.'

That summer another poet was in the East End, near where the Rosenbergs lived. Wilfred Owen, also thinking of enlisting ('*I now do most intensely want to fight*'), had been at a commercial fair in London on behalf of a Bordeaux scent manufacturer. Owen told his mother how, thinking 'a little ugliness would be refreshing', he'd walked down Fenchurch Street into Whitechapel Road. How wrong he'd been, for 'I never saw such beauty, in two hours, before that Saturday night. The Jews are a delightful people, at home, & that night I re-read some Old Testament with a marvellous great sympathy and cordiality.'

Owen's move towards war was linked to poetry. He told his mother in December 1914, from Bordeaux, 'Do you know what would hold me together on a battlefield? The sense that I was perpetuating the language in which Keats and the rest of them wrote! I do not know in what else England is greatly superior, or dearer to me, than another land and people ...' By February 1915, when dangers in the Channel still kept him in France, he was sure of his destiny. That month Owen wrote, again to his mother, always his greatest confidante, 'I seem without a footing in life; but I have one. It is as bold as any, and I have kept it for years. For years now. I was a boy when I first realized that the fullest life liveable was a Poet's.'

After the commercial fair, he went back to Bordeaux where the scent manufacturer asked him to be the firm's agent in the Middle East when the fighting ended. Owen resumed his tutoring work, thinking now of the Artists' Rifles or, if that failed, the Italian cavalry. His French pupils set off for an English boarding school in September 1915. On 21 October, aged twenty-two, Wilfred Owen joined the Artists' Rifles. In November he was in the Poetry Bookshop, buying a copy of the posthumous edition of Rupert Brooke's poems.

Brooke had become an even greater sensation in death than in life.

The sense of worthwhile sacrifice was needed. The retreat of August and September 1914, the death toll at Ypres, the stalemate in the trenches, had drained hope. Brooke's reputation had soared when Dean Inge of St Paul's read out the whole of 'The Soldier' in an Easter sermon that was delayed by a man standing up and speaking against the war. Inge took his text from the book of the prophet Isaiah ('thy dead men shall live, together with my dead body shall they arise. Awake and sing, ye that dwell in dust') and then moved on to Brooke's sonnet, the work (he said) of 'a young writer who would … take rank with our great poets'. The Dean praised this 'enthusiasm of a pure and elevated patriotism', even if it wasn't quite Christian to suggest that a soul survived only as 'a pulse in the eternal mind'.

Rupert Brooke, on Easter Sunday 1915, was already a sick man. He'd become ill, perhaps from sunstroke, in Egypt, where the expedition had stopped on its way to the Dardanelles. The force's commander, General Sir Ian Hamilton, came to see the poet, offering him a staff appointment – which Brooke refused. Hamilton told Brooke's senior officer, 'Mind you take care of him. His loss would be a national one,' and wrote in his diary of the invalid's 'knightly presence, stretched out there on the sand with the only world that counts at his feet'. Brooke ignored the suggestion that he stay in Egypt to recover and embarked with the force, resuming light duties on the ship.

A review in *The Times* praising the sonnets reached him and he thought it 'unperceptive'. Marsh sent an account of Dean Inge's sermon (the poet joked that he was sorry Inge didn't think him as good as Isaiah) and Henry James's appreciation of the poet's 'happy force and truth' that shone through some 'hackneyed' rhymes and clumsy phrasing. As the ship sailed among the Greek islands, officers read Homer and walked in olive groves on Skyros, with Brooke struggling to keep up. *New Numbers* was selling out, the paper shortage making further printing impossible. Brooke's lip began to swell, from a mosquito bite whose effect had been latent since Port Said. His temperature soared and he was transferred to a French hospital ship. Telegrams were sent. The Admiralty contacted his mother.

Rupert Brooke died on 23 April and was buried that night on Skyros. An obituary appeared in *The Times*, under Winston

Churchill's name but written by Marsh, that praised Brooke's 'very incomparable war sonnets', his sacrificial nobility and his courage. A last poem, found in manuscript, was more measured, more grimly foreboding: more appropriate also. By the end of June 1915, Brooke's battalion had lost eleven of its fifteen officers; only two of the five men who'd piled stones on the grave at Skyros were alive at the war's end. The attempt to force the Straits was disastrous, with troops pinned down on the beaches by the Turkish defenders after inept tactics and delay. The withdrawal began in December. Churchill's reputation sank. Hamilton was never given battle command again.

At first even those who'd scorned Brooke's emotional patriotism mourned: Maynard Keynes wept; D. H. Lawrence, who loathed the war, thought the death 'like madness'; the Dymock poets let loose verses by (among others) Abercrombie and Gibson; Robert Nichols, who'd met Brooke briefly, wrote an elegy ('Begin, O guns, your giant requiem / Over my lovely friend the Fiend has slain'). Eddie Marsh, devastated, began preparing *1914 and Other Poems*, to be published in June.

Then the fight against the myth began. There were early doubters among the poets. Isaac Rosenberg disliked the exultant language. To Sorley, Brooke's earlier, lighter poems were better, for the sonnets appeared too sentimental, 'far too obsessed with his own sacrifice', with 'preserving his own world'.

Phrases have lasted, if only as historical curiosities: 'swimmers into cleanness leaping', 'the red sweet wine of youth' and all of 'The Soldier', one of the most quoted poems of the twentieth century. Thomas Hardy had, in 'Drummer Hodge', written earlier of a British soldier who'd been killed in the Boer War and buried in 'an unknown plain' that 'will Hodge for ever be'; Brooke made the idea more sentimental, even strangely ideal. Throughout the sonnets there's a sense, as with many of the poets, that it's the land that is loved rather than contemporary England, or Britain, where Brooke had often felt unhappy and desperate.

In May, Edward Dent, who'd admired (perhaps loved) the earlier sardonic and witty Brooke, was publicly critical in the *Cambridge Magazine*. Dent – a sharp, cynical and brilliant Cambridge scholar of music – condemned the way that the 'romanticism he so hated came uppermost'. In August, E. M. Forster, who'd known Brooke at Cambridge, thought the sonnets 'inspired by romantic thoughts about war, not by his knowledge of it'. Brooke had been, Forster thought, 'essentially hard', although 'as charming an acquaintance as one could desire'. Like Dent, Forster looked back to the rebel, to the Fabian and admirer of Donne, the satirist and the cynic; how absurd it was that Brooke should go down as 'a sort of St Sebastian, haloed by the Dean of St Paul's, and hymned by the Morning Post as the evangelist of anti-Germanism ... how he would hate it, or rather laugh at it'. Such sentiments horrified Brooke's mother. Hadn't her son returned to her values, to the spirit of Rugby?

Julian Grenfell read 'The Soldier', telling his mother on 7 March 1915, 'I got Brooke's poem, and liked it very much – *awfully*', and sent her one of his own poems. Grenfell had mocked the idea of the Dardanelles expedition. Would it be better, he joked on 14 March, 'to disguise the Cavalry Corps as reindeer and to send them up by Norway, and in that way?' His brother Billy was now at the front, having joined up on 7 August 1914 and become a second lieutenant within a week.

Like Brooke, Julian Grenfell was offered a job on the staff of a general, a friend of his parents; like Brooke, he refused. While out of the line, he went to a boxing match in a town hall near Ypres, challenged anyone there, took on a huge man who'd been a professional boxer, and laid him out, giving his mother a detailed description of the fight. Grenfell was shocked by the destruction inflicted on Ypres and the high prices, amused that the girls said they had never had so much pleasure. Then came the trenches for five days, only fifty yards from the Germans, although quite quiet. 'You should have seen our men setting out from here for the trenches – absolutely radiant with excitement and joy to be getting back to the fight.'

He yearned for more solitary adventures: 'I wish they'd let me go and fight the Bosches on my own ...' At this time he wrote 'A Prayer for Those on the Staff', a mockery of those who were out of the fighting. A big attack was said to be planned for the spring. Grenfell doubted that the German lines could be broken. The Germans themselves had failed earlier at Ypres, with their greater artillery and shell power.

A diary begun in March shows more doubt than the letters: sex in Ypres ('a very hot day for me'), birdsong in the woods, leaving the front line ('although I like trenches, I love getting back'); fear after bombs and noise, so 'petrified' that he 'lost self-control'. Julian Grenfell's battalion stood in reserve near La Bassée during a British attack in March which led to 4,000 casualties. He went on leave to Paris in April, a 'divine' city whose people seemed so light-hearted, more natural than the British, real 'artists in fun': 'the biggest experience of New Things I've ever had in my life'. A photograph of a Parisian girl – Peggy – was found later in his wallet.

That month a German attack forestalled an Allied spring offensive, bringing the action that Grenfell had craved. The Germans used gas for the first time; French troops, terrified, fled; the next attack, against the Canadians, found the defenders prepared; and German awe at gas's success left them uncertain of what to do next. Shelling destroyed much of Ypres and reduced the salient held by the Allies. British counter-attacks kept the city from the Germans, at a high cost. The British had some 58,000 casualties against the German losses of 38,000.

Grenfell's detachment moved east of Poperinge, near Ypres, on 24 April. It was very cold at first before the weather changed to a warm spring. The poets learned those Flemish names – Poperinge, Vlamertinge, the Menin Road, Passchendaele – and also came to know the flat country where a mound or a sheltering coppice gave great advantage. On 29 April, Grenfell's brigade rested in a field near

Poperinge. Billeted in a farmhouse, he had 'wonderful sunny lazy days' sleeping outside to the sound of nightingales yet still 'longing to be up and doing something'. That day he noted, 'Wrote poem – Into Battle': a poem that glorifies courage, romantically linking it to the earth's spring and human and animal beauty. This was the passion of Grenfell's war. It seems true, then ends in ambiguity with a Death that alternately 'moans and sings'. Seeking her approval (for the war had ended Julian Grenfell's rebellion), he sent 'Into Battle' to his mother, saying that she could try to get the poem published. The regiment moved up to the second line of trenches, near Ypres.

Grenfell was on a small hill when he was knocked over by a shell blast. Recovering, he volunteered to take a message to the commander of troops in front of him, whom he approached, saying, 'You once gave me a mount with the Belvoir Hounds.' He was walking later on the same hill with a general when a shell landed near them and both were hit, Grenfell seriously.

From the casualty clearing station, he wrote a pencil note to his mother, saying that although the British had been 'practically wiped out' they had recovered ground. He had, he said, been wounded and 'my head and my skull is slightly cracked. But I'm getting on splendidly. I did awfully well.' He told her he was going to a hospital in Wimereux. 'Shall you be there?' In the event it was Boulogne. His parents came across, hope revived; then on 26 May Grenfell died, after moving his mother's hand to his lips. He had, she said, 'the most radiant smile' they had ever seen on his face. The next day, alongside the news of his death, *The Times* published 'Into Battle'.

As with Brooke, there was an outpouring. Julian Grenfell's poem and death were glorious to many, at that febrile time. Henry James thought 'Into Battle' 'extraordinarily living and breathing, ringing and stinging'. He told Grenfell's mother that he felt 'almost to have known your splendid son even though that ravaged felicity hasn't come my way … What great terrible and unspeakable things! But out of which, round his sublime young image, a noble and exquisite legend will flower.' Maurice Baring, novelist and friend of the family, had his sonnet 'Julian Grenfell' published in *The Times* in June. Lord Desborough, the poet's father, tried to direct the mourning away from too literary an atmosphere, as if to be a poet was not enough, even a little shameful. His son, Desborough said, 'did not look upon himself as a poet, but as essentially as a fighting man, boxer, steeple-chase rider and lover of animals ... He used to write verses when the spirit moved him, and very often threw them away. Whether he would have taken up writing seriously when he grew older and less absorbed in outdoor pursuits it is impossible to say.'

Charles Sorley was in France by June, writing that 'it is like a picnic' and 'the weather is of the best'. Out of the line, he found a strange calm: 'I have never felt more restful.' As if balancing between his two countries, he asked for Richard Jefferies's *Life in the Fields* and for Goethe's *Faust*. England took on a mythical aspect, one that he didn't want to see tarnished. Sorley planned to travel after the war, perhaps to Mexico, Russia or the Balkans: 'in England never. England remains the dream, the background: at once the memory and the ideal.' War had freed him, he thought; Oxford, the planned next stage, would have prolonged the imprisonment.

From the trenches, Sorley told the Master of Marlborough on 25 June that 'we have seen as yet neither horrors, nor heroism, nor suffering. The test still lies ahead.' The French locals were kind, 'almost German in their hospitality'; and the enemy was only a hundred yards away. Sorley, not yet twenty, grew harder in this 'incredibly peaceful' existence. He forgot dead comrades 'in a week', considered visiting generals to be 'bloody fools' and was thankful when a fallen body was dead for it wouldn't have to be carried in. He saved two lives during raids. By September he was a junior captain, about to take part in the battle of Loos.

Edward Thomas reviewed Rupert Brooke's *1914 and Other Poems* in June. He wrote that the book showed wonderfully 'the thought, the aspiration, the indignation of youth', with the last poems implying that a safe reputation would come only with death, as if their author knew he must go on striving. He didn't criticize the book's sense of what he called 'the very widespread idea that self sacrifice is the highest self indulgence'. He felt diminished by what the other poet had seen of the war. After all, as he told Frost, he himself hadn't 'enlisted or fought the keeper'.

Work on a commissioned life of the eighteenth-century general the Duke of Marlborough, a miserable grind, deepened Thomas's gloom. This volume was thought to have propaganda value through its reminder of Marlborough's victories in northern France and may have rubbed into Thomas his absence from the trenches. His poems, now coming in profusion, depicted the war at home, the changes it brought – 'In Memoriam (Easter, 1915)' and 'A Private' – and his sense of being out of it, as in 'The Owl' where the poet shelters in an inn, leaving 'soldiers and poor' outside, 'unable to rejoice'. 'The Unknown Bird' has the belief that he could reach new lands: 'I alone could hear him'. 'Home' (the first of two poems with that title) portrays the poet as a superfluous man.

While finishing another commission – *This England: An Anthology from her Writers* – Thomas wrote 'Lob', about the immortal countryman. It was set in Wiltshire, where he had walked in search of Richard Jefferies, and was not nationalistic but a romantic view of a vanishing world. The old life, or Thomas's idea of it, was what he was mourning, as in 'In Memoriam (Easter, 1915)', more than the war dead. In *This England* Thomas put two poems of his own – 'The Manor Farm' and 'Haymaking' – under the pseudonym of Edward Eastaway. Now he was a published poet. A trip to the Cotswolds in July may have banished thoughts of joining Frost in New Hampshire.

Edward Thomas enlisted in the Artists' Rifles in July 1915. He declared he was fighting for the landscape, for the English earth, as in 'For These', completed the day he passed his medical examination ('An acre of land between the shore and the hills, / Upon a ledge that shows my kingdoms three, / The lovely visible earth and sky and sea, / Where what the curlew needs not, the farmer tills …').

Siegfried Sassoon left the Yeomanry in April, to take a commission in the Royal Welsh Fusiliers, fixed for him by a neighbour in Kent. He went that summer for officer training to Cambridge, where he shared rooms with a charming fellow recruit, David Thomas – with whom he fell in love. The war scarcely impinges on Sassoon's poems of late 1914 and early 1915 which include a retired huntsman's long farewell to a fading world. At Cambridge he met Edward Dent, who found the young poet 'curious' and the possessor of 'the vitality and artistic enthusiasm of his race and without their bad qualities'. Dent was not impressed by Sassoon's privately printed verses.

The one war poem he wrote at this time – 'Absolution' – has a sense of Brooke's sonnets. The war came closer at the end of October when Sassoon's brother Hamo, an officer in the Royal Engineers and Siegfried's ally because of his homosexuality, was killed at Gallipoli. Sassoon left with his regiment for France on 17 November. In his diary on 28 November he wrote, 'Walked into Bethune for tea with Robert Graves, a young poet, Captain in the Third Battalion and very much disliked.'

Graves had been out since May 1915, just too late for a failed attack at Aubers Ridge. His battalion of the Royal Welsh Fusiliers was moved to a bad sector near Cuinchy, by some brickstacks where there was constant mining and sniping. In June, in training for Loos, he was near Vermelles, supposedly out of the line yet often shelled. The sceptical Graves, awed by the proximity of death, took Holy Communion in Vermelles church. By the time he met Sassoon, Graves had been through the battle of Loos and, although some nine years younger, could play the old soldier. When Sassoon showed him some poems, Graves said that these would change after his new friend had seen action. Both reported the meeting to their friend Eddie Marsh, each scornful of the other's verses.

Edmund Blunden, older than Graves but still only eighteen, had joined up in August 1915, cycling into Chichester to enlist in the Royal Sussex Regiment. It must have seemed natural to follow other boys leaving Christ's Hospital who were doing the same; fighting, and if necessary dying, for your country was part of the public school creed of duty. Such was the shortage of officers that within a fortnight Blunden had a commission, although his only military experience had been in the school Cadet Corps. He would not go to France until the spring of 1916. First there was training at Weymouth in Dorset and Shoreham in Kent (from where he'd walk the forty miles to his parents' home at Yalding) and in Ireland. Still constantly writing poetry, as he'd done at school, Blunden continued to look to rural England for inspiration. France and Belgium had hitherto lived for him only on maps or in books. He wrote later that 'I was not anxious to go.'

For the Allies, the year brought few successes. The Dardanelles turned out to be a disaster. The small British Expeditionary Force – Britain's regular army – had suffered heavy casualties in the west, straining manpower which depended more and more on volunteers. Attacks quickly became bogged down at Aubers Ridge and Festubert. A shell shortage crippled artillery support.

The battle of Loos, pushed by the French General Joffre, who wanted a sign of obvious British involvement, was an attempt to break the German line, across a jagged, easily defended landscape of slag heaps, coal mines and winding towers; Haig, then commander of the British First Army, opposed the plan. There was success at first, with some ground gained, then came the lack of shells, fierce enemy counter-attacks and exhaustion. The British had some 60,000 casualties, including three generals, against the German 20,000. The Allies had used gas for the first time, but wind had spoilt its effect. Bad weather set in after 13 October, preventing further attacks.

An experienced British officer identified flaws. To him, Gallipoli was 'the vital spot' (by this time its failure was clear) and Loos 'a waste', an attack on the Germans at their strong point to please the French. The Old Army, the BEF, had shown its mettle; and the new volunteers were brave. However, 'raw enthusiasts are ideal for a dashing attack, but when they've got to the limit they don't know what to do next; seasoned troops do'.

German counter-attacks throughout the war were startlingly effective. Lack of training was evident. Graves and Brooke were thrown in as officers much too soon; Blunden and Julian Grenfell's brother Billy got their commissions in weeks, even days; in David Jones's *In Parenthesis*, the officer, Mr Jenkins, is only twenty. Loos had been meant to restore the war of movement, to break out of the solidified trenches, and had failed. The experienced observer saw 'mismanagement at the top, inefficiency in the middle, want of training at the bottom'. To these Robert Graves added the superiority of German equipment: more shells, more artillery, better gas helmets, more telescopic sights for sniping. British flares were so bad that the enemy laughed at them.

Graves had waited in the trenches at Loos. The enemy was 300 yards away; shells crashed around them and they could hear the groans of the wounded and dying. He found a water bottle full of rum and drank about half a pint which soothed his nerves. Comrades fell near him; but he wasn't sent over the top. That night the dead and wounded were brought in, while the Germans humanely held fire. Gas was launched, and a patrol sent out to observe its effects was blown to bits. Graves drank about a bottle of whisky a day to keep his nerves from breaking. On 3 October, what was left of his unit withdrew from the front line.

Charles Sorley wrote to a friend two days later, 'on the eve of our crowning hour'. Earlier that year he'd written 'Such, Such is Death' and 'Saints Have Adored the Lofty Soul of You'. The end he saw as 'a merciful putting away of what has been': 'no triumph, no defeat': certainly now familiar as 'we see your straight and steadfast signpost there'. Sorley dreaded pain and showing himself to be a coward; to his father he said that he was sure the Germans were on their way home, although the journey would be a long one, through rain, dirt and cold. On 13 October, the British launched another attack. Sorley was killed by a sniper as he led his troops forward. The manuscript of 'When You See Millions of the Mouthless Dead' was found on his body – the sort of poem that Rupert Brooke might have written if he'd seen more of the war.

Loos needed a scapegoat. Sir John French, the BEF's commander, was called home, to be replaced by Haig. The battle broke another poet. Robert Nichols had been writing poetry since joining the army, imitating Brooke with 'Five Sonnets upon Imminent Departure', which were printed in *The Times* in May. He reached France in August 1915, as an officer in the Royal Field Artillery, some days after his elegy to Rupert Brooke had appeared. A publisher accepted Nichols's first collection, *Invocation*, at the end of August. He was now launched as a war poet.

Twenty-five years later he described how he'd felt, how he'd looked at death: 'exaltation. Beyond was a blank. How can a boy consider what he can't imagine?' Nichols thought of one 'decisive' image: 'the descent of a great beam of light' or resplendence. His poetry looked back to a scene in Dedham Vale near the family house, and the sound of church bells across the fields, 'a golden note, so calm so clear' in an ordered, historic England.

Nichols found incompetence rather than glory in France. Artillery was placed too near the trenches ('sheer foolery') so the shells might not even clear the British front line and the attacking enemy couldn't be fired on for fear of hitting British defenders. He thought of his feelings about the Germans as Loos began. Nichols had little hatred for them, rather a determination to see that British tolerance should outlast Prussian militarism; he was also fighting, he felt, for the men alongside him. He tried to catch this in the poem 'Battery Moving Up from Rest Camp'. Then his nerve broke in the bombardment and 'very hard fighting' around his battery, making him useless, although his commanding officer wrote that 'your heart was as big as a lion's'. He was just twenty-two. Nichols's poems of the war, such as 'The Day's March' and 'Thanksgiving', were based on his experience at Loos.

He went back to hospitals in England. In October he was diagnosed as suffering from 'neurasthenia'; this wasn't new for he'd had previous mental collapses. But news of the death of a friend that autumn seemed to make his nerves worse, with insomnia and irrational excitement. Nichols had also caught syphilis, either before going to France or after his return. His good looks and his personality – showing desperation, posturing romanticism, hysteria and sexual energy – became inseparable from an impassioned view of his poetic destiny. Later in the war, he was seen as a leader of the new soldier poets. His first book, *Invocation*, may have made little impression; the 1917 collection *Ardours and Endurances*, however, led to the idea (admittedly short-lived) that Robert Nichols was a genius.

The army, at least initially, brought exhilaration to most of the poets. Ivor Gurney said that after joining the Gloucestershire Regiment in February 1915 he was in a better state of mind than he had been for years. Gurney felt later that it would have been much worse not to have fought, cherishing particularly the comradeship of his fellow soldiers as an affirmation of human goodness. In April 1915, he said he couldn't have been happier anywhere else, although life was hard. He declared that autumn, 'I cannot remember a time when my health was better ...'

Gurney read Edward Thomas's review of Rupert Brooke's poems. He doubted if the poet would have improved had he lived, for the lines had come much too quickly from events not fully experienced. 'Rupert Brooke soaked it in quickly and gave it out with as great ease.' His own 'To the Poet Before Battle', written in July or early August, is Brooke-like. But Gurney read adventurously, ranging far. 'Have you read the Undying Past by Sudermann ...?' he asked a friend about a book by the nationalistic German writer Hermann Sudermann. 'I doubt whether any of our young men could touch it. It is German ... everything so intense and volcanic and half-mad ...'

Edward Thomas felt happy at Hare Hall Camp in Essex – where

Wilfred Owen had also been sent for training, although there's no record of them meeting. Thomas wrote 'Cock-Crow' soon after his enlistment in July, comparable to Hardy's 'Men Who March Away'. At Hare Hall, he said that he'd never been 'so well'. His first poem in the camp was 'There's Nothing Like the Sun' about the sun's kindness to all things that it touched, except snow, ending with the words 'till we are dead'. Owen wrote similarly in 'Futility', during the last spring of his life. 'This is No Case of Petty Right or Wrong', which Thomas wrote in December 1915, has 'God save England' not as a cry that might be made by 'one fat patriot' but as a celebration of the land: 'an England beautiful'.

Isaac Rosenberg joined the army not from pure patriotism but at least partly to bring financial help to his family. In October 1915, when he enlisted at a Whitechapel recruiting station, he felt that he was doing 'a criminal thing' in becoming part of the killing. When he told his mother he had joined up, she was upset. He wanted to escape poverty and, as he told Marsh in 1918, 'I thought if I'd join there would be a separate allowance for my mother.' This was never paid, although by January 1916 his mother was receiving half of Isaac's wages. Rosenberg had hoped not to be part of the fighting machine. But he was too short for the Royal Army Medical Corps and had to join a so-called bantam battalion that was part of the Suffolk Regiment.

The war of Ivor Gurney and Isaac Rosenberg was the private soldier's war, with worse food, worse conditions, worse pay, than the other poets who were officers. But officers went first over the top and were more likely to be killed. Rosenberg was bullied because of his Jewishness. At first, however, as with Gurney, the training and exercise made him healthier than he'd been in the Whitechapel smog. His apocalyptic imagination turned to the future, in the December poem 'Marching'. The vision is of machine-inflicted carnage, of a mythical war – the field of Mars and charging cavalry – turned into 'an iron cloud' that rains 'immortal darkness'. This wasn't the poetry through which the public, or most poets, saw the war in 1915. The dominant spirits were still those of Brooke and Grenfell. Sassoon hadn't yet written his satires. Owen wasn't yet in France. The huge offensive of the next year, 1916, would change everything.

1915 POEMS

The Unknown Bird

Three lovely notes he whistled, too soft to be heard
If others sang; but others never sang
In the great beech-wood all that May and June.
No one saw him: I alone could hear him
Though many listened. Was it but four years
Ago? or five? He never came again.

Oftenest when I heard him I was alone,
Nor could I ever make another hear.
La-la-la! he called, seeming far-off –
As if a cock crowed past the edge of the world,
As if the bird or I were in a dream.
Yet that he travelled through the trees and sometimes
Neared me, was plain, though somehow distant still
He sounded. All the proof is – I told men
What I had heard.

I never knew a voice,
Man, beast, or bird, better than this. I told
The naturalists; but neither had they heard
Anything like the notes that did so haunt me,
I had them clear by heart and have them still.
Four years, or five, have made no difference. Then
As now that La-la-la! was bodiless sweet:
Sad more than joyful it was, if I must say
That it was one or other, but if sad
'Twas sad only with joy too, too far off
For me to taste it. But I cannot tell
If truly never anything but fair
The days were when he sang, as now they seem.
This surely I know, that I who listened then,

Happy sometimes, sometimes suffering
A heavy body and a heavy heart,
Now straightway, if I think of it, become
Light as that bird wandering beyond my shore.

EDWARD THOMAS

Absolution

The anguish of the earth absolves our eyes
Till beauty shines in all that we can see.
War is our scourge; yet war has made us wise,
And, fighting for our freedom, we are free.

Horror of wounds and anger at the foe,
And loss of things desired; all these must pass.
We are the happy legion, for we know
Time's but a golden wind that shakes the grass.

There was an hour when we were loth to part
From life we longed to share no less than others.
Now, having claimed this heritage of heart,
What need we more, my comrades and my brothers?

SIEGFRIED SASSOON

To the Poet Before Battle

Now, youth, the hour of thy dread passion comes;
Thy lovely things must all be laid away;
And thou, as others, must face the riven day
Unstirred by rattle of the rolling drums,
Or bugles' strident cry. When mere noise numbs
The sense of being, the sick soul doth sway,
Remember thy great craft's honour, that they may say
Nothing in shame of poets. Then the crumbs
Of praise the little versemen joyed to take
Shall be forgotten; then they must know we are,
For all our skill in words, equal in might
And strong of mettle as those we honoured; make
The name of poet terrible in just war,
And like a crown of honour upon the fight.

IVOR GURNEY

Home

Often I had gone this way before:
But now it seemed I never could be
And never had been anywhere else;
'Twas home; one nationality
We had, I and the birds that sang,
One memory.

They welcomed me. I had come back
That eve somehow from somewhere far:
The April mist, the chill, the calm,
Meant the same thing familiar
And pleasant to us, and strange too,
Yet with no bar.

The thrush on the oaktop in the lane
Sang his last song, or last but one;
And as he ended, on the elm
Another had but just begun
His last; they knew no more than I
The day was done.

Then past his dark white cottage front
A labourer went along, his tread
Slow, half with weariness, half with ease;
And, through the silence, from his shed
The sound of sawing rounded all
That silence said.

EDWARD THOMAS

In Memoriam (Easter, 1915)

The flowers left thick at nightfall in the wood
This Eastertide call into mind the men,
Now far from home, who, with their sweethearts, should
Have gathered them and will do never again.

EDWARD THOMAS

Fragment

I strayed about the deck, an hour, to-night
Under a cloudy moonless sky; and peeped
In at the windows, watched my friends at table,
Or playing cards, or standing in the doorway,
Or coming out into the darkness. Still
No one could see me.

I would have thought of them
– Heedless, within a week of battle – in pity,
Pride in their strength and in the weight and firmness
And link'd beauty of bodies, and pity that
This gay machine of splendour 'ld soon be broken,
Thought little of, pashed, scattered ...

Only, always,
I could but see them – against the lamplight – pass
Like coloured shadows, thinner than filmy glass,
Slight bubbles, fainter than the wave's faint light,
That broke to phosphorous out in the night,
Perishing things and strange ghosts – soon to die
To other ghosts – this one, or that, or I.

RUPERT BROOKE

Thanksgiving

Amazement fills my heart to-night,
Amaze and awful fears;
I am a ship that sees no light,
But blindly onward steers.

Flung toward heaven's toppling rage,
Sunk between steep and steep,
A lost and wondrous fight I wage
With the embattled deep.

I neither know nor care at length
Where drives the storm about;
Only I summon all my strength
And swear to ride it out.

Yet give I thanks; despite these wars,
My ship – though blindly blown,
Long lost to sun or moon or stars –
Still stands up alone.
I need no trust in borrowed spars;
My strength is yet my own.

ROBERT NICHOLS

The Owl

Downhill I came, hungry, and yet not starved;
Cold, yet had heat within me that was proof
Against the North wind; tired, yet so that rest
Had seemed the sweetest thing under a roof.

Then at the inn I had food, fire, and rest,
Knowing how hungry, cold, and tired was I.
All of the night was quite barred out except
An owl's cry, a most melancholy cry.

Shaken out long and clear upon the hill,
No merry note, nor cause of merriment,
But one telling me plain what I escaped
And others could not, that night, as in I went.

And salted was my food, and my repose,
Salted and sobered too, by the bird's voice
Speaking for all who lay under the stars,
Soldiers and poor, unable to rejoice.

EDWARD THOMAS

Prayer for Those on the Staff

Fighting in mud, we turn to Thee
In these dread times of battle, Lord,
To keep us safe, if so may be,
From shrapnel, snipers, shell and sword.

Yet not on us – (for we are men
Of meaner clay, who fight in clay) –
But on the Staff, the Upper Ten,
Depends the issue of the Day.

The Staff is working with its Brains
While we are sitting in the trench;
The Staff the universe ordains
(Subject to Thee and General French).

God, help the Staff – especially
The young ones, many of them sprung
From our high aristocracy;
Their task is hard, and they are young.

O Lord, who mad'st all things to be,
And madest some things very good
Please keep the Extra A.D.C.
From horrid scenes, and sights of blood …

See that his eggs are newly laid,
Not tinged – as some of them – with green;
And let no nasty draughts invade
The windows of his limousine.

When he forgets to buy the bread,
When there are no more minerals,
Preserve his smooth well-oilèd head
From wrath of costive Generals.

O Lord, who mad'st all things to be,
And hatest nothing thou has made,
Please keep the Extra A.D.C.
Out of the sun and in the shade.

JULIAN GRENFELL

A Private

This ploughman dead in battle slept out of doors
Many a frozen night, and merrily
Answered staid drinkers, good bedmen, and all bores:
'At Mrs Greenland's Hawthorn Bush,' said he,
'I slept.' None knew which bush. Above the town,
Beyond 'The Drover', a hundred spot the down
In Wiltshire. And where now at last he sleeps
More sound in France – that, too, he secret keeps.

EDWARD THOMAS

Into Battle

(Flanders, April 1915)

The naked earth is warm with spring,
And with green grass and bursting trees
Leans to the sun's gaze glorying,
And quivers in the loving breeze;
And Life is Colour and Warmth and Light,
And a striving evermore for these;
And he is dead who will not fight;
And who dies fighting, has increase.

The fighting man shall from the sun
Take warmth, and life from the glowing earth;
Speed with the light-foot winds to run,
And with the trees to newer birth;
And find, when fighting shall be done,
Great rest, and fullness after dearth.

All the bright company of Heaven
Hold him in their high comradeship –
The Dog-star, and the Sisters Seven,
Orion's Belt and sworded hip.

The woodland trees that stand together,
They stand to him each one a friend;
They gently speak in the windy weather;
They guide to valley and ridge's end.

The kestrel hovering by day,
And the little owls that call by night,
Bid him be swift and keen as they,
As keen of sound, as swift of sight.

The blackbird sings to him, 'Brother, brother,
If this be the last song you shall sing,
Sing well, for you will not sing another;
Brother, sing!'

In dreary doubtful, waiting hours,
Before the brazen frenzy starts,
The horses show him nobler powers;
O patient eyes, courageous hearts!

And when the burning moment breaks,
And all things else are out of mind,
And joy of battle only takes
Him by the throat, and makes him blind,

Through joy and blindness he shall know
Not caring much to know, that still
Nor lead nor steel shall reach him, so
That it be not the Destined Will.

The thundering line of battle stands,
And in the air Death moans and sings;
But Day shall clasp him with strong hands,
And Night shall fold him in soft wings.

JULIAN GRENFELL

Battery Moving Up to a New Position
from Rest Camp: Dawn

Not a sign of life we rouse
In any square close-shuttered house
That flanks the road we amble down
Toward far trenches through the town.

The dark, snow-slushy, empty street ...
Tingle of frost in brow and feet ...
Horse-breath goes dimly up like smoke.
No sound but the smacking stroke

As a sergeant flings each arm
Out and across to keep him warm,
And the sudden splashing crack
Of ice-pools broken by our track.

More dark houses, yet no sign
Of life ... And axle's creak and whine ...
The splash of hooves, the strain of trace ...
Clatter: we cross the market place.

Deep quiet again, and on we lurch
Under the shadow of a church:
Its tower ascends, fog-wreathed and grim;
Within its aisles a light burns dim ...

When, marvellous! from overhead,
Like abrupt speech of one deemed dead,
Speech-moved by some Superior Will,
A bell tolls thrice and then is still.

And suddenly I know that now
The priest within, with shining brow,
Lifts high the small round of the Host.
The server's tingling bell is lost

In clash of the greater overhead.
Peace like a wave descends, is spread,
While watch the peasants' reverent eyes …

The bell's boom trembles, hangs, and dies.

O people who bow down to see
The Miracle of Calvary,
The bitter and the glorious,
Bow down, bow down and pray for us.

Once more our anguished way we take
Towards our Golgotha, to make
For all our lovers sacrifice.
Again the troubled bell tolls thrice.

And slowly, slowly, lifted up
Dazzles the overflowing cup.

O worshipping, fond multitude,
Remember us too, and our blood.

Turn hearts to us as we go by,
Salute those about to die,
Plead for them, the deep bell toll:
Their sacrifice must soon be whole.

Entreat you for such hearts as break
With the premonitory ache
Of bodies, whose feet, hands, and side,
Must soon be torn, pierced, crucified.

Sue for them and all of us
Who the world over suffer thus,
Who scarce have time for prayer indeed,
Who only march and die and bleed.

*

The town is left, the road leads on,
Bluely glaring in the sun,
Toward where in the sunrise gate
Death, honour, and fierce battle wait.

ROBERT NICHOLS

Marching – As Seen from the Left File

My eyes catch ruddy necks
Sturdily pressed back, –
All a red brick moving glint.
Like flaming pendulums, hands
Swing across the khaki –
Mustard-coloured khaki –
To the automatic feet.

We husband the ancient glory
In these bared necks and hands.
Not broke is the forge of Mars;
But a subtler brain beats iron
To shoe the hoofs of death,
(Who paws dynamic air now).
Blind fingers loose an iron cloud
To rain immortal darkness
On strong eyes.

ISAAC ROSENBERG

Such, Such is Death

Such, such is Death: no triumph: no defeat:
Only an empty pail, a slate rubbed clean,
A merciful putting away of what has been.

And this we know: Death is not Life effete,
Life crushed, the broken pail. We who have seen
So marvellous things know well the end not yet.

Victor and vanquished are a-one in death:
Coward and brave: friend, foe. Ghosts do not say,
'Come, what was your record when you drew breath?'
But a big blot has hid each yesterday
So poor, so manifestly incomplete.
And your bright Promise, withered long and sped,
Is touched, stirs, rises, opens and grows sweet
And blossoms and is you, when you are dead.

CHARLES SORLEY

Cock-Crow

Out of the wood of thoughts that grows by night
To be cut down by the sharp axe of light, –
Out of the night, two cocks together crow,
Cleaving the darkness with a silver blow:
And brought before my eyes twin trumpeters stand,
Heralds of splendour, one at either hand,
Each facing each as in a coat of arms:
The milkers lace their boots up at the farms.

EDWARD THOMAS

'When You See Millions of the Mouthless Dead'

When you see millions of the mouthless dead
Across your dreams in pale battalions go,
Say not soft things as other men have said,
That you'll remember. For you need not so.
Give them not praise. For, deaf, how should they know
It is not curses heaped on each gashed head?
Nor tears. Their blind eyes see not your tears flow.
Nor honour. It is easy to be dead.
Say only this, 'They are dead.' Then add thereto,
'Yet many a better one has died before.'
Then, scanning all the o'ercrowded mass, should you
Perceive one face that you loved heretofore,
It is a spook. None wears the face you knew.
Great death has made all his for evermore.

CHARLES SORLEY

The Redeemer

Darkness: the rain sluiced down; the mire was deep;
It was past twelve on a mid-winter night,
When peaceful folk in beds lay snug asleep;
There, with much work to do before the light,
We lugged our clay-sucked boots as best we might
Along the trench; sometimes a bullet sang,
And droning shells burst with a hollow bang;
We were soaked, chilled and wretched, every one;
Darkness; the distant wink of a huge gun.

I turned in the black ditch, loathing the storm;
A rocket fizzed and burned with blanching flare,
And lit the face of what had been a form
Floundering in mirk. He stood before me there;
I say that He was Christ; stiff in the glare;
And leaning forward from His burdening task,
Both arms supporting it; His eyes on mine
Stared from the woeful head that seemed a mask
Of mortal pain in Hell's unholy shine.

No thorny crown, only a woollen cap
He wore – an English soldier, white and strong,
Who loved his time like any simple chap,
Good days of work and sport and homely song;
Now he has learned that nights are very long,
And dawn a watching of the windowed sky.
But to the end, unjudging, he'll endure
Horror and pain, not uncontent to die
That Lancaster on Lune may stand secure.

He faced me, reeling in his weariness,
Shouldering his load of planks, so hard to bear.
I say that He was Christ, who wrought to bless
All groping things with freedom bright as air,
And with His mercy washed and made them fair.
Then the flame sank, and all grew black as pitch,
While we began to struggle along the ditch;
And someone flung his burden in the muck,
Mumbling: 'O Christ Almighty, now I'm stuck!'

SIEGFRIED SASSOON

This is No Case of Petty Right or Wrong

This is no case of petty right or wrong
That politicians or philosophers
Can judge. I hate not Germans, nor grow hot
With love of Englishmen, to please newspapers.
Beside my hate for one fat patriot
My hatred of the Kaiser is love true: –
A kind of god he is, banging a gong.
But I have not to choose between the two,
Or between justice and injustice. Dinned
With war and argument I read no more
Than in the storm smoking along the wind
Athwart the wood. Two witches' cauldrons roar.
From one the weather shall rise clear and gay;
Out of the other an England beautiful
And like her mother that died yesterday.
Little I know or care if, being dull,
I shall miss something that historians
Can rake out of the ashes when perchance
The phoenix broods serene above their ken.
But with the best and meanest Englishmen
I am one in crying, God save England, lest
We lose what never slaves and cattle blessed.
The ages made her that made us from dust:
She is all we know and live by, and we trust
She is good and must endure, loving her so:
And as we love ourselves we hate her foe.

EDWARD THOMAS

1916

THE BATTLE OF Verdun raged on France's eastern frontier. In the west the British, under pressure to relieve their ally, launched the huge offensive that became the battle of the Somme. Conscription was introduced in Britain, after the losses suffered by the original BEF and the new volunteer army. Isaac Rosenberg feared that this might show the enemy how desperate things were. Single men between eighteen and forty-one were called up in March 1916 – with exceptions for the unfit, the clergy, teachers and workers in industry; in May the draft was extended to married men. Ireland was exempted, the Asquith government recognizing that Irish nationalism might produce martyrs or rebellious conscripts. Even in Britain conscription was controversial, and in April 200,000 people demonstrated against it in Trafalgar Square. In the last months of the war the age was raised to fifty-one. Conscription lasted until 1920.

In 1916, more poets arrived in France. Edmund Blunden came out in the spring; Ivor Gurney arrived with the Gloucesters in May; Isaac Rosenberg disembarked at Le Havre in June; in December, Wilfred Owen was at Etaples.

There's doubt and pessimism in 1916. The heroine of Rose Macaulay's novel *Non-Combatants and Others* constantly sees headlines about British failures to hold trenches, British troops moving back, German counter-attacks regaining ground. H. G. Wells's Mr Britling is perplexed. In war, he thinks, with horror, that perhaps German cruelty has logic, even 'a stupid rightness', if only in reaction to British indolence that is 'at least equally stupid'. The most popular poem of the war – 'In Flanders Fields' by the

Canadian John McCrae – was published anonymously in *Punch* in December 1915. It would be reproduced often and translated into many languages (far more than Sassoon or Owen) and its author (after his name had been revealed) inundated with letters. The British government used the poem to encourage recruitment and to sell war bonds. Its tone, however, was mournful, if patriotic – and the line about crosses 'row on row' grimly prophetic.

Siegfried Sassoon's letter to his mother of 9 December 1915 showed exhaustion. Written eighteen miles from Amiens ('very fine country ... rather like parts of East Kent'), a few weeks after his first sight of trench warfare, it said, 'We had an awful time moving: 10 hours in the train, & then 16 mile march & got here at 7 am, dead beat. Love from Sig. Send a pair of slippers & a plum pudding. Don't want any more underclothes.'

Sassoon thought later that Robert Graves was his greatest influence during the next year; for Graves it was Charles Sorley's *Marlborough and Other Poems*, published posthumously early in 1916 and giving a cool view of the war. 'It seems ridiculous to fall in love with a dead man, as I have found myself doing,' Graves wrote of Sorley, 'but he seems to have been one so entirely after my own heart in his loves and hates, besides having been just my own age ...'

The war released more of Sassoon's poetry, first in excitement, then in anger. In March 1916, the death of David Thomas, whom he'd loved, brought a change: 'since they shot Tommy,' Sassoon wrote, 'I would gladly stick a bayonet into a German by daylight'. But in May he told his uncle, 'These six months have been miles the best I have ever struck. In fact I find it very hard to take it all in; there is so much, and it is mostly beautiful or terrifying, or both. And the excitement of things bursting is positively splendid: I had no idea I should enjoy it so much.'

This was Sassoon's dilemma – his wish to be a good officer and his revulsion at the war. 'The Redeemer', his first realistic war poem, was written in November 1915, yet in January 1916 he had the euphoric 'To Victory' published in *The Times* and was writing similar verses that month. Graves may have directed him to Charles Sorley. By May Sassoon had read and admired his fellow old Marlburian's poems.

After leave at the end of February – some of it spent hunting, some in London with his new friend, Oscar Wilde's former lover Robbie Ross – Sassoon returned to France. Graves told Marsh, 'I think S.S.'s verses are getting infinitely better than the first crop I saw, much freer and more Georgian. What a terrible pity he didn't start earlier!' It was Graves's sharp-edged opinions, not his poetry, which influenced Sassoon, who let Marsh know that he found this new friend's poems disappointing.

Graves, his nerves shredded by Loos, left the trenches in January 1916 to be an instructor at base camp and in March went to England, to have an operation on his nose. Time in hospital and at the regimental depot and leave let him miss the start of the Somme. Some fellow officers, who disliked his tactlessness and German blood, remarked caustically on this.

In March 1916, Siegfried Sassoon began his forays, often alone, into no man's land. He claimed that these expeditions were partly to get poets a good name; but after David Thomas's death there was also 'hate' and 'the lust to kill'. His poems began to be published by the anti-militarist *Cambridge Magazine*: first 'The Redeemer' and then the bloodthirsty 'The Kiss', distinctly (although Sassoon denied this) sado-masochistic in tone.

He told Marsh how the trenches had changed him. 'O yes, this is some life – the men almost make me weep sometimes, so patient and cheery & altogether dear. And chasing Germans in the moonshine with bombs is no mean sport, & has brought me prestige ...' In May, Sassoon was in the line, near Fricourt, after a month away on a course. Disobeying his commanding officer, he took part in a raid, winning the Military Cross for rescuing a wounded man from a crater. He had joined Julian Grenfell as a hero poet.

The western front was now full of rumours about the coming offensive. Constant activity was thought to be vital and officers led parties to reconstruct damaged trenches, repair wire and bury the dead. This was what Edmund Blunden found when he arrived in France in May.

Blunden was already a poet of immense fluency. One long pre-trench poem, finished in March, was a disquieting account of cruelty's consequences called 'The Silver Bird of Herndyke Mill'. A dark atmosphere threatens an English churchyard, stream and wood in the kind of Georgian scene that always inspired Blunden. Early in 1916, with artillery rumbling from across the Channel, death must have seemed near, even in the tranquil Kentish fields.

After some training in the camp at Etaples – where a sergeant major was killed by a faulty grenade – Blunden joined his battalion of the Royal Sussex Regiment at La Touret, not far from Béthune. It could seem idyllic until heavy guns and mines exploded, let off by both sides. Festubert was within reach, where Sassoon and Graves had been at the end of 1915, and Blunden looked for the local orchards, finding a chapel dedicated to the Virgin Mary, a peaceful place away from the guns. Like Sassoon, he went off on a course; then saw the La Bassée canal, a Red Cross barge on it, the rich summer landscape and the now ruined village of Cuinchy, near the treacherous brickstacks. He was close to Neuve Chapelle by the end of June.

Ivor Gurney was near by. The comradeship of the army impressed Gurney, who suffered all his life from a sense of isolation, because of his extraordinary gifts and difficult personality. When, soon after enlisting, he arrived at Northampton in February 1915 with his unit, the 2/5th Gloucesters, to find a whole division assembled, others from Gloucestershire crowded round and 'it gave me a thrill such as I have not had for a long time'. They moved to Chelmsford in April, for training and work on the trench system meant to protect London; 'nowhere', he wrote to a friend from his days as a music student, 'could I be happier than where I am (except perhaps at sea)'. A torrent of letters began, to friends like Marion Scott and the composer Herbert Howells.

Rupert Brooke. Virginia Woolf thought him beautiful and 'the most restless, complex and analytic of human beings'.

Julian (*centre inset and left*) and Billy Grenfell (*right*) with their mother, Lady Desborough. Julian Grenfell thought 'one loves one's fellow man so much more when one is bent on killing him.'

The Royal Naval Division, ready for the Dardanelles. Rupert Brooke is in the middle row, second from the left.

Siegfried Sassoon. He thought courage was 'the only thing that mattered' in war.

Charles Sorley. Although an admirer of Germany and its culture, Sorley joined up promptly in 1914, declaring that 'since getting a commission I have become a terror'.

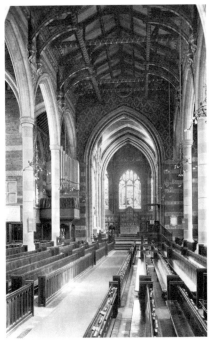

Rugby chapel. The public schools instilled a belief in the nobility of patriotic sacrifice.

Isaac Rosenberg. 'Death does not conquer me, I conquer death, I am the master.'

Jewish Whitechapel: the market in Goulston Street, near where Rosenberg grew up.

Ivor Gurney. He felt intensely moved
by the comradeship that he found on the
western front.

Edward Thomas. 'I was born
to be a ghost.'

Ivor Gurney's
'noble and golden'
Gloucestershire.

Robert Nichols after the war. He wrote of the shock of battle, 'How can a boy consider what he can't imagine?'

Edmund Blunden and his first wife, Mary. Blunden wrote later that 'I was not anxious to go' to the war, yet thought 'when will kindness have such power again?'

Robert Graves as a young officer. He was proud of having fought but thought his own war poems 'journalistic'.

Wilfred Owen in uniform. He told his mother from the front that 'I cannot do a better thing or be in a better place'.

Wilfred Owen and Laurent Tailhade. The Frenchman was the first poet that Owen knew well.

Anthem for Dead Youth.

What passing-bells for these who die so fast?
— Only the {solemn monstrous anger of the guns.
Let the majestic insults of their mouths
Be as the priest-words of their burials.
Of choristers and holy music, none;
Nor any voice of mourning, save the wail
The long-drawn wail of high far-sailing shells.

What candles may we hold for these lost souls?
— Not in the hands of boys, but in their eyes
Shall many candle-flames:
And Women's wide-spreaded arms shall be their wreaths,
And pallor of girls' cheeks shall be their palls.
Their flowers, the tenderness of minds,
And each slow Dusk, a drawing-down of blinds.

First Draft
(With Sassoon's amendments.)

The first draft of Wilfred Owen's 'Anthem for Doomed Youth',
with Siegfried Sassoon's amendments.

The New Menin Gate at Ypres. Unveiled as a war memorial in 1927, it was derided by Siegfried Sassoon as a pompous 'sepulchre of crime'.

Edmund Blunden (*left*), Siegfried Sassoon (*centre*), and Dennis Silk at Heytesbury, where the ageing Sassoon sought refuge from the modern world.

Like the painter and poet Isaac Rosenberg, Ivor Gurney practised two arts: poetry and music. Already he'd written *Five Elizabethan Songs* and hoped to match Schubert or Mozart – and Rupert Brooke's war sonnets made him think that he could improve on these as well. Like Brooke, Ivor Gurney was moved to warrior-like emotion, in the martial sonnet 'To the Poet Before Battle' and in a Hilaire Belloc-like ballad of the Cotswolds. Gloucestershire became a sacred place for this lonely man, the names of its villages, towns, rivers and hills as consoling as prayer.

By February 1916, still in training, Gurney was thinking of death, of which 'I am not greatly afraid'. He felt that one should submit to destiny, as Tolstoy had taught in *War and Peace*. He trained on Salisbury Plain, in mud like Flanders, on route marches sometimes twenty miles long and nights spent in trenches. He walked across the Malvern Hills during some leave in April, reaching Ryton near Dymock, searching in vain for the poet Lascelles Abercrombie who was by then working in a Liverpool munitions factory. Gurney sent a postcard to Herbert Howells on the evening of 23 May: 'We go tomorrow.'

Gurney's unit was sent south-west of Ypres. They learned trench skills from the London Welsh near Riez Bailleul, coming up through the fretwork of paths within sight of Neuve Chapelle. Gurney was amused that these and the trenches were named after public schools: 'curious names … Eton Road, Cheltenham Road, Rugby Road …'. On 15 June, near Laventie, the battalion was in the front line for five days, in danger from snipers, raids and shells that reached the support trenches, even the rest areas. Gurney missed the start of the Somme.

Isaac Rosenberg was out of it as well. Unlike Gurney, Rosenberg had come to dislike this new world of the army (although he admitted he felt well). He'd told Schiff in December 1915, while training at Bury St Edmunds, 'This kind of life does not bother me much. I sleep soundly on boards in the cold; the drills I find fairly interesting …' But in the spring of 1916 Rosenberg wrote, 'Believe me the army is the most detestable invention on this earth and nobody but a private in the army knows what it is to be a slave.'

He complained about the food and the anti-Semitism, telling his Jewish patron Schiff that 'my being a Jew makes it bad among these wretches'; the poet's awkward manner and scruffiness (remembered later by other soldiers) didn't help. Rosenberg's lack of illusions or romantic patriotism meant that he had no dramatic fall into bitterness. At the end of 1915, some of the bantam unit were transferred from the 12th Suffolks to the 12th South Lancashires in preparation for France. There was more training at Blackdown Camp in Surrey where protests against the conditions verged on mutiny and were put down by troops using bayonets.

Marsh had sent Rosenberg's work to Lascelles Abercrombie, who wrote to its author that although 'not quite certain of themselves' some poems had 'remarkable' phrases which no poet could 'help envying'. Marsh and Abercrombie were smooth Georgians, keener on clarity than Rosenberg with his sense of chaos and implacable power, but they felt awe at the unique vision. The war seemed yet more justification of the existence of a malign God. The poetry reflects this – the verse drama 'Moses', and the poem 'Spring 1916' which challenges the idea of the season as a time of hope.

Rosenberg was transferred again, this time to the King's Own (Royal Lancaster Regiment). Rumours of departure grew. On leave in May 1916, he attended to the publication of his new book of poems, entitled *Moses* and printed by a long-time supporter, the East End printer Reuben 'Crazy' Cohen. By far the longest poem in this (taking up eighteen of the book's twenty-six pages) is the verse drama 'Moses', not obviously influenced by the First World War – and begun before it – but depicting God as 'a rotting deity' and also celebrating brave resistance to state power. 'Marching' is among the eight other works; the book is too early for Rosenberg's other great poems about the war. Marsh had doubts about 'Moses', as did Laurence Binyon and the poet Gordon Bottomley, criticizing the shapelessness but praising its ambition. A bleak epic tone – evident in 'Marching' – suffuses the poet's more recent work (not in the 1916 book), 'A Worm Fed on the Heart of Corinth', that compares England's likely fall with dead empires, her power like a corpse fed on by worms.

Isaac Rosenberg arrived in France on 3 June 1916. His poem 'The Troop Ship' evokes soldiers packed in, sleepless in the 'wet wind' or dozing until woken by the cold or a man's feet in your face. Rosenberg still hadn't told his mother where he was going, and when he did, while writing to ask her for socks, she wept. He still drew in France; a self-portrait shows a tough-eyed warrior in a steel helmet.

Rosenberg was sent to trenches near Loos, which kept him from the first weeks of the Somme. As a private soldier, he shared rat-infested, water-logged dug-outs, with much less privacy than the officers, less likely too to get food parcels from home, yet not expected to go first over the top so in less danger although always vulnerable to shelling. At this time came the ironical 'Break of Day in the Trenches' where a rat roams across both sides, like Donne's flea which thoughtlessly took blood from anyone. The poppy held by the poet shows renewal that even industrial warfare couldn't stop. Rosenberg moved to a Salvage Office in August, working to retrieve what was left in the wreckage. The rest of his battalion went to another sector, among slag heaps near Lens.

Robert Graves's first book of poems, *Over the Brazier*, had come out in May 1916, just before the Somme. Published by Monro's Poetry Bookshop, it had a cover illustration by Claud Lovat Fraser of the Menin Gate at Ypres. The title poem is a meditation on what to do in peacetime: for the poet a cottage in Wales 'full of books'; for others gathered round the brazier a new start in Canada or on a southern island: then death wrecks these dreams. 'It's a Queer Time' showed, as Graves admitted later, how soldier poets could exaggerate. This 'realistic' poem had been written at the regimental depot in Wales 'some weeks before I had a chance of verifying my facts'.

The origin of the Allies' Somme offensive lay in the plan to draw the enemy away from Verdun, on France's eastern frontier, where the Germans hoped to break the French army. Reluctant to attack at least until August – because he believed that the new British troops weren't ready – Haig gave way to the War Cabinet who felt pressure from the French. He planned the July launch with Henry Rawlinson, the commander of the Fourth Army. The heaviest possible artillery barrage would precede the greatest British offensive of the war, first by infantry and then by cavalry to exploit an inevitable breakthrough. The troops were told that the artillery had already blasted the German defences apart.

Haig ordered a front of twenty miles; Rawlinson had wanted more limited attacks. But the artillery wasn't sufficiently concentrated, or given enough shells, to break up the strong defences. The German machine-gun emplacements, well dug in, stayed comparatively intact, ready for the infantry that came across no man's land on 1 July. Haig believed the untried troops were not ready for fast movement – or attacks in conjunction with artillery – and might break into disconnected groups, so he insisted on a slow walk forward, without covering shellfire. In the south, the French, moving faster and using artillery, made greater gains.

In reserve, Siegfried Sassoon watched the attack on 1 July as if, he thought, from an opera box. The day was sunny but confusing; there were rumours of success, that the village of Fricourt had been taken.

Sassoon moved with his battalion into the front line on 3 July, to a trench opposite Mametz Wood, passing a mass of corpses. By 4 July, rain had come and mud; and Sassoon saw panic (he threatened to shoot an officer who was hysterical) and men killed. In an act of solitary courage – like Julian Grenfell's war – he charged a German trench in daylight, throwing bombs and shouting hunting cries at fifty or sixty retreating enemy and then sat on the trench's fire step before going back to report.

His commanding officer was furious. Why hadn't Sassoon

reported earlier so that the captured trench could be consolidated? The artillery bombardment had been held up for three hours as it was thought that his patrol was still out there – so the charge had been what Graves called 'a pointless feat'. Sassoon and his badly hit battalion were withdrawn to marshy ground by the River Ancre. Then he was moved again, to look after the transport near Meaulté, with time to read Thomas Hardy.

He saw Robert Graves, back in France since June, and they talked about what they would do after the war – poetry and travel. That the men loved him was Sassoon's consolation; he longed for books and music, not, however, for a return to his pre-war world of cricket, hunting and sexual frustration. The battle went on, raging round certain vantage points like the notorious High Wood, where Graves's battalion was ordered to be in reserve for an attack on 20 July. Relentless German shelling caused Graves to be very badly wounded. Taken to a dressing station, and lying unconscious for twenty-four hours, he was given up for dead and put on the regimental casualty list – which Sassoon saw with horror, writing desperately to Marsh, 'Won't they leave us anyone we are fond of?' In fact Graves survived, and was taken across the Channel to hospital in north London. By August both the poets were in England: Sassoon with fever and dysentery, Graves with wounds in the chest, thigh, shoulder and above one eye.

What happened at High Wood is typical of the heavy cost of the Somme for little obvious gain. It was captured in July, after bad casualties; then the Germans counter-attacked and weren't evicted until 15 September, after two months of battle.

Edmund Blunden was left out of a diversionary attack made by part of his regiment on 30 June, south-west of Neuve Chapelle. His battalion moved up to Cambrin, where there was shrapnel, shelling and exploding mines. On 20 July they went back to trenches near Neuve Chapelle recently occupied by Ivor Gurney, still under bombardment and making dangerous night patrols. By August they were at Cuinchy, in trenches near the brickstacks.

The names of the trenches amused Blunden (as they had Gurney): not taken from public schools this time but still an attempt to bring England to northern France: Windy Corner, Orchard Road, Queen's Road, Hatfield Road, one called Ducks' Bill because of its shape. His colonel revealed that he was a literary man who'd read a good review in the *Times Literary Supplement* of Blunden's first book of poems.

Reinforcements were needed to the south on 11 August, in the worst part of the Somme battle. To many of the men it seemed 'death-news', as in Blunden's later poem 'Two Voices', and he sought calm again in the summer landscape, reminded of his happy earlier life. He had his worst-yet war experience near Beaumont Hamel, as field-works officer leading bomb-carrying parties. Known as 'rabbit' because of his fast pace, alertness and small size, he brought up his bombs in the confusion of battle and saw men break in bursts of terror. Edmund Blunden won the Military Cross for his courage at this time.

His battalion came under shellfire, even after withdrawing into billets. It was back in the front line by 16 September, quiet until an attack on Thiepval, captured by the British eleven days later. Blunden stayed at the front, with breaks of only a few days, through the last Somme offensive – five terrible November days of fighting, through drizzling rain and a barrage when 'never had shells seemed so torrentially swift, so murderous'. Blunden got lost, until a crucifix loomed between Thiepval and Grandcourt, and he raced with his runner, Private Johnson, through shellfire by the glittering River Ancre back to the British line where they were welcomed 'as Lazarus was'. The battalion left the Somme two days later, moving to what was to be a place of even greater danger: the land round Ypres.

In England since July, first with fever in hospital and then at the regimental depot in the Liverpool suburb of Litherland or in London or at home in Kent, Siegfried Sassoon had news from his battalion about fighting round Delville Wood and High Wood and the many woundings and deaths. His poetry became more fierce – as in 'They' or 'Blighters' – influenced by Hardy's satires, often with a knock-out blow in the last lines, these javelin-like verses sharpened by guilt at not being in the trenches.

To describe pain, Sassoon still used lyricism, as in 'The Death Bed'. On a visit to Cambridge, he met Professor Sorley, Charles Sorley's father, and shocked the musical scholar Dent – the friend from Sassoon's training days at Pembroke College in 1915 who'd scorned Brooke's emotional patriotism – with stories of rough army life. Like most soldiers, Sassoon had contempt for those on the Home Front, however terrible he found the war.

The Somme had been horrific, for the Germans and for the British. The waves of July had changed into a series of smaller attacks, with not much ground gained. The British had had 82,000 casualties by the end of August; but Haig went on, insisting that the enemy was about to collapse. In September the tactic of the creeping barrage and the introduction of tanks had disappointing results because of technical hitches and too wide-ranging artillery. Rain came in October and November, bringing back the mud. By the end in November the British had had some 450,000 casualties, the French 200,000 and the Germans 400,000.

The enemy had suffered, as the writer Ernst Jünger, a German officer, admitted. Edmund Blunden thought that he'd seen a British 'feat of arms vying with any recorded', feeling pride and 'exaltation' and the sense that he and the troops could now bear anything. Another young officer, Charles Carrington, not at all a reckless warrior, held that the men's spirits were much lower away from the sound of guns than in the front line. To Carrington 'the Somme raised the morale of the British army' and, although not an outright victory, gave the British a sense of superiority, man to man.

Glorification of patriotic duty hadn't died with Rupert Brooke. In 1916, Lady Desborough completed her memorial to her two dead sons, Julian and Billy Grenfell. Entitled *Pages from a Family Journal 1888–1915*, the thick book was produced, appropriately enough, by the Eton College printers and written at the suggestion of one former Prime Minister, Lord Rosebery, with an early copy sent to another, Arthur Balfour. Lady Desborough had planned fifty copies; but this was extended to 250, privately printed at a cost of what today would be about £20,000. Consisting principally of extracts from her sons' letters (Billy had been killed, leading a charge, a few months after Julian) with linking passages by her, it tells of two brilliant boys, wayward sometimes but bound tightly to their background. There was an understandable doctoring of material to show immense filial devotion. As Julian dies, he smiles at his mother in a sunlit hospital room, saying his mysterious last words 'Phoebus Apollo'.

Balfour, a cool man, wrote admiringly, but not effusively, of the book. There was, however, admiration from many, including Kipling and John Buchan, although others, especially some of the boys' contemporaries, thought much had been missed out, notably the ambiguity and desperation which had tormented Julian Grenfell. To the pacifists, the book was a nightmare, Lytton Strachey thinking that the boys came across as brave savages who enjoyed killing and Lady Ottoline Morrell, an unconventional aristocrat, seeing contempt for the less fortunate and a sense that, for the Grenfells, joy was a right.

The book became a pattern for later memoirs of dead aristocratic sons – but never, after what had happened under the leadership of the old governing class, could this world be quite so admired again. More bitter poets like Sassoon, Owen and Rosenberg – not the exultant Grenfell – came to be seen as the true voices of the war.

In August 1916, Isaac Rosenberg was near Loos, out of the front line but within range of shells. He took the wounded to hospital in handcarts, telling Gordon Bottomley, 'It's a toss up whether you're going to be the carried or the carrier.' Poetry came painfully and included the jingoistic 'Pozières', which he submitted as the divisional Christmas card, but it was rejected.

Rosenberg was back in the line by the last half of August. He marched with his brigade to an area near Beaumont Hamel on 11 November, to cold and wet trenches. There was a break for training in December, then back to the Somme area, near Bray, into land devastated by shellfire, with mud and broken trenches and excreta left unburied by the French. The historian of Rosenberg's division wrote later, 'Now began three months in the most God-forsaken and miserable area in France, bar, possibly, the salient of Ypres. The whole country-side was a churned-up, yeasty mass of mud, as a result of the vile weather and of the battle which even yet had not petered out. The weather was awful. Constant rain was varied by spells of intensely cold weather and some very heavy snowfalls. Mud and dirt were everywhere ...'

Isaac Rosenberg would be taken out of the line early in 1917, probably after Marsh had written to the War Office about this 'budding genius'. This meant that, aged twenty-six, he would go to a works battalion, mending roads, still under shellfire. The private soldier's war was one of drudgery. It was luck what officer you had, if he cared for your welfare (as Siegfried Sassoon did) and avoided dangerous adventures. Rosenberg in 1915 wrote that 'we have pups for officers'.

There was brutality; a Coldstream Guards corporal who had been in the fighting since Mons in the first month of the war, told Ivor Gurney in May 1916 that you should never take prisoners for all Germans should be killed. Gurney had been in Laventie, away from the Somme. Here, though, he could be in trenches only a few yards away from the enemy, near enough for bombs to be thrown. No man's land was full of the stinking dead. The men brought him happiness. He liked watching the French children in the villages, the women's faces etched with character; and the country could look like the Stroud valley. Some June days in a dug-out with Welsh soldiers whom his battalion was relieving were 'the happiest for years', with good talk; 'war's damned interesting', Gurney thought, and this brought the post-war poem 'First Time In'. He heard a cuckoo; 'what could I think of but Framilode, Minsterworth, Cranham, and the old haunts of home?' A Welshman said that the 'damned bird' had sung constantly during the bombardment.

Gurney endured mortar and shell attacks and saw the deaths of comrades but wrote again in June, 'Floreat Gloucestriensis! It was a great time; full of fear of course, but not so bad as neurasthenia ...' A rumour came that he'd been recommended for the Distinguished Conduct Medal ('my dear lady,' he told Marion Scott, 'I am pleased with myself'). There was exasperation, as when he exploded that 'the Army is an awful life for an artist, even if he has such experiences as we had with the Welsh. Either it is slogging along uselessly with a pack or doing nothing but hang about after – or boredom and hell in the trenches. Very little between.' He thought, however, that 'it is much better out here than in England ...'

Gurney dreamed of finding a profitable line in Brooke- or Grenfell-like verses: 'a delight of rolling country, of a lovely river, and trees, trees, trees. Après la guerre, it must be that I write piffle under the name of Rupert de Montvilliers Fortescue-Carruthers or some such name, to rake in the good gold in exceeding abundance, to see the earth and the glories thereof and develop a paunch ...' He set five songs to music in the trenches: one by Masefield, others by his friend F. W. Harvey, by Raleigh, by Yeats, and then his own 'Song' ('Only the wanderer knows').

Marion Scott cherished the poems that he sent her; and in 1917 she and others persuaded Sidgwick and Jackson, Rupert Brooke's publisher, to take Gurney's first collection *Severn and Somme*. In this were 'Requiem', written east of Laventie in November 1916; 'Strange Service', a hymn to Gloucestershire, from the summer; and 'Bach and the Sentry', about memories of a Bach prelude as fog lifted across no man's land.

In October 1916, Gurney's battalion marched through Albert, where a damaged statue of the Virgin and Child was poised precariously on the church's tower; by 22 November they were in the line, in mud and shelling so bad that he told Marion Scott, 'We suffer pain out here, and for myself it sometimes comes that death would be preferable to such a life.' But he thought, 'It is better to live a grey life in mud and danger, so long as one uses it – as I trust I am doing – as a means to an end ...' Not until 30 December was Ivor Gurney safe, out of the line and training in biting cold.

That day Second Lieutenant Wilfred Owen reached the base camp at Etaples. Owen's military career had strangely prospered, first at Hare Hall Camp in Essex, then at the officers' school at Romford and on a course in London, after which he'd been offered a commission in the Lancashire Fusiliers. Losses brought about by Loos and the relentless shelling on the western front had opened up the class structure of the military. At first he'd refused promotion, thinking that he hadn't enough experience, but he soon changed his mind, becoming an officer in the Manchester Regiment in June. A camp at Milford in Surrey and courses at Aldershot, Oswestry, Southport and Fleetwood followed. At intervals there'd been leave, at home in Shrewsbury or in London, where in March 1916 he took a room in the Poetry Bookshop and gave his poems to Harold Monro. After some anxious days, Monro responded, with criticism and praise. Wilfred Owen was at the Hotel Metropole in Folkestone in December, awaiting embarkation for France.

Owen could seem vulnerable. In February 1916, his younger brother Harold thought 'how physically unsophisticated, almost helpless he seemed ... I could feel only a desperate sort of protective urge towards him, not pity – he never engendered that – but a compelling wish that I might somehow help this hunched-up little figure sitting next to me ...' But Owen coped well when pitched into military life, noting that class distinction in the army could be banished by only two things, 'animal sports and mortal danger', and 'neither religion, nor Love, nor Charity, nor Community of Interests, nor Socialism, nor Conviviality can do it at all ...'.

Edward Thomas was still in England. The artist Paul Nash was with him at Hare Hall and remembered the 'always humorous interesting and entirely loveable' poet, and Thomas wrote of the kindness that he found there, made even better by visits to a literary admirer, Edna Clark Hall, who lived near by. Others, however, recalled 'the most depressed man they ever met', showing how fast his mood could change.

'Rain' was written in a hut in the camp, conveying fear of a ruined land and culture and also the power of memory to keep goodness alive. In March came 'Home', about his life as a soldier. In May the poem 'The Sun Used to Shine' evokes escape into a rosy past; 'As the Team's Head-Brass' tells how the war touched each field and village. Thomas decided to take a commission; and in July, in spite of his occasional diabetes, was accepted by the artillery. Looking back, he told Frost that 'I don't believe I often had as good times as I have had, one way and another, these past 13 months.'

Thomas now wanted to be at the war: to 'run risks, to be put through it', for (as he told Frost) 'this waiting troubles me'. An officer cadet in the Royal Artillery, he went to Bloomsbury for training, then in September to Trowbridge barracks in Wiltshire, where he wrote 'The Trumpet', worthy of Rupert Brooke. Helen and the younger children moved to Essex – after Thomas had left. By November 1916, the month of 'Lights Out' with its title taken from a bugle call, he knew that he wanted to risk his life.

1916 POEMS

August 1914

What in our lives is burnt
In the fire of this?
The heart's dear granary?
The much we shall miss?

Three lives hath one life –
Iron, honey, gold.
The gold, the honey gone –
Left is the hard and cold.

Iron are our lives
Molten right through our youth.
A burnt space through ripe fields,
A fair mouth's broken tooth.

ISAAC ROSENBERG

Rain

Rain, midnight rain, nothing but the wild rain
On this bleak hut, and solitude, and me
Remembering again that I shall die
And neither hear the rain nor give it thanks
For washing me cleaner than I have been
Since I was born into this solitude.
Blessed are the dead that the rain rains upon:
But here I pray that none whom once I loved
Is dying to-night or lying still awake
Solitary, listening to the rain,
Either in pain or thus in sympathy
Helpless among the living and the dead,
Like a cold water among broken reeds,
Myriads of broken reeds all still and stiff,
Like me who have no love which this wild rain
Has not dissolved except the love of death,
If love it be towards what is perfect and
Cannot, the tempest tells me, disappoint.

EDWARD THOMAS

The Troop Ship

Grotesque and queerly huddled
Contortionists to twist
The sleepy soul to a sleep,
We lie all sorts of ways
And cannot sleep.
The wet wind is so cold,
And the lurching men so careless,
That, should you drop to a doze,
Wind's fumble or men's feet
Is on your face.

Isaac Rosenberg

A Worm Fed on the Heart of Corinth

A worm fed on the heart of Corinth,
Babylon and Rome.
Not Paris raped tall Helen,
But this incestuous worm,
Who lured her vivid beauty
To his amorphous sleep.
England! famous as Helen
Is thy betrothal sung.
To him the shadowless,
More amorous than Solomon.

Isaac Rosenberg

Home

Fair was the morning, fair our tempers, and
We had seen nothing fairer than that land,
Though strange, and the untrodden snow that made
Wild of the tame, casting out all that was
Not wild and rustic and old; and we were glad.

Fair, too, was afternoon, and first to pass
Were we that league of snow, next the north wind.

There was nothing to return for, except need,
And yet we sang nor ever stopped for speed,
As we did often with the start behind.
Faster still strode we when we came in sight
Of the cold roofs where we must spend the night.
Happy we had not been there, nor could be,
Though we had tasted sleep and food and fellowship
Together long.
'How quick', to someone's lip
The words came, 'will the beaten horse run home.'

The word 'home' raised a smile in us all three,
And one repeated it, smiling just so
That all knew what he meant and none would say.
Between three counties far apart that lay
We were divided and looked strangely each
At the other, and we knew we were not friends
But fellows in a union that ends
With the necessity for it, as it ought.

Never a word was spoken, not a thought
Was thought, of what the look meant with the word
'Home' as we walked and watched the sunset blurred.
And then to me the word, only the word,
'Homesick', as it were playfully occurred:
No more.

If I should ever more admit
Than the mere word I could not endure it
For a day longer: this captivity
Must somehow come to an end, else I should be
Another man, as often now I seem,
Or this life be only an evil dream.

EDWARD THOMAS

The Kiss

To these I turn, in these I trust –
Brother Lead and Sister Steel.
To his blind power I make appeal,
I guard her beauty clean from rust.

He spins and burns and loves the air,
And splits a skull to win my praise;
But up the nobly marching days
She glitters naked, cold and fair.

Sweet Sister, grant your soldier this:
That in good fury he may feel
The body where he sets his heel
Quail from your downward darting kiss.

SIEGFRIED SASSOON

The Festubert Shrine

A sycamore on either side
In whose lovely leafage cried
   Hushingly the little winds –
Thus was Mary's shrine descried.

'Sixteen Hundred and Twenty-Four'
Legended above the door,
   'Pray, sweet gracious Lady, pray
For our souls,' – and nothing more.

Builded of rude gray stones and these
Scarred and marred from base to frieze
   With the shrapnel's pounces – ah,
Fair she braved War's gaunt disease:

Fair she pondered on the strange
Embitterments of latter change,
   Looking fair towards Festubert,
Cloven roof and tortured grange.

Work of carving too there was,
(Once had been her reredos),
   In this cool and peaceful cell
That the hoarse guns blared across.

Twisted oaken pillars graced
With oaken amaranths interlaced
   In oaken garlandry, had borne
Her holy niche – and now laid waste.

Mary, pray for us? O pray!
In thy dwelling by this way
    What poor folks have knelt to thee!
We are no less poor than they.

EDMUND BLUNDEN

As the Team's Head-Brass

As the team's head-brass flashed out on the turn
The lovers disappeared into the wood.
I sat among the boughs of the fallen elm
That strewed the angle of the fallow, and
Watched the plough narrowing a yellow square
Of charlock. Every time the horses turned
Instead of treading me down, the ploughman leaned
Upon the handles to say or ask a word,
About the weather, next about the war.
Scraping the share he faced towards the wood,
And screwed along the furrow till the brass flashed
Once more.

The blizzard felled the elm whose crest
I sat in, by a woodpecker's round hole,
The ploughman said. 'When will they take it away?'
'When the war's over.' So the talk began –
One minute and an interval of ten,
A minute more and the same interval.
'Have you been out?' 'No.' 'And don't want to, perhaps?'
'If I could only come back again, I should.
I could spare an arm, I shouldn't want to lose
A leg. If I should lose my head, why, so,
I should want nothing more ... Have many gone
From here?' 'Yes.' 'Many lost?' 'Yes, a good few.
Only two teams work on the farm this year.
One of my mates is dead. The second day
In France they killed him. It was back in March,
The very night of the blizzard, too. Now if
He had stayed here we should have moved the tree.'
'And I should not have sat here. Everything

Would have been different. For it would have been
Another world.' 'Ay, and a better, though
If we could see all all might seem good.' Then
The lovers came out of the wood again:
The horses started and for the last time
I watched the clods crumble and topple over
After the ploughshare and the stumbling team.

EDWARD THOMAS

The Sun Used to Shine

The sun used to shine while we two walked
Slowly together, paused and started
Again, and sometimes mused, sometimes talked
As either pleased, and cheerfully parted

Each night. We never disagreed
Which gate to rest on. The to be
And the late past we gave small heed.
We turned from men or poetry

To rumours of the war remote
Only till both stood disinclined
For aught but the yellow flavorous coat
Of an apple wasps had undermined;

Or a sentry of dark betonies,
The stateliest of small flowers on earth,
At the forest verge; or crocuses
Pale purple as if they had their birth

In sunless Hades fields. The war
Came back to mind with the moonrise
Which soldiers in the east afar
Beheld then. Nevertheless, our eyes

Could as well imagine the Crusades
Or Caesar's battles. Everything
To faintness like those rumours fades –
Like the brook's water glittering

Under the moonlight – like those walks
Now – like us two that took them, and
The fallen apples, all the talks
And silences – like memory's sand

When the tide covers it late or soon,
And other men through other flowers
In those fields under the same moon
Go talking and have easy hours.

EDWARD THOMAS

Break of Day in the Trenches

The darkness crumbles away.
It is the same old Druid Time as ever,
Only a live thing leaps my hand,
A queer sardonic rat,
As I pull the parapet's poppy
To stick behind my ear.
Droll rat, they would shoot you if they knew
Your cosmopolitan sympathies.
Now you have touched this English hand
You will do the same to a German
Soon, no doubt, if it be your pleasure
To cross the sleeping green between.
It seems, odd thing, you grin as you pass
Strong eyes, fine limbs, haughty athletes,
Less chanced than you for life,
Bonds to the whims of murder,
Sprawled in the bowels of the earth,
The torn fields of France.
What do you see in our eyes
At the shrieking iron and flame
Hurled through still heavens?
What quaver – what heart aghast?
Poppies whose roots are in man's veins
Drop, and are ever dropping,
But mine in my ear is safe –
Just a little white with the dust.

ISAAC ROSENBERG

Strange Service

Little did I dream, England, that you bore me
Under the Cotswold Rills beside the water meadows,
To do you dreadful service, here, beyond your borders
And your enfolding seas.

I was a dreamer ever, and bound to your dear service,
Meditating deep, I thought on your secret beauty,
As through a child's face one may see the clear spirit
Miraculously shining.

Your hills not only hills, but friends of mine and kindly,
Your tiny knolls and orchards hidden beside the river
Muddy and strongly flowing, with shy and tiny streamlets
Safe in its bosom.

Now these are memories only, and your skies and rushy sky-pools
Fragile mirrors easily broken by moving airs …
But deep in my heart for ever goes on your daily being,
And uses consecrate.

Think on me too, O Mother, who wrest my soul to serve you
In strange and fearful ways beyond your encircling waters;
None but you can know my heart, its tears and sacrifice;
None, but you, repay.

IVOR GURNEY

The Death Bed

He drowsed and was aware of silence heaped
Round him, unshaken as the steadfast walls;
Aqueous like floating rays of amber light,
Soaring and quivering in the wings of sleep.
Silence and safety; and his mortal shore
Lipped by the inward, moonless waves of death.

Someone was holding water to his mouth.
He swallowed, unresisting; moaned and dropped
Through crimson gloom to darkness; and forgot
The opiate throb and ache that was his wound.
Water – calm, sliding green above the weir.
Water – a sky-lit alley for his boat,
Bird-voiced, and bordered with reflected flowers
And shaken hues of summer; drifting down,
He dipped contented oars, and sighed, and slept.

Night, with a gust of wind, was in the ward,
Blowing the curtain to a glimmering curve.
Night. He was blind; he could not see the stars
Glinting among the wraiths of wandering cloud;
Queer blots of colour, purple, scarlet, green,
Flickered and faded in his drowning eyes.

Rain – he could hear it rustling through the dark;
Fragrance and passionless music woven as one;
Warm rain on drooping roses; pattering showers
That soak the woods; not the harsh rain that sweeps
Behind the thunder, but a trickling peace,
Gently and slowly washing life away.

He stirred, shifting his body; then the pain
Leapt like a prowling beast, and gripped and tore
His groping dreams with grinding claws and fangs.
But someone was beside him; soon he lay
Shuddering because that evil thing had passed.
And death, who'd stepped toward him, paused and stared.

Light many lamps and gather round his bed.
Lend him your eyes, warm blood, and will to live.
Speak to him; rouse him; you may save him yet.
He's young; he hated War; how should he die
When cruel old campaigners win safe through?

But death replied: 'I choose him.' So he went,
And there was silence in the summer night;
Silence and safety; and the veils of sleep.
Then, far away, the thudding of the guns.

SIEGFRIED SASSOON

The Trumpet

Rise up, rise up,
And, as the trumpet blowing
Chases the dreams of men,
As the dawn glowing
The stars that left unlit
The land and water,
Rise up and scatter
The dew that covers
The print of last night's lovers –
Scatter it, scatter it!

While you are listening
To the clear horn,
Forget, men, everything
On this earth newborn,
Except that it is lovelier
Than any mysteries.
Open your eyes to the air
That has washed the eyes of the stars
Through all the dewy night:
Up with the light,
To the old wars;
Arise, arise!

EDWARD THOMAS

Lights Out

I have come to the borders of sleep,
The unfathomable deep
Forest where all must lose
Their way, however straight,
Or winding, soon or late;
They cannot choose.

Many a road and track
That, since the dawn's first crack,
Up to the forest brink,
Deceived the travellers,
Suddenly now blurs,
And in they sink.

Here love ends,
Despair, ambition ends,
All pleasure and all trouble,
Although most sweet or bitter,
Here ends in sleep that is sweeter
Than tasks most noble.

There is not any book
Or face of dearest look
That I would not turn from now
To go into the unknown
I must enter and leave alone,
I know not how.

The tall forest towers;
Its cloudy foliage lowers
Ahead, shelf above shelf;
Its silence I hear and obey
That I may lose my way
And myself.

EDWARD THOMAS

Bach and the Sentry

Watching the dark my spirit rose in flood
On that most dearest Prelude of my delight.
The low-lying mist lifted its hood,
The October stars showed nobly in clear night.

When I return, and to real music-making,
And play that Prelude, how will it happen then?
Shall I feel as I felt, a sentry hardly waking,
With a dull sense of No Man's Land again?

IVOR GURNEY

1917

To the poet David Jones, 'the wholesale slaughter' and impersonality of the war's later years began with the Somme. Previously there'd been a sense of tradition stretching back to the Peninsula, to Marlborough's campaigns, even to Agincourt. Now the war became more mechanical, harder, more horrifically modern.

The direction of Britain's war changed in December 1916 when David Lloyd George, the Minister of Munitions and former Chancellor of the Exchequer, succeeded Asquith – never a natural war leader – as Prime Minister. It was a huge leap for the country to be led by a man who'd not been to a public school or university. Having grown up in a cottage in north Wales, where his uncle was a cobbler, Lloyd George had made a virtue out of this, even exaggerating his early poverty, proclaiming his mission to aid the poor, particularly at the expense of inheritors of great wealth. He owed his advancement not only to his own dynamism but also to a deadlocked war.

Gallipoli had failed; the Somme battles had gained only a few miles; the Royal Navy had been brought to a dead heat, arguably a defeat, at Jutland; U-boats were menacing British supply routes; the Russians, effective against the Austrians, couldn't match the Germans who'd conquered Romania and still occupied Belgium and much of northern France. The cold winter further sapped morale.

The new Prime Minister was not impressed by Douglas Haig and the British High Command, particularly after the Somme. For the planned 1917 spring offensive, Lloyd George infuriated Haig by putting the British army under the temporary control of the persuasive, English-speaking French General Nivelle who'd done well at Verdun.

The British role was to advance on a front stretching from Bapaume in the south up to Arras. The main force would come from a massive French attack on the Chemin des Dames, a surge uphill against well-dug-in German machine guns. The Germans, through captured papers, knew of the plan. There followed, in March 1917, what seemed like a retreat, as the Germans withdrew, wrecking the country that they left behind, taking up positions in the well-fortified so-called Hindenburg Line. This was a strategic move, not a flight. It determined the fate of the Allies' spring offensive that was meant to win the war.

In January 1917, Wilfred Owen was with the 2nd Battalion, the Manchester Regiment in the transit camp at Etaples. Here he was hit, during bombing practice, by a fragment which grazed his thumb, letting him coax out one drop of blood, a glimpse of what it was to be a warrior. 'There is a fine heroic feeling about being in France,' Owen told his mother on New Year's Day, 'and I am in perfect spirits. A tinge of excitement is about me, but excitement is always necessary to my happiness.' He wrote again ten days later, 'Have no anxiety. I cannot do a better thing or be in a righter place ...'

He'd been under shellfire in the snow at Bertrancourt by 4 February. The ugliness of the trenches cut into the crimson aestheticism, nurtured by Tailhade and the reading of Wilde. 'I suppose I can endure cold, and fatigue, and face-to-face death, as well as another; but extra for me there is the universal perversion of *Ugliness*,' he told his mother. 'Hideous landscapes, vile noises, foul language and nothing but foul, even from one's own mouth (for all are devil-ridden), everything unnatural, broken, blasted; the distortion of the dead, whose unburiable bodies sit outside the dug-outs all day, all night, the most execrable sights on earth.' Owen claimed that he'd been too busy surviving to be frightened: 'I cannot say I felt any fear.' That day he arrived at Abbeville to take a transport course. Another offensive was only two months away.

Edward Thomas had his last leave in England over the weekend of 6 January. There was snow and mist round the cottage that his family had taken near High Beech Camp in Essex. He read stories to his children, bathed them in a tub in front of the fire and sang folk songs, showing great tenderness to them yet impatient with Helen his wife, talking briskly about life assurance documents, arguing over possible improvements to the house. After a day in London – away from her – he was loving on their last night, carrying Helen to bed in his greatcoat and saying 'remember that, whatever happens, all is well between us for ever and ever'. As Edward strode away the next morning, soon invisible in the mist, he called out, 'Coo-ee!' and she answered, before running up a hill, hoping to see him but, as she wrote later, 'There was nothing but the mist and the snow and the silence of death.' He was in France as an artillery officer by the end of January, near the guns and regretting the absence of birdsong.

Thomas's poetry was starting to be noticed. Harriet Monroe, an American patron of writers, took three of his poems for her Chicago magazine *Poetry* in February; by then he knew that his first collection had been accepted by publishers in the United States (pushed by Frost) and in Britain. But the war cut into Thomas's writing and he could read only sporadically, finding it hard to concentrate on a volume of Shakespeare's sonnets given to him by Helen.

His battery was outside Arras by the second week of February 1917, in snow and only a mile from the Germans. A fortnight later he was sent to the headquarters of the Heavy Artillery Group, three miles back, where, as a skilled map-reader, he worked on reconnaissance reports and photographs. 'Am I to stay on here and do nothing but have cold feet?' Thomas wrote in his diary.

As if in answer, the enemy fired in his direction while he was out inspecting a gun position; then a British shell narrowly missed him. Thomas told Frost he was happy but confided his confusion to his wife. How hard it was to think about anything other than this new world, although he felt strangely detached from it, as if sitting in a railway waiting room. To Walter de la Mare he wrote that he doubted his chances. Danger came when at a crossroads near Arras he climbed a disused factory chimney to use it as an observation post, moving slowly up rickety steps until shells bursting near by sent him back down. That earlier failure returned. 'It was', he told Frost, 'just another experience like the gamekeeper.'

Siegfried Sassoon returned to France in February. While in England, he'd seen much of Robbie Ross, Wilde's friend who scorned jingoism, and it was to Ross that Sassoon wrote from a Rouen hospital, while recovering from German measles, that 'I haven't met anyone yet who has any faith in "the purpose of war" ...' He moved up with the 2nd Battalion, the Royal Welsh Fusiliers and passed through country destroyed by the retiring Germans, seeing futile discipline when a general publicly humiliated the battalion's colonel. Encouraged by new friends that his poetry had brought him – by Ross and the pacifists Philip and Lady Ottoline Morrell – doubt seeped into Sassoon about the war.

The battle of Arras, the British part of the Nivelle offensive, began on Easter Monday, 9 April, following a five-day bombardment. As on the Somme's first day, good news drifted back to Sassoon who was still out of the line; a huge mining operation had stunned the enemy. On 8 April, a dud shell had fallen near Edward Thomas and he was teased, one man saying that this meant Thomas's luck would always hold. But the next day he fell, the breath sucked out of him by a blast that left no mark on his body.

Among the last words in his diary were 'I never understood quite what was meant by God'; also a sentence about the air and the landscape: 'The morning chill and clear hurts my skin while it delights my mind.' Then a sketch of a French village scene: 'Neuville in early morning with its flat straight crest with trees and houses – the beauty of this silent empty scene of no inhabitants and hid troops, but don't know why I could have cried and didn't.' Edward Thomas's last three lines of verse were:

Where any turn may lead to Heaven
Or any corner may hide Hell
Roads shining like river up hill after rain.

Siegfried Sassoon was in peril some seven days later. His company entered the front line on 15 April and General Pinney, a later target of Sassoon's satire, ordered a suicidal attack of a hundred bombers. Sassoon was told to take command of this and, after rallying the troops in dark, hellish, corpse-filled trenches, he looked over the parapet and was shot by a German sniper. The wound, between the shoulders, narrowly missing the jugular vein and the spine, was bad enough for him to be sent back to England, though he'd wanted to go on, feeling 'capable of the most suicidal exploits'.

Arras brought humiliation for Wilfred Owen. He returned to his company in March and, when with a working party, fell into a hole which brought mild concussion and a visit to a casualty clearing station at Gailly on the Somme canal where he passed his twenty-fourth birthday. Here Owen thought of his future; perhaps after the war he might live in a cottage in southern England with an orchard, or so he told his brother Colin, 'and give my afternoons to the care of pigs. The hired labour would be very cheap, 2 boys could tend 50 pigs. And it would be the abruptest change' from the writing that would be 'my morning's work'.

He came into the front line again near Saint Quentin on 3 April where there was still snow, and lay four days and four nights without relief in the open, kept going by brandy and the fear of death. On 14 April, Owen led his section in an attack on the German trenches under fire and shelling, later telling his brother Colin that 'going over the top' was 'about as exhilarating as going over a precipice', that he'd wished for a bugle and drum and had kept chanting 'Keep the line straight! Not so fast on the left! Steady on the left' before the 'tornado' of shells.

The imagery of the 1918 poems goes back to this, and to the horror of a few days later, indelibly marking the literature of war.

Owen's battalion stayed in the line around Savy, lying again in holes where 'for twelve days I did not wash my face, nor take off my boots nor sleep a deep sleep …'. A shell hit a bank, just two yards from his head, and he was blown into the air, ending up in a hole just big enough to shelter him, with the dead body of a comrade near by, covered with earth. There followed a collapse, then possible imputations of cowardice from his commanding officer who judged that Owen was no longer fit to lead men and ordered him back to the casualty clearing station. The diagnosis was 'neurasthenia', or shell shock, although he assured his mother that he hadn't had a breakdown. A medical report stated that on 1 May he was found to be 'shaky and tremulous and his conduct and manner were peculiar and his memory confused'. By the end of June Owen was in Craiglockhart, a hospital housed in a dark, converted Victorian hydro in Slateford, a suburb of Edinburgh.

There was no breakthrough. The Canadians took Vimy Ridge, at a high cost, but the French offensive on the Chemin des Dames became a massacre that led to outbreaks of mutiny. Stalemate returned to the western front. One good omen did come, unconnected to military strategy or brilliance. In April the United States entered the war, provoked by German unrestricted submarine warfare, the sinking of the passenger liner *Lusitania* by a U-boat and the Zimmermann telegram (from which Germany had seemed to be plotting with Mexico against the US). The vast American reserves of manpower and equipment would take time to reach Europe in great enough numbers. For the Central Powers – Germany and the Austro-Hungarian empire – the chances of victory had become more doubtful, and needed to be seized quickly, but they were still there.

Isaac Rosenberg wrote often to Eddie Marsh, who did his best for this poet, believing him to be a flawed genius. The transfer to a works battalion had taken Rosenberg back from the line; then he moved again at the start of 1917, this time to a trench mortar battery, a small unit that may have been thought likely to be more sympathetic, particularly as it was commanded by a Jewish officer who'd been asked by the colonel (to whom Marsh had written) to take on this unusual soldier. His new commander – later recalling a 'completely hopeless' soldier and a 'miserable-looking fellow, normal above the waist but short in the legs' – made him an assistant cook and was even more unimpressed when Rosenberg showed him some odd verses that included 'something to do with a rat': one of the greatest poems of the war, 'Break of Day in the Trenches'.

Another transfer came, back to a works battalion, then to the Royal Engineers. The work on roads, bridges, wire and railways was hard but Rosenberg drafted two verse plays, like 'Moses' on Old Testament themes – 'Adam and Lilith' and 'The Amulet', both abandoned. By now, though, he wanted to show the real war. 'Louse Hunting', which Bottomley had encouraged him to write after getting a letter that described frenzied men trying to catch and burn the lice with candles, is like a dark scene from Goya or Daumier. 'Returning We Hear the Larks' was written in the spring or early summer, a pastoral poem that jerks quickly out of romanticism. 'Dead Men's Dump' in May has the earth coldly taking in the dead as their souls rise, a sign of nature's obliviousness to human destruction reminiscent of the pitiless world of Charles Sorley's 'All the Hills and Vales Along'.

In June, the centre of the war moved north for the British army, back to Ypres. Although shells still reached him, Rosenberg finished what he thought of as his best poem, 'Daughters of War', a depiction of mythical goddesses who lead the dead into Valhalla. He told Marsh that the poem's ending was meant to show 'the severance of all human relationship and the fading away of human love'. 'Daughters of War' reflects an ambiguity about the war, for the Amazonian goddesses are magnificent as well as implacable purveyors of destruction. Gordon Bottomley thought it a masterpiece. To Marsh, however, the poem was discordant and obscure, and, to its author's disappointment, he left it out of the third volume of *Georgian Poetry* which was published in November.

In September, during the battle of Passchendaele, Rosenberg went to London on leave. He found, as those away from the front often did, that home was an anti-climax, a disappointment, partly because no civilian could imagine war's 'elemental' life. An East End revolutionary, Joseph Leftwich, wrote of seeing the poet at this time: of how Rosenberg, obviously much improved physically, seemed 'more boisterously happy than I had known him before' and anxious to contradict rumours that he 'hated the army' as 'he liked the life and the boys, and he had to fight. He wasn't going to let these people go about spreading rumours that he was funking it.' Such views come into the poem 'Soldier Twentieth Century', about an unbroken line between great captains like Napoleon and Caesar and the troops in the trenches.

In February 1917, Ivor Gurney, in reserve at Raincourt, saw an increase in shelling as the Germans let off surplus ammunition before moving back. He entered the abandoned land in March, where villages had been wrecked, crossroads mined and wells destroyed; and on 31 March his battalion attacked and took the village of Bihecourt.

A bullet went through Gurney's right arm just below the shoulder, giving bad pain for half an hour before fading, enough to be sent to hospital in Rouen, not the coveted 'Blighty'. As the fighting got worse, he thought back to the country where he'd once walked with his friend and fellow poet, F. W. 'Will' Harvey: 'I cannot keep out of mind what April has meant to me in past years – Minsterworth, Framilode, and his companionship.' He needed these, 'for Beauty's sake; and the hope of joy'. In hospital, he dreamed of the Cotswolds and 'a garden to dig in, and music and books in a house of one's own, set in a little valley from whose ridges one may see Malverns and the Welsh Hills, the plane of the Severn and the Severn Sea', where he was free from 'the drill-sergeant and the pack'.

'Pain', 'Ballad of the Three Spectres' (its conclusion prophetic of Gurney's post-war suffering), 'Servitude' (about how comradeship

and 'England' made the 'heavy servitude' bearable), 'Time and the
Soldier' (on the slowness of the war), 'After-Glow' (recalling Will
Harvey after he'd heard a rumour that Harvey had been killed),
'Song' and 'Song and Pain' all date from this time. When the
anthology *Soldier Poets* reached him in May, Gurney found in it
'precious little of value but much of interest', with Julian Grenfell's
'Into Battle' 'easily the best' and Sorley's translation of part of *Faust*
also fine. The death of Edward Thomas at Arras was 'a great loss'.
'Have you seen any verse by a man named Sassoon?' he asked
Marion Scott. 'I remember having seen quite good stuff,' particu-
larly 'Stretcher Case' ('it is very good').

Gurney was back in France in July, preparing for the next offen-
sive which became the third battle of Ypres, or Passchendaele. By
then he'd heard about Sidgwick and Jackson's offer for his poems:
not enough money, he thought, as the poems suited the increas-
ingly dark view of the war. The collection was, he judged, 'very
interesting, very true, very coloured', without enough sustained
'melody', perhaps slovenly in workmanship and lacking original
thought, although its beauty surprised him. He saw in *Severn and
Somme* 'hardly any of the devotion of self sacrifice, the splendid
readiness for death that one finds in Grenfell, Brooke, Nichols
etc', and wondered if this was because he was even more fragile
than they were. Gurney doubted that artists should risk death when
they could contribute to their country in other ways; 'such is my
patriotism, and I believe it to be the right kind'.

Severn and Somme is introverted: more about the poet's turmoil
and memories of Gloucestershire than about the war itself. Sieg-
fried Sassoon's *The Old Huntsman*, published on 8 May 1917, has
much more the feel of the trenches, although it included peacetime
work like the long Georgian title poem. 'It is good news that you
have Sassoon's book,' Gurney wrote to Marion Scott on 31 July
1917, 'which sounded interesting and sincere. Please tell me about
it.' In August he was with a machine-gun unit, supposedly for his
shooting ability. The country, even in its war-torn state, moved him,

'a darling land' of 'salt of the earth' peasants, without, he thought, the curse of England's 'ugly towns and commodious villas, born of vulgarity, sluggish liver, greed and all uncharitableness'. He still looked to 'noble and golden' Tewkesbury or Frampton on Severn, for 'villages of the hills also are precious and clean'.

Towards the end of August Gurney wrote, 'I hope you will send some more Sassoon, for his touch of romance and candour I like. He is one who tries to tell Truth, though perhaps not a profound truth.' Further reading of *The Old Huntsman* made him critical. The poet, he felt, could sacrifice meaning to beauty and be too journalistic or slack in technique. Gurney wondered if Sassoon wrote sometimes 'to free himself from circumstance. They are charms to magic him out of the present. Cold feet, lice, sense of fear – all these are spurs to create Joy ... Beauty is the only comfort.'

Was Sassoon 'the half poet, the borrower of magic'? Ivor Gurney thought about this in 'country like the last hell of desolation'. In the second week of September, he inhaled gas and collapsed. On 26 September, he wrote to Marion Scott from a hospital at Bangour in the Scottish borders. Craiglockhart – where, that month, Sassoon and Owen were patients – wasn't far away.

Sassoon's 'The General' was written in hospital, scathing about inept commanders, aimed particularly at Pinney who'd ordered the last attack that had nearly killed the poet. The reviews of *The Old Huntsman* began to come, sometimes shocked, mostly favourable, accompanied by respectful if surprised letters from comrades at the front who'd got hold of the book; and, as a soldier poet, he met writers and intellectuals like H. G. Wells, Arnold Bennett, Bertrand Russell and Middleton Murry. The artist Glyn Philpot thought Sassoon Byronic when he painted his portrait, which pleased the sitter. Immersed in fame and flattery, Sassoon discussed with the pacifists Russell and Murry the idea of a public protest against the continuation of the war. Both of them, and the Morrells, were sure that this would have a great effect if it came from an officer who'd won the Military Cross.

The war, Sassoon declared in his statement (which accompanied a letter to his commanding officer), had become one of 'aggression and conquest', and there should be immediate peace negotiations. Those at home showed, he believed, 'a callous complacence' about the 'agonies' at the front; and he was no longer prepared to fight. This was mutiny. Friends like Marsh were horrified; Robbie Ross, although in agreement, considered a public protest most unwise. Siegfried Sassoon's brother officers, from the front, admired the courage but not the sense.

Robert Graves thought it 'completely mad'. He and Sassoon had stayed in close touch after their time together on the Somme and Graves's near-death at High Wood in July 1916. It had taken time for the army to realize that Graves was still alive; his pay had been stopped, notices had appeared in *The Times* and his family had received many letters of sympathy.

Graves left hospital in the late summer of 1916 and went to his family home near Harlech, then in September 1916 to stay with Sassoon in Kent where he heard Siegfried's mother attempting to contact the spirit of her dead son Hamo, who'd been killed at Gallipoli in 1915. He rejoined his regiment in the freezing weather of January 1917, but was still thought not to be fit for the front line. By March he was judged to be exhausted, suffering from bronchitis, perhaps also the after-effects of his 1916 wounds. He was sent back to England, first to hospital at Somerville College, Oxford (where he fell in love with a girl for the first time), then for convalescence to the huge mansion built by Queen Victoria at Osborne on the Isle of Wight. It was at Osborne that Graves heard of Sassoon's protest. He became determined to try to save his friend from prosecution for mutiny, for which the sentence was death.

The outcome shows Sassoon's high reputation as an officer and also, possibly, the army's fear of the publicity that might accompany any trial. He was detained, in an oddly half-hearted way, at Litherland, the regimental depot near Liverpool. Meanwhile Graves got permission to leave Osborne and go north. But the authorities had little wish to prosecute; Graves persuaded Sassoon that he would not be made a martyr and should accept a diagnosis of shell shock. On 23 July, Sassoon arrived for treatment at Craiglockhart, supposedly escorted by Graves who, apparently in a worse state of nerves, had missed the train.

Sassoon had protested against the political, not the military, side of the war. The British had made secret treaties – as if to bear out his charge of 'aggression' and 'conquest' – with their allies (French and Russian) about new colonies to be carved out of the Ottoman empire in the event of victory. But he was wrong in thinking that this was the reason for continuing the war. The Germans still occupied neutral Belgium and much of northern France and their High Command, having stifled peace moves in the Reichstag, felt that, with Russia on the brink of revolution, the Central Powers could still win before enough American troops arrived. In June 1917, the Allies would be negotiating from weakness after a failed offensive and French mutinies, with British shipping still menaced by U-boats and the Americans cautious about what they might offer Britain and France, imperial powers historically distrusted in the United States. Better perhaps, like H. G. Wells's Mr Britling, to 'see it through'.

It was true, however, that the end of the war seemed no nearer. The emphasis, after the French failure of the Chemin des Dames, was again on Haig and the British. At Messines, ground was gained in June and July before the rain came; and by the end of a wet August there'd been some 60,000 casualties. In a dry September there was an advance; then, as autumn drew on, stalemate in the mud of Passchendaele. As on the Somme, Haig, feeling an unreal optimism and obligation to his allies, inflicted on his troops what Edmund Blunden thought was the worst part of the war. It was at Ypres (where, as we shall see, he believed 'we should all die') that Blunden read Sassoon. Here at last, he thought, was a poet who told the truth.

It wasn't pacifism that made Blunden think this. He remained loyal to his regiment, to those he was fighting alongside, and to his colonel, who stayed a friend; never, he thought later, would he meet such kindness again. Wilfred Owen was also no pacifist. In June he told his mother that his 'aim in war' was 'extinction of Militarism beginning with Prussian'. It was necessary to fight for this, even through 'unnameable tortures'. In Craiglockhart, in August, Owen read a life of Tennyson. He felt that the Victorian laureate was 'a great child' and 'so should I have been, but for Beaumont Hamel'.

By then he'd had a revelation. 'I have just been reading Siegfried Sassoon, and am feeling at a very high pitch of emotion,' he told his mother. 'Nothing like his trench life sketches has ever been written or ever will be written. Shakespeare reads vapid after these. Not of course because Sassoon is a greater artist, but because of the subjects, I mean. I think if I had the choice of making friends with Tennyson or with Sassoon I should go to Sassoon.' In the second week of August Owen approached his hero, bringing copies of *The Old Huntsman* for signature.

Siegfried Sassoon, engaged in polishing his golf clubs, looked at this 'modest and ingratiating' visitor, taking in his occasional stammer, 'border Welsh' accent and gushing idolatry. 'The Death Bed', Owen said, was the finest poem in the book; its author would have liked this, wishing to be known for his lyrical works rather than his satires. The visitor said he too was a poet. What, Sassoon wondered, could this 'interesting little chap' have written?

They were together for some two months. Craiglockhart was busy by day – with doctors' appointments, games and clubs for bee-keeping, photography, acting, music, the running of a magazine (the *Hydra*, which Owen edited) and debating; but at night the former hydro became a world of nightmares and cries of terror while enfeebled wills fought for calm. News of the war came by post or from visitors. Sassoon heard what his regiment was enduring at Passchendaele. He felt love for these men, and also shame not to be with them, writing in 'Banishment', 'Love drove me to rebel / Love drives me back to grope with them through hell; / And in their tortured eyes I stand forgiven.'

Dr Rivers – Siegfried Sassoon's physician and new father figure – seized on these urges. Rivers – a monkish, ruthless man – had heard terrible stories from his patients, like that of a soldier who'd been knocked out by a shell's blast and regained consciousness to find his mouth full of the contents of a dead German's stomach. He saw hysteria as a return to infantilism; traumas should be confronted, even if some repression was needed to preserve civilization. War took men back to childhood, to a more primitive life. To Rivers, Sassoon, as an ex-public schoolboy, was prone to guilt about letting his men down, about not protecting them, about being a shirker or failing to be a man. The doctor thought there was one cure. To satisfy himself, Siegfried Sassoon had to go back to the front, possibly to be killed. He had to leave this place of casualties and weakness.

Wilfred Owen told his mother how young Sassoon looked, how he 'talks as badly as Wells writes' and often seemed bored; then this changed to reports of a wish to 'cut capers of pleasure' in Sassoon's company even though 'he is not a cheery dog himself'.

They showed each other their work: Sassoon's poems that would make up his next collection *Counter-Attack* (including the title poem, which Owen found more frightening than battle's reality), and Owen at first some old verses, then the newer 'Antaeus' and 'Song of Songs', finally drafts for some of his last poems like 'Anthem for Doomed Youth', 'Dulce et Decorum Est' and 'The Chances'. Owen took on the need to break from artificial phrases, lush words reminiscent of the 1890s like 'viols' and 'murmurous hearts' and 'dawn singing' – to use everyday language; Sassoon too may have been influenced, by the rich imagery (again a *fin-de-siècle* throwback) or use of half-rhyme. Both were homosexuals – Owen possibly more experienced than the virginal Sassoon; both were well read, both realistic about the war but not pacifists. Owen told his mother in September, 'I hate washy pacifists as temperamentally as I hate whiskied prussianists.'

It was 'Anthem for Doomed Youth' which made Sassoon urge

Owen towards early publication. Robert Graves arrived in Edin-
burgh to see Siegfried and, characteristically, took this stranger in
hand, saying he could be 'damn fine' but was too lax in metre,
'careless ... too Sassoonish'. Owen, now more confident, thought he
didn't need instruction from 'Captain Graves'.

At the start of November, Wilfred Owen left Edinburgh, with
money from Sassoon and an introduction to Robert Ross. A week
later he told his mother he'd met Ross, Arnold Bennett and H. G.
Wells at the Reform Club. Sassoon had said he would get William
Heinemann to publish his new friend. On the last day of 1917,
Owen could say 'I go out of this year a Poet, my dear Mother, as
which I did not enter it. I am held peer by the Georgians; I am a
poet's poet.'

Graves, Owen and Sassoon had missed what was happening
around Ypres. Of the poets, it was Edmund Blunden who went
through this. From July until November Blunden was with his
battalion of the Royal Sussex as the fighting crossed the Flemish
landscape, by places like Vlamertinge, Van Heule Farm, the River
Steenbeek and the ruined Ypres.

Morale and the weather worsened; Blunden had to threaten a
mutinous warrant officer with arrest. A move to the Yser canal
brought greater safety, then some leave which ended in August and
a course at a wireless school at Zuytpeene before a return to the
transport lines, where he had to take up the rations: once 'almost a
laughing matter' but now dangerous in mud and shellfire. For
Blunden third Ypres, or Passchendaele, meant sheltering in tunnels
and trenches, edging out to reconnoitre through the mud, deep
pools and rain of churned-up fields, shattered settlements and
blasted trees that showed civilization's end.

On 1 November, his twenty-first birthday, he supervised trench
digging. He felt overcome by 'the general grossness of the war. The
uselessness of the offensive, the contrast in the quality of ourselves
with the quality of the year before, the conviction that the civilian
population realised nothing of our state, the rarity of thought, the

growing intensity and mood of destructive forces – these brought on a mood of selfishness. We should all die, presumably, round Ypres.'

Sent to the Army Signal School for two months, Edmund Blunden missed the end of the Ypres battles and Cambrai – where the success of the new tanks died out in enemy counter-attacks. He came back to his battalion in January 1918. After two days, he went to England on leave, ignoring the suggestion of his battalion's temporary commander that he should stay in Flanders. Already Blunden's time in the trenches had been long, and he'd been brave. While in France, he wrote poetry constantly. By May and June 1916 the war started to feature in these as well, seen often through a contrasting pastoral or romantic mood that accentuated the pain. 'Vlamertinghe: Passing the Chateau' (with its first line from Keats emphasizing sacrifice) was written in July. Like Owen, he read Sassoon, finding an astonishing sense of how the war felt, also a resemblance to sketches by Goya and, in the poems' conversational style, to Hardy and to Browning.

War poetry was, by 1917, an established genre, its best-sellers now mostly forgotten, apart from John McCrae's 'In Flanders Fields'. A successful grocer called William Dunkerley, writing under the name of John Oxenham, had published *All's Well* in November 1915 and sold 75,000 copies by July 1916. Other Oxenham books, sometimes in pamphlet form, reached hundreds of thousands of readers, his hymn 'For the Men at the Front' touching eight million. Christian works, aware of war's pain, these also had nostalgia for a settled world. Another popular poet was Robert Service, admired by Blunden for his poems about country life.

Of the more literary writers, it was Robert Nichols who achieved both praise and sales. Declared permanently unfit for military service at home or abroad, he worked for the Ministry of Labour, then the Foreign Office, unable to take anything too demanding because of treatment for neurasthenia. Nichols's new collection, *Ardours and Endurances*, published in the summer of

1917, propelled him into the public eye. Some thirty poems tell – romantically yet also in evocations of suffering – what he'd seen in France, how he responded to the war; some pre-war lyrics are also in the book, often about his old subjects such as fauns and love. The best poems include observations of batteries on the move and elegies to the dead, as in a memory of an Oxford contemporary:

> I mind how we sat one winter night
> While past his open window raced the bright
> Snow-torrent golden in the hot firelight ...
> I see him smiling at the streamered air ...

By the time the book came out, Nichols had met Marsh, who was ecstatic about it, comparing the poems to those by his beloved Rupert Brooke and putting eight of them into his latest Georgian anthology, which was published in November 1917. There was much praise; Charles Scott Moncrieff, later the translator of Proust, said that the book defined the times, and Graves, who later mocked Nichols's short service at the front and taste for prostitutes, joined in, as did the ageing critic Edmund Gosse, writing of Nichols's 'mournful passion'. John Masefield wrote that 'Nichols, Graves and Sassoon are singing together like morning stars.' The book had a first printing of 1,000, then a second of another 1,000, followed by a third in October of 500 and another 1,000 in early 1918.

Robert Nichols could persuade others of his pain. Blunden recalled Graves claiming that Nichols, he (Graves) and Sassoon were the three most important poets of the war. Sassoon would have hallucinations about the book in his hospital bed in 1918. Its author began a new life as a reciter and lecturer, his performances high-flown and theatrical.

In September 1917, Ivor Gurney fell in love with a nurse at Bangour hospital who liked but did not love him. The reviews of *Severn and Somme* in November were good enough to let Gurney think of himself as a war poet. The book's last section, entitled 'Sonnets 1917', was dedicated 'To the Memory of Rupert Brooke', a not entirely ironical tribute to the poet whose work had set him thinking about the best way to write about the war.

Gurney glanced wryly at Brooke's sales. 'When Rupert Brooke went abroad,' he wrote to Marion Scott on 21 November, 'he left his copyrights equally between Gibson, Abercrombie, and De la Mare. They have had £2,000 each! ... Poetry pays – it took a war to make it ...' At Bangour, he wrote 'To the Prussians of England', another blast against what was said about the war's purpose at home when Gurney and others were fighting to make their country a better place.

Robert Graves's *Fairies and Fusiliers* was published in November 1917, dedicated to the Royal Welsh Fusiliers. It includes a verse letter to Siegfried Sassoon, written 'from bivouacs at Mametz Wood, July 13th 1916', and another to Robert Nichols, showing the regard Graves had for him. Graves had a paternalistic feeling for his men and he felt that Sassoon's protest had let the men down. The two were never so close again. Sassoon told Lady Ottoline Morrell in November, from Craiglockhart, 'I don't think R.G. feels things as deeply as some – certainly not as much as Nichols – with all his egotism.'

Owen had been transformed by Craiglockhart. Early in November, his poem 'Miners' was accepted by the *Nation*; later that month he visited his cousin and former literary confidant Leslie Gunston, displaying a new confidence by writing mockingly to Siegfried Sassoon about Gunston's tame verses and sexual innocence. In November, he rejoined the 5th Battalion, the Manchester Regiment, at Scarborough, still thought capable only of light duties.

Officers were leaving for the front, which made Owen think of his duty as a poet and a man. Living in a tower room in a hotel near the sea, he remembered the look of those in the camp at Etaples, 'an incomprehensible look', he told his mother, 'not despair or terror, it was more terrible than terror, for it was a blindfold look, and without expression, like dead rabbit's. It will never be painted, and no actor will ever seize it. And to describe it, I think I must go back and be with them.' Avoiding the interminable games of bridge in the mess, Owen wrote 'Hospital Barge' (remembering the casualty clearing station at Gailly), the ninetyish fragment 'I Saw his Round Mouth's Crimson' and 'Apologia Pro Poemate Meo' (perhaps responding to Graves's instruction that he should write more optimistically). He heard that Sassoon had rejoined his regiment.

Nineteen-seventeen brought two new anthologies. *The Muse at Arms*, edited by E. B. Osborne ('an attempt to show the British warrior's soul'), offered a conventional view, with stirring verses and not much to stir the thoughts; Sassoon was represented by 'Absolution' (a call to arms of 1915) and 'The Redeemer', a frontline work but less sharp than the later 'Blighters'. Osborne gave Robert Nichols more poems than any other writer, reflecting the view that this was the new Rupert Brooke.

Edward Marsh's new *Georgian Poetry* was more adventurous. His 1915 volume, too early for war poetry, had sold 19,000 copies, a startling amount, and was dedicated to two poets who had died that year, Brooke and James Elroy Flecker. In 1917 the editor's taste for verse drama is shown in an extract from 'Moses' by Isaac Rosenberg, and there were also war poems by Sassoon, Graves and Robert Nichols, the Sassoon selection including 'They', 'The Kiss', 'The Death Bed' and 'In the Pink' and only one 'happy warrior' work, 'To Victory'. Marsh showed his reverence for rank with an embarrassingly bad poem by the former Prime Minister's son Raymond Asquith, who'd been killed on the Somme.

The poets began to be lionized. Sassoon and Nichols read in November in the drawing room of the London hostess Mrs Colefax, the poems interspersed by Ivor Novello at the piano; and in December, Nichols read at Mrs Colefax's again, this time with Osbert and Sacheverell Sitwell, T. S. Eliot and Aldous Huxley. A young officer in the audience, Bernard Freyberg, who'd won the Victoria Cross, disapproved; it was 'offensive,' Freyberg declared, for Siegfried Sassoon 'to come back and say, I can't lead men to their death any more', which claimed 'a monopoly of virtue, as if other officers liked doing it, because they acquiesced in their duty'. Nichols, by this time an experienced and keen reader, didn't always impress. Huxley was scathing, declaring that he 'raved and screamed and hooted his filthy war poems like a lyceum villain who hasn't learnt how to act'.

Aldous Huxley was moving towards pacifism; Nichols, Sassoon and Owen weren't pacifists. All, however, wanted the war to end. In Britain there was some movement towards this. H. G. Wells's Mr Britling pleads for some form of world government, or at least an understanding of German demands. In August 1917, Professor Alfred Pollard, an eminent constitutional historian, said that wartime controls were making Britain as regimented as Prussia. In November, Lord Lansdowne, a former Foreign Secretary, Leader of the House of Lords and Viceroy of India, wrote to the *Daily Telegraph* calling for a negotiated peace.

For peace, there had to be a response from the other side. Germany seemed strong at the end of 1917, with all her troops fighting on foreign soil. After the Bolshevik revolution of October the Germans began negotiations for a treaty with the new Soviet Russia that would take vast swathes of land and release the armies from the eastern front. In the Middle East, the Turks had humiliated the British; in Flanders, the Ypres and Passchendaele offensive had ended inconclusively at huge cost. The military dictators that ruled Germany – Hindenburg, Ludendorff and their cipher the Emperor – still thought the war could be won before enough Americans came over. The quickest and surest way for the Allies to end the fighting was to surrender.

The war was becoming a test of endurance, with the grind at the front ever more relentless. In November, Isaac Rosenberg was at Cambrai, back with the 11th King's Own, which attacked Bourlon Wood when flu kept the poet in hospital. He read Marsh's new Georgian anthology, with his piece from 'Moses' and eight poems by Siegfried Sassoon, and reflected that 'Sassoon has power.' From his sick bed, Rosenberg asked for watercolours so that he might paint; and wrote 'Girl to Soldier on Leave' and a fresh version of a verse play. By the start of January 1918, he was well enough to return to the line. 'I am back in the trenches which are terrible now,' he told Marsh. 'We spend most of our time pulling each other out of the mud. I am not fit at all.' Christ, he thought, had not suffered as much as this.

1917 POEMS

After-Glow

(To F. W. Harvey)

Out of the smoke and dust of the little room
With tea-talk loud and laughter of happy boys,
I passed into the dusk. Suddenly the noise
Ceased with a shock, left me alone in the gloom,
To wonder at the miracle hanging high
Tangled in twigs, the silver crescent clear.
Time passed from mind. Time died, and then we were
Once more at home together, you and I.

The elms with arms of love wrapped us in shade
Who watched the ecstatic west with one desire,
One soul uprapt; and still another fire
Consumed us, and our joy yet greater made:
That Bach should sing for us, mix us in one
The joy of firelight and the sunken sun.

IVOR GURNEY

174

Song

Only the wanderer
    Knows England's graces,
Or can anew see clear
    Familiar faces.

And who loves joy as he
    That dwells in shadows?
Do not forget me quite,
    O Severn meadows.

IVOR GURNEY

Soldier: Twentieth Century

I love you, great new Titan!
Am I not you?
Napoleon or Caesar
Out of you grew.

Out of the unthinkable torture,
Eyes kissed by death,
Won back to the world again,
Lost and won in a breath,

Cruel men are made immortal.
Out of your pain born.
They have stolen the sun's power
With their feet on your shoulders worn.

Let them shrink from your girth,
That has outgrown the pallid days,
When you slept like Circe's swine,
Or a word in the brain's ways.

Isaac Rosenberg

Blighters

The House is crammed: tier beyond tier they grin
And cackle at the Show, while prancing ranks
Of harlots shrill the chorus, drunk with din;
'We're sure the Kaiser loves our dear old Tanks!'

I'd like to see a Tank come down the stalls,
Lurching to rag-time tunes, or 'Home, sweet Home',
And there'd be no more jokes in Music-halls
To mock the riddled corpses round Bapaume.

SIEGFRIED SASSOON

Ballad of the Three Spectres

As I went up by Ovillers
   In mud and water cold to the knee,
There went three jeering, fleering spectres,
   That walked abreast and talked of me.

The first said, 'Here's a right brave soldier
   That walks the dark unfearingly;
Soon he'll come back on a fine stretcher,
   And laughing for a nice Blighty.'

The second, 'Read his face, old comrade,
   No kind of lucky chance I see;
One day he'll freeze in mud to the marrow,
   Then look his last on Picardie.'

Though bitter the word of these first twain
   Curses the third spat venomously;
'He'll stay untouched till the war's last dawning
   Then live one hour of agony.'

Liars the first two were. Behold me
   At sloping arms by one – two – three,
Waiting the time I shall discover
   Whether the third spake verity.

IVOR GURNEY

Servitude

If it were not for England, who would bear
This heavy servitude one moment more?
To keep a brothel, sweep and wash the floor
Of filthiest hovels were noble to compare
With this brass-cleaning life. Now here, now there
Harried in foolishness, scanned curiously o'er
By fools made brazen by conceit, and store
Of antique witticisms thin and bare.

Only the love of comrades sweetens all,
Whose laughing spirit will not be outdone.
As night-watching men wait for the sun
To hearten them, so wait I on such boys
As neither brass nor Hell-fire may appal,
Nor guns, nor sergeant-major's bluster and noise.

IVOR GURNEY

Louse Hunting

Nudes – stark aglisten
Yelling in lurid glee. Grinning faces of fiends
And raging limbs
Whirl over the floor one fire,
For a shirt verminously busy
Yon soldier tore from his throat
With oaths
Godhead might shrink at, but not the lice.
And soon the shirt was aflare
Over the candle he'd lit while we lay.
Then we all sprang up and stript
To hunt the vermin brood.
Soon like a demons' pantomime
The place was raging.
See the silhouettes agape,
See the gibbering shadows
Mixed with the battled arms on the wall.
See gargantuan hooked fingers
Dug in supreme flesh
To smutch the supreme littleness.
See the merry limbs in hot Highland fling
Because some wizard vermin
Charmed from the quiet this revel
When our ears were half lulled
By the dark music
Blown from Sleep's trumpet.

ISAAC ROSENBERG

Dead Man's Dump

The plunging limbers over the shattered track
Racketed with their rusty freight,
Stuck out like many crowns of thorns,
And the rusty stakes like sceptres old
To stay the flood of brutish men
Upon our brothers dear.

The wheels lurched over sprawled dead
But pained them not, though their bones crunched,
Their shut mouths made no moan,
They lie there huddled, friend and foeman,
Man born of man, and born of woman,
And shells go crying over them
From night till night and now.

Earth has waited for them,
All the time of their growth
Fretting for their decay:
Now she has them at last!
In the strength of their strength
Suspended – stopped and held.

What fierce imaginings their dark souls lit
Earth! have they gone into you?
Somewhere they must have gone,
And flung on your hard back
Is their soul's sack,
Emptied of God-ancestralled essences.
Who hurled them out? Who hurled?

None saw their spirits' shadow shake the grass,
Or stood aside for the half used life to pass
Out of those doomed nostrils and the doomed mouth,
When the swift iron burning bee
Drained the wild honey of their youth.

What of us who, flung on the shrieking pyre,
Walk, our usual thoughts untouched,
Our lucky limbs as on ichor fed,
Immortal seeming ever?
Perhaps when the flames beat loud on us,
A fear may choke in our veins
And the startled blood may stop.

The air is loud with death,
The dark air spurts with fire,
The explosions ceaseless are.
Timelessly now, some minutes past,
Those dead strode time with vigorous life,
Till the shrapnel called 'an end!'
But not to all. In bleeding pangs
Some borne on stretchers dreamed of home,
Dear things, war-blotted from their hearts.

A man's brains splattered on
A stretcher-bearer's face;
His shook shoulders slipped their load,
But when they bent to look again
The drowning soul was sunk too deep
For human tenderness.

They left this dead with the older dead,
Stretched at the cross roads.

Burnt black by strange decay
Their sinister faces lie
The lid over each eye,
The grass and coloured clay
More motion have than they,
Joined to the great sunk silences.

Here is one not long dead;
His dark hearing caught our far wheels,
And the choked soul stretched weak hands
To reach the living word the far wheels said,
The blood-dazed intelligence beating for light,
Crying through the suspense of the far torturing wheels
Swift for the end to break,
Or the wheels to break,
Cried as the tide of the world broke over his sight.

Will they come? Will they ever come?
Even as the mixed hoofs of the mules,
The quivering-bellied mules,
And the rushing wheels all mixed
With his tortured upturned sight,
So we crashed round the bend,
We heard his weak scream,
We heard his very last sound,
And our wheels grazed his dead face.

ISAAC ROSENBERG

The General

'Good-morning, good-morning!' the General said
When we met him last week on our way to the line.
Now the soldiers he smiled at are most of 'em dead,
And we're cursing his staff for incompetent swine.
'He's a cheery old card,' grunted Harry to Jack
As they slogged up to Arras with rifle and pack.

But he did for them both by his plan of attack.

SIEGFRIED SASSOON

Returning, We Hear the Larks

Sombre the night is.
And though we have our lives, we know
What sinister threat lurks there.

Dragging these anguished limbs, we only know
This poison-blasted track opens on our camp –
On a little safe sleep.

But hark! joy – joy – strange joy.
Lo! heights of night ringing with unseen larks.
Music showering our upturned list'ning faces.

Death could drop from the dark
As easily as song –
But song only dropped,
Like a blind man's dreams on the sand
By dangerous tides,
Like a girl's dark hair for she dreams no ruin lies there,
Or her kisses where a serpent hides.

ISAAC ROSENBERG

Sergeant-Major Money

It wasn't our battalion, but we lay alongside it,
  So the story is as true as the telling is frank.
They hadn't one Line-officer left, after Arras,
  Except a batty major and the Colonel, who drank.

'B' Company Commander was fresh from the Depot,
  An expert on gas drill, otherwise a dud;
So Sergeant-Major Money carried on, as instructed,
  And that's where the swaddies began to sweat blood.

His Old Army humour was so well-spiced and hearty
  That one poor sod shot himself, and one lost his wits;
But discipline's maintained, and back in rest-billets
  The Colonel congratulates 'B' Company on their kits.

The subalterns went easy, as was only natural
  With a terror like Money driving the machine,
Till finally two Welshmen, butties from the Rhondda,
  Bayoneted their bugbear in a field-canteen.

Well, we couldn't blame the officers, they relied on Money;
  We couldn't blame the pitboys, their courage was grand;
Or, least of all, blame Money, an old stiff surviving
  In a New (bloody) Army he couldn't understand.

ROBERT GRAVES

To Any Dead Officer

Well, how are things in Heaven? I wish you'd say,
Because I'd like to know that you're all right.
Tell me, have you found everlasting day,
Or been sucked in by everlasting night?
For when I shut my eyes your face shows plain;
I hear you make some cheery old remark –
I can rebuild you in my brain,
Though you've gone out patrolling in the dark.

You hated tours of trenches; you were proud
Of nothing more than having good years to spend;
Longed to get home and join the careless crowd
Of chaps who work in peace with Time for friend.
That's all washed out now. You're beyond the wire:
No earthly chance can send you crawling back;
You've finished with machine-gun fire –
Knocked over in a hopeless dud-attack.

Somehow I always thought you'd get done in,
Because you were so desperate keen to live:
You were all out to try and save your skin,
Well knowing how much the world had got to give.
You joked at shells and talked the usual 'shop,'
Stuck to your dirty job and did it fine:
With 'Jesus Christ! when *will* it stop?
Three years ... It's hell unless we break their line.'

So when they told me you'd been left for dead
I wouldn't believe them, feeling it *must* be true.
Next week the bloody Roll of Honour said
'Wounded and missing' – (That's the thing to do

When lads are left in shell-holes dying slow,
With nothing but blank sky and wounds that ache,
Moaning for water till they know
It's night, and then it's not worth while to wake!)

Good-bye, old lad! Remember me to God,
And tell Him that our Politicians swear
They won't give in till Prussian Rule's been trod
Under the Heel of England ... Are you there? ...
Yes ... and the War won't end for at least two years;
But we've got stacks of men ... I'm blind with tears,
Staring into the dark. Cheero!
I wish they'd killed you in a decent show.

SIEGFRIED SASSOON

Vlamertinghe: Passing the Chateau

(July 1917)

'And all her silken flanks with garlands drest' –
But we are coming to the sacrifice.
Must those have flowers who are not yet gone West?
May those have flowers who live with death and lice?
This must be the floweriest place
That earth allows; the queenly face
Of the proud mansion borrows grace for grace
Spite of those brute guns lowing at the skies.

Bold great daisies, golden lights,
Bubbling roses' pinks and whites –
Such a gay carpet! poppies by the million;
Such damask! such vermilion!
But if you ask me, mate, the choice of colour
Is scarcely right; this red should have been much duller.

EDMUND BLUNDEN

Counter-Attack

We'd gained our first objective hours before
While dawn broke like a face with blinking eyes,
Pallid, unshaved and thirsty, blind with smoke.
Things seemed all right at first. We held their line,
With bombers posted, Lewis guns well placed,
And clink of shovels deepening the shallow trench.
The place was rotten with dead; green clumsy legs
High-booted, sprawled and grovelled along the saps
And trunks, face downward, in the sucking mud,
Wallowed like trodden sand-bags loosely filled;
And naked sodden buttocks, mats of hair,
Bulged, clotted heads slept in the plastering slime.
And then the rain began, – the jolly old rain!

A yawning soldier knelt against the bank,
Staring across the morning blear with fog;
He wondered when the Allemands would get busy;
And then, of course, they started with five-nines
Traversing, sure as fate, and never a dud.
Mute in the clamour of shells he watched them burst
Spouting dark earth and wire with gusts from hell,
While posturing giants dissolved in drifts of smoke.
He crouched and flinched, dizzy with galloping fear,
Sick for escape, – loathing the strangled horror
And butchered, frantic gestures of the dead.

An officer came blundering down the trench:
'Stand-to and man the fire-step!' On he went ...
Gasping and bawling, 'Fire-step ... counter-attack!'
Then the haze lifted. Bombing on the right
Down the old sap: machine-guns on the left;

And stumbling figures looming out in front.
'O Christ, they're coming at us!' Bullets spat,
And he remembered his rifle ... rapid fire ...
And started blazing wildly ... then a bang
Crumpled and spun him sideways, knocked him out
To grunt and wriggle: none heeded him; he choked
And fought the flapping veils of smothering gloom,
Lost in a blurred confusion of yells and groans ...
Down, and down, and down, he sank and drowned,
Bleeding to death. The counter-attack had failed.

SIEGFRIED SASSOON

To the Prussians of England

When I remember plain heroic strength
And shining virtue shown by Ypres pools,
Then read the blither written by knaves for fools
In praise of English soldiers lying at length,
Who purely dream what England shall be made
Gloriously new, free of the old stains
By us, who pay the price that must be paid,
Will freeze all winter over Ypres plains.
Our silly dreams of peace you put aside
And Brotherhood of man, for you will see
An armed Mistress, braggart of the tide
Her children slaves, under your mastery ...
We'll have a word there too, and forge a knife,
Will cut the cancer threatens England's life.

IVOR GURNEY

Anthem for Doomed Youth

What passing-bells for these who die as cattle?
– Only the monstrous anger of the guns.
Only the stuttering rifles' rapid rattle
Can patter out their hasty orisons.
No mockeries now for them; no prayers nor bells;
Nor any voice of mourning save the choirs, –
The shrill, demented choirs of wailing shells;
And bugles calling for them from sad shires.

What candles may be held to speed them all?
Not in the hands of boys but in their eyes
Shall shine the holy glimmers of good-byes.
The pallor of girls' brows shall be their pall;
Their flowers the tenderness of patient minds,
And each slow dusk a drawing-down of blinds.

WILFRED OWEN

To his Love

He's gone, and all our plans
Are useless indeed.
We'll walk no more on Cotswold
Where the sheep feed
Quietly and take no heed.

His body that was so quick
Is not as you
Knew it, on Severn River
Under the blue
Driving our small boat through.

You would not know him now ...
But still he died
Nobly, so cover him over
With violets of pride
Purple from Severn side.

Cover him, cover him soon!
And with thick-set
Masses of memoried flowers –
Hide that red wet
Thing I must somehow forget.

IVOR GURNEY

I Saw his Round Mouth's Crimson

I saw his round mouth's crimson deepen as it fell,
    Like a sun, in his last deep hour;
Watched the magnificent recession of farewell,
    Clouding, half gleam, half glower,
And a last splendour burn the heavens of his cheek.
    And in his eyes
The cold stars lighting, very old and bleak,
    In different skies.

WILFRED OWEN

Photographs (To Two Scots Lads)

Lying in dug-outs, joking idly, wearily;
Watching the candle guttering in the draught;
Hearing the great shells go high over us, eerily
Singing; how often have I turned over, and laughed

With pity and pride, photographs of all colours,
All sizes, subjects: khaki brothers in France;
Or mothers' faces worn with countless dolours;
Or girls whose eyes were challenging and must dance,

Though in a picture only, a common cheap
Ill-taken card; and children – frozen, some
(Babies) waiting on Dicky-bird to peep
Out of the handkerchief that is his home

(But he's so shy!). And some with bright looks, calling
Delight across the miles of land and sea,
That not the dread of barrage suddenly falling
Could quite blot out – not mud nor lethargy.

Smiles and triumphant careless laughter. O
The pain of them, wide Earth's most sacred things!
Lying in dugouts, hearing the great shells slow
Sailing mile-high, the heart mounts higher and sings.

But once – O why did he keep that bitter token
Of a dead Love? – that boy, who, suddenly moved,
Showed me, his eyes wet, his low talk broken,
A girl who better had not been beloved.

IVOR GURNEY

1918

In January 1918, Robert Graves married Nancy Nicholson in London, and Wilfred Owen came down from Scarborough for the wedding. Here he met Eddie Marsh and Charles Scott Moncrieff who later put it about that he'd seduced this 'quiet little person'. Scott Moncrieff tried to fix a home posting for his new friend but the trail to France opened up when a medical board upgraded Owen in early March. He moved to the northern command depot in Ripon, arriving there on 12 March and renting a room in the Yorkshire cathedral city.

Wilfred Owen wrote many of the great poems of his last year at Scarborough and Ripon, perhaps because the front-line traumas of 1917 could be recalled in the comparative calm of a home posting (and a room of his own) alongside the extraordinary stimulation given by Sassoon. Some, like 'Dulce et Decorum Est', 'The Dead Beat' (criticized by Sassoon and later redrafted), 'The Sentry' and possibly 'Insensibility', were begun in 1917 at Craiglockhart, then worked on at Scarborough and Ripon and, after August 1918, in France. 'Spring Offensive' was based on what he'd seen on the western front in April 1917; 'Strange Meeting' came in Scarborough and Ripon from January to March 1918. In May, in Ripon, he probably began a draft of the preface that would appear in collections of his poetry.

Such graphic, compassionate work was timely, for the spring brought another huge attack in the west. The treaty of Brest Litovsk with the new Soviet Russia had led to large German gains that reached into the Baltic States and what are now Poland, Belarus and western Ukraine. It also released troops from the eastern front. German strength in the west increased by some 30 per cent after November 1917, and Allied forces declined, after Passchendaele and Cambrai. The German General Ludendorff knew that speed was vital. He chose the British as the weakest point, where they joined the French part of the line.

On 21 March, the Germans attacked along a front of some fifty-five miles, beginning with a creeping barrage and infiltration of infantry through a morning mist. The British retreat fell into chaos, even though the attack had been expected, failing to destroy bridges and roads, letting the enemy surge even faster forward. Ernst Jünger wrote of joyful hysteria, of how 'the immense desire to destroy that overhung the battlefield precipitated a red mist in our brains. We called out sobbing and stammering fragments of sentences to one another, and an impartial observer might have concluded that we were all ecstatically happy.' The giant rail junction at Amiens was under threat by 25 March, with the British some twenty-four miles back from what four days earlier had been their front line.

Isaac Rosenberg dreamed of getting into a Jewish battalion that was bound for the Middle East. Marsh tried to fix this but failed, and on 8 March – in reserve, repairing roads and bringing up supplies – Rosenberg wrote of his dread of wet weather, for 'We will become like mummies – look warm and lifelike, but a touch and we will crumble to pieces.' His ambition was to finish another verse drama, 'The Unicorn', that would show war and the forces let loose 'by an ambitious and unscrupulous will' or a pitiless God.

Rosenberg was back in the front line when the Germans attacked. His unit retreated into reserve, then further back, and in the turmoil he wrote 'Through These Pale Cold Days'. This, his last poem, could refer to the longed-for Jewish battalion: the 'dark faces' that 'burn / out of three thousand years, / and their wild eyes yearn': the end hinting at a premonition of his own death. Isaac Rosenberg was killed by a sniper or a raiding party at dawn on 1 April. Some words were found among his effects: 'How small a thing is art. A little pain; disappointment, and any man feels a depth – a boundlessness of emotion, inarticulate thoughts no poet has ever succeeded in imaging. Death does not conquer me, I conquer death, I am the master.'

Siegfried Sassoon was sent to Palestine that spring. The journey went, strangely, through Ireland after Craiglockhart. Stationed with his regiment in Limerick, Sassoon hunted, moved among the gentry, feeling oddly in limbo, and avoided the IRA in a country still simmering after the Easter Rising of 1916. On 11 February, he left for the Middle East to join General Allenby's Egyptian Expedition Force.

On the voyage out, Sassoon met soldiers from a Jewish volunteer battalion (perhaps the one that Rosenberg had tried to join) at Taranto and, as if forgetting his own Jewish roots, let slip some mild anti-Semitism in his diary. In Palestine, he found desolate hills, a sunlit landscape and, for a change, victory. Jerusalem and Jericho had fallen to Allenby's forces, 'Johnny Turk' was on the run and Sassoon's commanding officer joked about shooting prisoners. Then reports came of the German offensive on the western front and loss of most of the ground gained since the Somme.

Reinforcements were needed in France. Sassoon went first to Alexandria in Egypt, where he had hoped – but failed – to see E. M. Forster, who was working there for the Red Cross. Forster now dreaded what might happen after the war, for so much jingoism and false feeling, so much hatred, had been released. Any new peaceful Britain must, the novelist felt, be worse than the country he'd known in 1914.

Sassoon and his battalion reached the south of France, leaving Marseilles by train on 9 May to go north to the front. Much had happened since the launch of the German offensive. Harsh terms had been imposed on Romania, giving Germany and Austria-Hungary control over the country's oil fields for ninety-nine years, again showing how demanding the Germans would be in any peace negotiations. In April, however, an attack on the Lys spread their forces too thinly. On 3 April the Allies rallied with a new unified command under the French Marshal Foch. An officer friend told Ivor Gurney of the improvement: how much better the French staff was than the British. Even the dour Haig rose to the crisis, issuing a stirring statement on 11 April: 'With our backs to the wall and believing in the justice of our cause each one of us must fight on to the end.' The writer Vera Brittain, nursing at the front – and no fan of the High Command – wrote after reading this, 'I knew I should go on, whether I could or not.'

The German successes of March – 140 square miles seized in only twenty-four hours, with 39,000 casualties, as against 98 square miles gained by the Allies in 1916 on the Somme, over 140 days, with 1.5 million casualties – hid hunger and despair within Germany and dwindling manpower, even with the arrival of troops from the east. American entry into the war led to an intensification of the economic blockade, made worse by bad harvests in 1916 and 1917. German troops on leave were sick of fighting and disheartened by the worsening conditions at home; of those transferring to the west from Russia up to 10 per cent deserted on the way. Industrial unrest spread through the factories. The offensives led to drawn-out supply lines and exhaustion. In July the French began the Allied counter-attack on the Marne.

Wilfred Owen waited to go out. At Ripon in May, he made plans for a post-war world, a traditional vision: blank-verse plays on old Welsh themes, looking to Tennyson and Yeats; a *Collected Poems* in 1919; *Perseus*, a volume presumably inspired by myth, and another entitled *Idylls in Prose*.

There's a voluptuousness in the Ripon and Scarborough poems, a richness of detail and emotion, which shows the influence not only of Keats and Shelley but of the 1890s. Owen sent some drafts to Siegfried Sassoon who, on the evidence of these, wondered later why at Craiglockhart he'd thought this young man to be merely promising. Perhaps it had been the artlessness of the eager disciple or that effusive 'border-Welsh temperament'; now he saw the power of 'my little friend Wilfred'. Later Sassoon doubted if he'd had much effect on Owen, or had achieved anything beyond giving encouragement. Owen might, Sassoon thought, 'have done just as well if he had never met me. He was a born poet, & had he lived, would have produced some of the most beautiful & original poetry of his time.' What Siegfried Sassoon and Wilfred Owen might have achieved together haunted the survivor.

In May 1918, Sassoon arrived again on the western front. To begin with, he was out of the line, near Crécy, site of an English victory during the Hundred Years War, where he trained troops and felt overcome with sympathy for them. The fighting had moved across the old Festubert line, with the Germans still making gains. Until July Sassoon was in billets near Domvast, among beechwoods, bluebells, orchards and hawthorns, writing fatalistically to Graves to say that he'd left him £250 a year and that Robert Nichols ('the best poet of the three') must write an elegy about him if he was killed.

Like Forster, Sassoon wondered what peace might bring. The omens were bad. Robbie Ross's London had descended into turmoil as Lord Alfred Douglas, once (like Ross) Oscar Wilde's lover, embarked upon a campaign of public abuse against former friends of Wilde and homosexuals in general. 'Robbie' had introduced Sassoon to greater literary and sexual frankness; now this was threatened by intolerance and a home front of attention-seeking and ignorance. In March the police raided Ross's flat; in June a maverick member of parliament, Noel Pemberton Billing, claimed that the Germans had a black book of some 47,000 British homosexuals whom Billing would name. It seemed to Sassoon, Forster and others that to their own country they were now the enemy within.

As he moved into the front line, Siegfried Sassoon's second wartime collection of poems was published, entitled *Counter-Attack*, some of which he'd shown to Owen at Craiglockhart. The print run of 1,500 showed that sales of *The Old Huntsman* had been good, although not on the scale of Oxenham or even Nichols: that Sassoon was now famous as a rebel hero. The Cambridge academic

Edward Dent, who'd loathed the war and its jingo patriotism from the start, thought that the book was devastating; Sassoon's doctor at Craiglockhart, Rivers, however, worried about the poet's 'damned hankering after death'. Thomas Hardy especially liked the title piece and 'To Any Dead Officer'. In November 1917, Edmund Blunden had left the line near Ypres to go on a signalling course – a routine set up at least partly to give soldiers a useful rest – returning to his battalion in the New Year before going on leave on 13 January 1918. It was in England that Blunden read *Counter-Attack*, impressed by the collection not only as 'a portrait of war' but also because of the 'recollected charm of peace': an illustration of how soldiers needed to think of home.

There was some criticism. Middleton Murry said in the *Nation* that Sassoon's torment and suffering were more significant than his poetry, which was mere floating verses without deep thought, far from Wordsworth's classic definition of 'emotion recollected in tranquillity'. To Bertrand Russell, Murry's opinions showed the 'safe smugness' of the Bloomsbury conscientious objectors who, in contrast to Russell's time in jail for his anti-war protests, had safe billets working fitfully on farms. 'Ouf! I hate all the Bloomsbury crew, with their sneers at anything that has live feeling in it,' he told Lady Ottoline Morrell. '*Beastly* of them to be down on S.S.'

The Murry review came out on 11 July, the day that Sassoon, in the line near Saint Floris, had a direct hit on his dug-out. Having resumed his patrols in no man's land, he went out the next day with a corporal for over two hours. Returning in the early morning of 13 July, he stood up to look back and, having been mistaken for a German by a British soldier, was shot in the head. Robert Nichols, typically melodramatic, claimed that the High Command had ordered Siegfried Sassoon's execution because of his views on the war. Sassoon was taken to the American Red Cross Hospital in London, where he wrote his 'Letter to Robert Graves', a disjointed poem of suffering and shock that lets him be claimed for modernism.

Five days after Sassoon had been wounded, on 18 July, the French counter-attacked on the Marne; and on 8 August the British, Australians and Canadians advanced at Amiens. These months of fighting were as hard as any that had gone before, but Haig at last succeeded in combining devastating artillery firepower with carefully measured infantry attacks on a retreating enemy.

Siegfried Sassoon wasn't the only war poet to suffer from what Russell called Bloomsbury 'sneers'. Working under the strain of trying to please the poet's puritanical mother – who gave him the most depressing time of his life – Edward Marsh edited Rupert Brooke's *Collected Poems*. This was published in the summer of 1918 – and included his own memoir of Brooke – and, that August, Virginia Woolf reviewed the book in the *Times Literary Supplement*. Even those like Woolf who had detested the war (and Rupert Brooke's attitude to it) remained impressed by the man. Woolf said, however, that Marsh's memoir was incomplete and gently mocked its occasionally gushing tone while scarcely mentioning the poems. To Brooke's contemporaries (she added) it didn't seem to matter that he wrote poetry; the looks, the intellectual vigour and curiosity about writing and life, even his diet and clothes, were much more his point. For Virginia Woolf the question was not what he'd written but 'what would he have been'. She thought that this 'most restless, complex and analytic of human beings' would have become a modern writer of 'subtle, analytic poetry, or prose perhaps, full of intellect and full of his keen unsentimental curiosity'. To her diary, however, she was more scathing, calling the book 'a disgraceful sloppy sentimental rhapsody' that left its subject 'rather tarnished', yet she recorded, while staying with Lytton Strachey, 'a great deal of talk about Rupert'.

Virginia Woolf never met and at that date had never heard of Wilfred Owen. But Owen's version of the war would grow slowly to eclipse that of Brooke which, as her comments show, was already (as early as August 1918) starting to fade into historical curiosity. Owen's spring and early summer had been spent at Ripon, then back at Scarborough in June, and had seen the publication of 'Song of Songs' in the *Bookman* and 'Hospital Barge' and 'Futility' in the *Nation*.

Owen saw Ross and Scott Moncrieff in London in May and met Osbert Sitwell, another poet who'd been at the front. The Sitwells – Osbert and his sister Edith – wanted Owen's poems for *Wheels*, a journal started by them at least partly in opposition to Georgian pastoral nostalgia. Owen was again in London on 12 August, visiting Sassoon in hospital and seeing the Sitwells; on 31 August during his last hours before leaving for France, he saw the Harrow boy bathing near him in the Channel, a magnificent 'piece' of England. The day before Owen had quoted, to his mother, the Indian writer Rabindranath Tagore's words, 'When I go from hence let this be my parting word, that what I have seen is unsurpassable.'

The way to the front went through Etaples, then to Amiens to join his battalion and from Amiens to Vendelles before preparations for an attack. In France Owen completed 'The Sentry', 'Exposure' and 'Spring Offensive'. Of the fighting, he told his mother, 'I lost all my earthly faculties, and fought like an angel.' Doubts about his courage vanished when, with a corporal, he captured a German machine-gun post, writing that 'I only shot one man with my revolver (at about 30 yards!). The rest I took with a smile.' Wilfred Owen won a Military Cross.

He knew that he had a mission now, to care for and to record what his men endured, how 'every word, every figure of speech must be matter of experience', must be conveyed so that any soldier could understand. 'I came out in order to help these boys,' he told his mother, 'directly by leading them as well as an officer can; indirectly by watching their sufferings that I may speak of them as a pleader can. I have done the first.' What he wrote would fulfil the second.

The end came on 4 November, during an attack across the Sambre–Oise canal when three Victoria Crosses were won. Owen was last seen trying to cross the canal on a raft under heavy enemy fire. The engagement was his unit's last time in action, the heroism perhaps encouraged by a sense that victory was near. Showing the static nature of the western front, the 2nd Manchesters found themselves on Armistice Day – 11 November 1918 – in billets to the south of Landrecies, where they'd been on 18 August 1914, on their way to Mons.

The confirmation of Owen's Military Cross occurred some four days after he had been killed. One of the myths of the armistice is of the bells of Shrewsbury ringing out in celebration as the telegram boy knocked on the door of the Owen home with the news of Wilfred's death. It's ironic that the last letter to his mother from a poet whose work shows so powerfully the pain of war should say, 'It is a great life ... Of this I am certain, you could not be visited by a band of friends so fine as surround me here.'

There was muted joy for the poets when victory came. On 11 November, Siegfried Sassoon was staying with the Morrells at Garsington, in a literary house party. The four years had transformed him from a shy, obscure, fox-hunting versifier into a poet and hero, the prey of lion hunters. Relieved to be alone in nearby water meadows when the church bells rang, he went later that day to a rainy, hysterical London, attending a dinner party where the guests, mostly non-combatants, exhibited the same patriotic ecstasy as the crowds outside. To Sassoon, the festivities seemed 'a loathsome ending to the loathsome tragedy of the last four years'.

Edmund Blunden, now married to a Suffolk girl, was about to cross the Channel for the first time since February, expecting to see more fighting. Instead he became part of the forces of peace and, billeted near Arras later that year, reached into a recess beside his bed and found a book: Edward Thomas's study of John Keats. Thomas had been killed near by in 1917. Could it be the author's own copy? Holding the book, Blunden imagined 'the tall, Shelley-like figure of the poet gathering together his equipment for the last time, hastening out of this ruined building to join his men and march into battle ...'.

Ivor Gurney was at home in Gloucester, increasingly resented by his family as one who couldn't (or wouldn't) help himself after a mental breakdown. He'd been in England since September 1917 and the gassing, obviously unfit for the front, his despair great enough in June 1918 for him to write to Marion Scott from a hospital in Warrington to say that he would kill himself.

Clearly he'd had another breakdown, reverting to his disturbed and wayward pre-war state. The symptoms were a mixture of self-starvation and compulsive eating, also voices in the head – perhaps a legacy from his work as a signaller – and garbled references to some hurtful incident in the Bangour hospital during the last months of 1917. Work in the Gloucester docks and a munitions factory helped, after his release from hospital. On 2 November he told Marion Scott, 'I am glad to tell you that I am better myself, after a fortnight's hauling of heavy things ...' But the atmosphere at home was so tense that he thought of going away to sea.

For Gurney, the armistice coincided with at least some good news: that he would get a small war pension; that his first book, *Severn and Somme*, was to be reprinted; that Sidgwick and Jackson would publish *War's Embers*. As if in response, his music and poetry poured forth while his family, whom he hardly mentions in his letters, became even more estranged from him.

Robert Graves, unfit for front-line service since his wound in July 1916, had been training recruits or performing garrison duties in depots at Litherland, Oswestry and Rhyl. A possible posting to Egypt or Gibraltar didn't happen but marriage did, and Graves wrote almost apologetically to Sassoon about his new wife Nancy Nicholson (who became pregnant in May 1918), telling also of his plans for post-war farming with which 'you'll have to promise to help us out if we get into a hole, with some of your Persian gold'. Resentment at such requests comes in Sassoon's verse letter with the line, 'Why keep a Jewish friend unless you bleed him?' He thought Graves's recent poems were too soft, implying that marriage had been bad for the poet. On Armistice Day, the Graveses were living in a cottage in Rhuddlan, and Robert walked alone over the Welsh hills, 'cursing and sobbing and thinking of the dead'.

Robert Nichols was in New York on 11 November, lecturing on shell shock and poetry on a tour arranged by the British Foreign Office to foster closer relations between the Allies. Nichols read his own work and that of Graves, Sassoon and Charles Sorley, thinking the city beautiful but American women like 'icebergs'. The poet had at least one fan: the rich Mrs Lamont who believed in his genius, found the war poets fascinating and was coming to England. She would, Nichols told Marsh, 'very much I think like to meet Siegfried if she can – do you think you could manage it?' This was the poet as Byron – a romance of danger, suffering, courage and youthful sacrifice: a rare English epic, strengthening as, gradually, the myths of the war began.

1918 POEMS

Insensibility

1

Happy are men who yet before they are killed
Can let their veins run cold.
Whom no compassion fleers
Or makes their feet
Sore on the alleys cobbled with their brothers.
The front line withers.
But they are troops who fade, not flowers,
For poets' tearful fooling:
Men, gaps for filling:
Losses, who might have fought
Longer; but no one bothers.

2

And some cease feeling
Even themselves or for themselves.
Dullness best solves
The tease and doubt of shelling,
And Chance's strange arithmetic
Comes simpler than the reckoning of their shilling.
They keep no check on armies' decimation.

3

Happy are these who lose imagination:
They have enough to carry with ammunition.
Their spirit drags no pack.
Their old wounds save with cold can not more ache.
Having seen all things red,
Their eyes are rid
  Of the hurt of the colour of blood for ever.
And terror's first constriction over,
Their hearts remain small-drawn.
Their senses in some scorching cautery of battle
Now long since ironed,
Can laugh among the dying, unconcerned.

4

Happy the soldier home, with not a notion
How somewhere, every dawn, some men attack,
And many sighs are drained.
Happy the lad whose mind was never trained:
His days are worth forgetting more than not.
He sings along the march
Which we march taciturn, because of dusk,
The long, forlorn, relentless trend
From larger day to huger night.

5

We wise, who with a thought besmirch
Blood over all our soul,
How should we see our task
But through his blunt and lashless eyes?
Alive, he is not vital overmuch;
Dying, not mortal overmuch;
Nor sad, nor proud,
Nor curious at all.
He cannot tell
Old men's placidity from his.

6

But cursed are dullards whom no cannon stuns,
That they should be as stones.
Wretched are they, and mean
With paucity that never was simplicity.
By choice they made themselves immune
To pity and whatever mourns in man
Before the last sea and the hapless stars;
Whatever mourns when many leave these shores;
Whatever shares
The eternal reciprocity of tears.

WILFRED OWEN

Dulce et Decorum Est

Bent double, like old beggars under sacks,
Knock-kneed, coughing like hags, we cursed through sludge,
Till on the haunting flares we turned our backs
And towards our distant rest began to trudge.
Men marched asleep. Many had lost their boots
But limped on, blood-shod. All went lame; all blind;
Drunk with fatigue; deaf even to the hoots
Of tired, outstripped Five-Nines that dropped behind.

Gas! Gas! Quick, boys! – An ecstasy of fumbling,
Fitting the clumsy helmets just in time;
But someone still was yelling out and stumbling,
And flound'ring like a man in fire or lime …
Dim, through the misty panes and thick green light,
As under a green sea, I saw him drowning.

In all my dreams, before my helpless sight,
He plunges at me, guttering, choking, drowning.

If in some smothering dreams you too could pace
Behind the wagon that we flung him in,
And watch the white eyes writhing in his face,
His hanging face, like a devil's sick of sin;
If you could hear, at every jolt, the blood
Come gargling from the froth-corrupted lungs,
Obscene as cancer, bitter as the cud
Of vile, incurable sores on innocent tongues, –
My friend, you would not tell with such high zest
To children ardent for some desperate glory,
The old Lie; Dulce et Decorum est
Pro patria mori.

WILFRED OWEN

Strange Meeting

It seemed that out of battle I escaped
Down some profound dull tunnel, long since scooped
Through granites which Titanic wars had groined.

Yet also there encumbered sleepers groaned,
Too fast in thought or death to be bestirred.
Then, as I probed them, one sprang up, and stared
With piteous recognition in fixed eyes,
Lifting distressful hands as if to bless.
And by his smile, I knew that sullen hall, —
By his dead smile I knew we stood in Hell.

With a thousand pains that vision's face was grained;
Yet no blood reached there from the upper ground,
And no guns thumped, or down the flues made moan.
'Strange, friend,' I said, 'here is no cause to mourn.'
'None,' said the other, 'Save the undone years,
The hopelessness. Whatever hope is yours,
Was my life also; I went hunting wild
After the wildest beauty in the world,
Which lies not calm in eyes, or braided hair,
But mocks the steady running of the hour,
And if it grieves, grieves richlier than here.
For by my glee might many men have laughed,
And of my weeping something had been left,
Which must die now. I mean the truth untold,
The pity of war, the pity war distilled.
Now men will go content with what we spoiled.
Or, discontent, boil bloody, and be spilled.
They will be swift with swiftness of the tigress,
None will break ranks, though nations trek from progress.

Courage was mine, and I had mystery,
Wisdom was mine, and I had mastery:
To miss the march of this retreating world
Into vain citadels that are not walled.
Then, when much blood had clogged their chariot-wheels
I would go up and wash them from sweet wells,
Even with truths that lie too deep for taint.
I would have poured my spirit without stint
But not through wounds; not on the cess of war.
Foreheads of men have bled where no wounds were.

'I am the enemy you killed, my friend.
I knew you in this dark; for so you frowned
Yesterday through me as you jabbed and killed.
I parried; but my hands were loath and cold.
Let us sleep now ...'

WILFRED OWEN

The Secret

Suddenly with a shy, sad grace
She turns to me her lighted face,
And I who hear some idle phrase
   Watch how her wry lips move,
And guess that the poor words they frame
Mean nought, for they would speak the same
Message I read in the dark flame
   Within her eyes, which say, 'I love.'
     But I can only turn away ...

I, that have heard the deep voice break
Into a sing-song sobbing shake,
Whose flutter made my being quake,
   What ears have I for women's cries?
I, that have seen the turquoise glaze
Fixed in the blue and quivering gaze
Of one whom cocaine cannot daze,
   How can I yield to women's eyes?
     I, who can only turn away.

I, that have held strong hands which palter,
Borne the full weight of limbs that falter,
Bound live flesh on the surgeon's altar,
   What need have I of woman's hand?
I, that have felt the dead's embrace;
I, whose arms were his resting-place;
I, that have kissed a dead man's face;
   Ah, but how should you understand?
     Now I can only turn away.

ROBERT NICHOLS

Through These Pale Cold Days

Through these pale cold days
What dark faces burn
Out of three thousand years,
And their wild eyes yearn,

While underneath their brows
Like waifs their spirits grope
For the pools of Hebron again –
For Lebanon's summer slope.

They leave these blond still days
In dust behind their tread
They see with living eyes
How long they have been dead.

ISAAC ROSENBERG

Exposure

Our brains ache, in the merciless iced east winds that knive us …
Wearied we keep awake because the night is silent …
Low drooping flares confuse our memory of the salient …
Worried by silence, sentries whisper, curious, nervous,
        But nothing happens.

Watching, we hear the mad gusts tugging on the wire,
Like twitching agonies of men among its brambles.
Northward, incessantly, the flickering gunnery rumbles,
Far off, like a dull rumour of some other war.
        What are we doing here?

The poignant misery of dawn begins to grow …
We only know war lasts, rain soaks, and clouds sag stormy.
Dawn massing in the east her melancholy army
Attacks once more in ranks on shivering ranks of grey,
        But nothing happens.

Sudden successive flights of bullets streak the silence.
Less deadly than the air that shudders black with snow,
With sidelong flowing flakes that flock, pause, and renew;
We watch them wandering up and down the wind's nonchalance,
        But nothing happens.

Pale flakes with lingering stealth come feeling for our faces –
We cringe in holes, back on forgotten dreams, and stare, snow-dazed,
Deep into grassier ditches. So we drowse, sun-dozed,
Littered with blossoms trickling where the blackbird fusses.
        – Is it that we are dying?

Slowly our ghosts drag home: glimpsing the sunk fires, glozed
With crusted dark-red jewels; crickets jingle there;
For hours the innocent mice rejoice: the house is theirs;
Shutters and doors, all closed: on us the doors are closed, –
        We turn back to our dying.

Since we believe not otherwise can kind fires burn;
Now ever suns smile true on child, or field, or fruit.
For God's invincible spring our love is made afraid;
Therefore, not loath, we lie out here; therefore were born,
        For love of God seems dying.

To-night, this frost will fasten on this mud and us,
Shrivelling many hands, puckering foreheads crisp.
The burying-party, picks and shovels in shaking grasp,
Pause over half-known faces. All their eyes are ice,
        But nothing happens.

WILFRED OWEN

Dawn on the Somme

Last night rain fell over the scarred plateau,
And now from the dark horizon, dazzling, flies
Arrow on fire-plumed arrow to the skies,
Shot from the bright arc of Apollo's bow;
And from the wild and writhen waste below,
From flashing pools and mounds lit one by one,
Oh, is it mist, or are these companies
Of morning heroes who arise, arise
With thrusting arms, with limbs and hair aglow,
Toward the risen god, upon whose brow
Burns the gold laurel of all victories,
Hero and heroes' god, th' invincible Sun?

ROBERT NICHOLS

Arms and the Boy

Let the boy try along this bayonet-blade
How cold steel is, and keen with hunger of blood;
Blue with all malice, like a madman's flash;
And thinly drawn with famishing for flesh.

Lend him to stroke these blind, blunt bullet-leads
Which long to muzzle in the hearts of lads.
Or give him cartridges of fine zinc teeth
Are sharp with sharpness of grief and death.

For his teeth seem for laughing round an apple.
There lurk no claws behind his fingers supple;
And God will grow no talons at his heels,
Nor antlers through the thickness of his curls.

WILFRED OWEN

Futility

Move him into the sun –
Gently its touch awoke him once,
At home, whispering of fields half-sown.
Always it woke him, even in France,
Until this morning and this snow.
If anything might rouse him now
The kind old sun will know.

Think how it wakes the seeds –
Woke once the clays of a cold star.
Are limbs, so dear achieved, are sides
Full-nerved, still warm, too hard to stir?
Was it for this the clay grew tall?
– O what made fatuous sunbeams toil
To break earth's sleep at all?

WILFRED OWEN

Preface

This book is not about heroes. English poetry is not yet fit to
    speak of them.

Nor is it about deeds, or lands, nor anything about glory,
    honour, might, majesty, dominion or power, except War.

Above all I am not concerned with Poetry.

My subject is War, and the pity of War.

The Poetry is in the pity.
Yet these elegies are to this generation in no sense consolatory.

They may be to the next. All a poet can do today is warn. That
    is why true Poets must be truthful.

(If I thought the letter of this book would last, I might have
used proper names; but if the spirit of it survives – survives
Prussia – my ambition and those names will have achieved
fresher fields than Flanders ...)

WILFRED OWEN

A Terre

(Being the philosophy of many Soldiers.)

Sit on the bed; I'm blind, and three parts shell.
Be careful; can't shake hands now; never shall.
Both arms have mutinied against me, – brutes.
My fingers fidget like ten idle brats.

I tried to peg out soldierly, – no use!
One dies of war like any old disease.
This bandage feels like pennies on my eyes.
I have my medals? – Discs to make eyes close.
My glorious ribbons? – Ripped from my own back
In scarlet shreds. (That's for your poetry book.)

A short life and a merry one, my buck!
We used to say we'd hate to live dead-old, –
Yet now ... I'd willingly be puffy, bald,
And patriotic. Buffers catch from boys
At least the jokes hurled at them. I suppose
Little I'd ever teach a son, but hitting,
Shooting, war, hunting, all the arts of hurting.
Well, that's what I learnt, – that, and making money.

Your fifty years ahead seem none too many?
Tell me how long I've got? God! For one year
To help myself to nothing more than air!
One Spring! Is one too good to spare, too long?
Spring wind would work its own way to my lung,
And grow me legs as quick as lilac-shoots.

My servant's lamed, but listen how he shouts!
When I'm lugged out, he'll still be good for that.

Here in this mummy-case, you know, I've thought
How well I might have swept his floors for ever.
I'd ask no nights off when the bustle's over,
Enjoying so the dirt. Who's prejudiced
Against a grimed hand when his own's quite dust,
Less live than specks that in the sun-shafts turn,
Less warm than dust that mixes with arms' tan?
I'd love to be a sweep, now, black as Town,
Yes, or a muckman. Must I be his load?

O Life, Life, let me breathe, – a dug-out rat!
Not worse than ours the lives rats lead –
Nosing along at night down some safe rut,
They find a shell-proof home before they rot.
Dead men may envy living mites in cheese,
Or good germs even. Microbes have their joys,
And subdivide, and never come to death.
Certainly flowers have the easiest time on earth.
'I shall be one with nature, herb, and stone,'
Shelley would tell me. Shelley would be stunned:
The dullest Tommy hugs that fancy now.
'Pushing up daisies' is their creed, you know.

To grain, then, go my fat, to buds my sap,
For all the usefulness there is in soap.
D'you think the Boche will ever stew man-soup?
Some day, no doubt, if ...
                                    Friend, be very sure
I shall be better off with plants that share
More peaceably the meadow and the shower.
Soft rains will touch me, – as they could touch once,
And nothing but the sun shall make me ware.
Your guns may crash around me. I'll not hear;
Or, if I wince, I shall not know I wince.

Don't take my soul's poor comfort for your jest.
Soldiers may grow a soul when turned to fronds,
But here the thing's best left at home with friends.

My soul's a little grief, grappling your chest,
To climb your throat on sobs; easily chased
On other sighs and wiped by fresher winds.

Carry my crying spirit till it's weaned
To do without what blood remained these wounds.

WILFRED OWEN

Disabled

He sat in a wheeled chair, waiting for dark,
And shivered in his ghastly suit of grey,
Legless, sewn short at elbow. Through the park
Voices of boys rang saddening like a hymn,
Voices of play and pleasure after day,
Till gathering sleep had mothered them from him.

About this time Town used to swing so gay
When glow-lamps budded in the light blue trees,
And girls glanced lovelier as the air grew dim, –
In the old times, before he threw away his knees.
Now he will never feel again how slim
Girls' waists are, or how warm their subtle hands.
All of them touch him like some queer disease.

There was an artist silly for his face,
For it was younger than his youth, last year.
Now, he is old; his back will never brace;
He's lost his colour very far from here,
Poured it down shell-holes till the veins ran dry,
And half his lifetime lapsed in the hot race
And leap of purple spurted from his thigh.

One time he liked a blood-smear down his leg,
After the matches, carried shoulder-high.
It was after football, when he'd drunk a peg,
He thought he'd better join. – He wonders why.
Someone had said he'd look a god in kilts,
That's why; and maybe, too, to please his Meg,
Aye, that was it, to please the giddy jilts
He asked to join. He didn't have to beg;
Smiling they wrote his lie: aged nineteen years.

Germans he scarcely thought of; all their guilt,
And Austria's, did not move him. And no fears
Of Fear came yet. He thought of jewelled hilts
For daggers in plaid socks; of smart salutes;
And care of arms; and leave; and pay arrears;
Esprit de corps; and hints for young recruits.
And soon, he was drafted out with drums and cheers.

Some cheered him home, but not as crowds cheer Goal.
Only a solemn man who brought him fruits
Thanked him; and then enquired about his soul.

Now, he will spend a few sick years in institutes,
And do what things the rules consider wise,
And take whatever pity they may dole.
Tonight he noticed how the women's eyes
Passed from him to the strong men that were whole.
How cold and late it is! Why don't they come
And put him into bed? Why don't they come?

WILFRED OWEN

Letter to Robert Graves

24 July 1918   American Red Cross Hospital, No. 22
                                 98–99 Lancaster Gate, W.2

Dear Roberto,
I'd timed my death in action to the minute
(The *Nation* with my deathly verses in it).
The day told off – 13 – (the month July) –
The picture planned – O Threshold of the dark!
And then, the quivering songster failed to die
Because the bloody Bullet missed its mark.

Here I am; they *would* send me back –
Kind M.O. at Base; Sassoon's morale grown slack;
Swallowed all his proud high thoughts and acquiesced.
O Gate of Lancaster, O Blightyland the Blessed.

No visitors allowed
Since Friends arrived in crowd –
Jabber–Gesture–Jabber–Gesture–Nerves went phut and failed
After the first afternoon when MarshMoonStreetMeiklejohn
    ArdoursandernduranSitwellitis prevailed,
Caused complications and set my brain a-hop;
Sleeplessexasperuicide, O Jesu make it stop!

But yesterday afternoon my reasoning Rivers ran solemnly in,
With peace in the pools of his spectacled eyes and a wisely
    Omnipotent grin;
And I fished in that steady grey stream and decided that I
After all am no longer the Worm that refuses to die.
But a gallant and glorious lyrical soldjer;
    Bolder and bolder; as he gets older;

Shouting 'Back to the Front
For a scrimmaging Stunt.'
(I wish the weather wouldn't keep on getting colder.)

Yes, you can touch my Banker when you need him.
Why keep a Jewish friend unless you bleed him?

Oh yes, he's doing very well and sleeps from Two till Four.
And there was Jolly Otterleen a knocking at the door,
But Matron says she mustn't, not however loud she knocks
(Though she's bags of golden Daisies and some Raspberries in a box),
Be admitted to the wonderful and wild and wobbly-witted
    sarcastic soldier-poet with a plaster on his crown,
Who pretends he doesn't know it (he's the Topic of the Town).

My God, my God, I'm so excited; I've just had a letter
From Stable who's commanding the Twenty-Fifth Battalion.
And my company, he tells me, doing better and better,
Pinched six Saxons after lunch,
And bagged machine-guns by the bunch.

But I – wasn't there –
O blast it isn't fair,
Because they'll all be wondering why
Dotty Captain wasn't standing by
When they came marching home.

But I don't care; I made them love me
Although they didn't want to do it, and I've sent them a
    Glorious Gramophone and God send you back to me
Over the green eviscerating sea –
And I'm ill and afraid to go back to them because those
    five-nines are so damned awful.
When you think of them all bursting and you're lying on your bed,

With the books you loved and longed for on the table; and your head
All crammed with village verses about Daffodils and Geese –
… O Jesu make it cease …

O Rivers please take me. And make me
Go back to the war till it break me.
Some day my brain will go BANG,
And they'll say what lovely faces were
The soldier-lads he sang

Does this break your heart? What do I care?
Sassons

SIEGFRIED SASSOON

Crickley Hill

The orchis, trefoil, harebells nod all day,
High above Gloucester and the Severn Plain.
Few come there, where the curlew ever and again
Cries faintly, and no traveller makes stay,
Since steep the road is,
And the villages
Hidden by hedges wonderful in late May.

At Buire-au-Bois a soldier wandering
The lanes at evening talked with me and told
Of gardens summer blessed, of early spring
In tiny orchards, the uncounted gold
Strewn in green meadows,
Clear-cut shadows
Black on the dust and gray stone mellow and old.

But these were things I knew, and carelessly
Heard, while in thought I went with friends on roads
White in the sun and wandered far to see
The scented hay come homeward in warm loads.
Hardly I heeded him;
While the coloured dim
Evening brought stars and lights in small abodes.

When on a sudden, 'Crickley' he said. How I started
At that old darling name of home! and turned
Fell into a torrent of words warm-hearted
Till clear above the stars of summer burned
In velvety smooth skies.
We shared memories
And the old raptures from each other learned.

O sudden steep! O hill towering above!
Chasm from the road falling suddenly away!
Sure no two men talked of you with more love
Than we that tender-coloured ending of day.
(O tears! Keen pride in you!)
Feeling the soft dew,
Walking in thought another Roman way.

You hills of home, woodlands, white roads and inns
That star and line our darling land, still keep
Memory of us; for when first day begins
We think of you and dream in the first sleep
Of you and yours –
Trees, bare rock, flowers
Daring the blast on Crickley's distant steep.

IVOR GURNEY

AFTERMATH

AT THE ARMISTICE, the emotion of 1914 seemed far away, after so much pain and so many deaths, and a huge change in the perception of war. That first enthusiasm could easily be shown as absurd. Were Rupert Brooke's poems now merely a symbol of distant naivety?

At first it seemed as if Brooke's war would survive well, partly because Eddie Marsh was quick to build a shrine with the 1918 *Collected Poems* and memoir. In March 1919, a tablet was unveiled at Rugby – the place to whose values he'd returned at the end – in the form of a medallion of Brooke's head, looking eager and very young, on a wall of the enormous Victorian chapel. The commander of the doomed Gallipoli expedition, General Sir Ian Hamilton, gave a eulogy, underlining the political significance of those 1914 sonnets. Brooke, Hamilton said, had had every gift – 'youth, charm, beauty, genius' – and 'had it in his magic pen' to show 'the significance of the Dardanelles to the people of the empire'. Instead he'd died 'not with the shout of victory ringing in his ears, but for nothing – so it may have seemed – ah, but not so really', for his pen had 'already ennobled the theme' of war.

After the Somme and Passchendaele, these words came from a dead world. Soon the criticism, the mocking, began. Yet some, like Graves, Nichols and Sassoon, stayed admirers, at least of the idea of Brooke. In the 1920s, Virginia Woolf told a friend that she didn't think much of the poems and perhaps this 'ablest of men' had been more suited to public life than to writing. Rupert Brooke might have become Prime Minister for he had 'such a gift with people, and such sanity and force'. This seems unlikely; and Brooke has remained a poet. 'The Soldier' is perhaps the best-known sonnet of the twentieth century. The poems still sell, even if, as with Byron, much of the interest is in the romance of the poet's life. Brooke's version of war seems increasingly a distant curiosity.

Siegfried Sassoon was put up against Rupert Brooke, as a realist who understood war's tragedy. In peacetime, however, Sassoon lost his anger. Heinemann published a selection of his war poems in 1919, which sold well, with critical opinion divided: the *Nation* writing of 'A great pamphlet against the war', and the *London Mercury* of mere 'journalism'. In April 1919, Sassoon's 'Everyone Sang' conveyed hope for freedom and change, not wholly realized by the poet. Propelled by his fame, and by mentors like Marsh and the priapic Cambridge musicologist Dent, Sassoon began a decade of guilt-ridden socializing and sex, briefly at Oxford before becoming literary editor of the *Daily Herald* and, billed as a hero poet, following Nichols on a lecture tour of the United States. Awkward in the public gaze, yet craving praise, he reverted to private publication of his poems. His post-war satires had too blunt an edge, or were too mild, even if influenced by the poet's new left-wing views. Eventually Sassoon found a quiet lyricism which he stuck to for the rest of his life.

Robert Graves too went to Oxford, where he'd been about to go in 1914. He lived with Nancy and their child on Boar's Hill and saw Edmund Blunden, who was also at the university, Graves noting the other poet's drinking, shakiness and emotional talk of the trenches. It was at the *Daily Herald* that Sassoon first met Blunden, who'd sent him some poems, mostly set in the Kentish landscape, thus beginning what was for both of them a vital, if unequal, post-war friendship. Blunden's post-war poetry had two main themes: loving evocations (Georgian in style, often quaint in language) of a passing country world and an obsessive remembering of the trenches. Even 'Almswomen' of 1920 – set in a sweet English village – shows the war's shadow in a lament about death's separation. As early as 1918, Blunden began a prose memoir.

A gap opened between those who'd fought and those who hadn't. Before 1914, Britain and the new art of continental Europe had been getting closer; now, for many, the Continent meant death, obliteration and, even in peace, rumours of chaos. Some – mostly non-combatants like Eliot, James Joyce and Pound – still looked to modernism, to abstract art, to writing without clear narrative, whereas Sassoon and Blunden, even the more adventurous Graves, stuck to tradition, often yearning for an imagined, calm past. They had tried to tell of war's reality, Wilfred Owen writing that 'every word, every figure of speech must be a matter of experience' and 'I don't want to write anything to which a soldier would say No compris'. Owen had known nothing of Eliot or Pound.

Ivor Gurney's gentle father died in May 1919, and Ivor quarrelled with his strong-willed mother and scarcely spoke to his brother Ronald. Gurney's genius didn't impress the hard-working Ronald, who'd also fought in the war. He saw in Ivor only selfishness, arrogance, self-indulgence, even malingering.

Gloucestershire was what Gurney had dreamed of, in hospital and in France. How could he leave it again? 'Crickley Hill' shows how a name could set off rapturous memories. But in peace the old places couldn't work enough magic against deepening depression and, like many landscapes, they were perhaps better in memory or in dreams. He rejoiced, however, in his friend Will Harvey's return from a prisoner-of-war camp in Germany; and at a concert at Stroud, where Harvey read and sang his poems and Gurney played the piano, a member of the audience thought Ivor 'wonderfully normal and well'.

Gurney stayed with the Harveys, happier away from his family, then worked briefly on a farm. In May 1919, he went back to London, to take up his scholarship at the Royal College of Music and study under Ralph Vaughan Williams. There was hope that a new London life, some success and the end of the war might help.

Ivor Gurney's second collection, *War's Embers*, came out in 1919. It didn't sell well, perhaps because Gurney was still unknown in the little magazines that were then important in literary life. Escaping from home and family while at the Royal College of Music, he revived old friendships in or near London. Like many of those who fought, Ivor Gurney felt anxious and lost in a civilian world, as 'The Interview' and 'Laventie', written in 1921–2, show. 'After War' is about rest out of the line rather than a new peacetime life. His music and poetry went on bringing back the war. 'The Silent One' is about the distance, suggested in the accent and absurd courtesy, between a polite public school officer and his men.

Gurney got a job in the income tax office in Gloucester with Marsh's help, but his bad breakdown made such work impossible. His family endured further threats of suicide, garbled stories of interior voices, a refusal to eat or to sleep, rages and abuse of his brother Ronald for being crazy enough to work.

In September 1922, Ronald Gurney wrote despairingly to Marion Scott. The family couldn't cope. Ivor Gurney entered asylums, first in Gloucester, then in Kent; and after December 1922 he never saw Gloucestershire again. Poems and music still came, sometimes published or performed, and there were still admirers like Marion Scott and the composer Gerald Finzi. The asylum poems go over the past, as in 'It is Near Toussaints', 'The Interview', 'The Bohemians', 'First Time In' (remembering his battalion's welcome into the trenches from the Welsh troops, how the Welsh songs had never sounded more beautiful than 'here under the guns' noise') and 'Memory', written between 1922 and 1925. 'War Books' declared that he'd written from 'heart's sickness', to escape hunger or the worst of the war and to bring back the Cotswolds. Ivor Gurney recalled the 'needing and loving-of-action body' that he'd been. The war could seem preferable to a grim present, even if his life had been at risk.

Edward Thomas never fell into obscurity. His 1920 *Collected Poems* had as its frontispiece a romantic photograph of the poet looking down in melancholy, and there was a list of his twenty-three books and two edited anthologies. Walter de la Mare wrote a foreword, declaring, in an attack on modernism, that Thomas had 'detested mere cleverness', that he had resembled, perhaps even surpassed, Clare and Cobbett, Morland and Hardy, Hudson and Doughty, for 'England's roads and heaths and woods, its secret haunts and solitudes, its houses, its people – themselves resembling its thorns and juniper – its very flints and dust, were his freedom and peace'. There was, de la Mare thought, 'nothing precious, elaborate, brilliant, esoteric, obscure in his work'. The description of Thomas's looks, abruptness, yearning for solitude and dislike of being confined in a city portrays the poet as a solitary, mysterious outsider. Robert Frost, increasingly famous in the United States, praised his old friend's work, helping it to become known there.

Helen Thomas broke down after Edward's death. In the early 1920s, she published a memoir with frank depictions of her husband's early sexual innocence that annoyed some of his friends, including Frost. Helen yearned for living memories of him. Ivor Gurney had set some of Thomas's poems to music, and mentioned him in his post-1918 poem 'The Mangel-Bury' ('Edward Thomas had fallen at Arras') about the war dead and also in 'I Saw England – July Night' where home is 'a village of lovely knowledge' that held Thomas, Shakespeare, Hardy and Borrow. In 1932, Helen Thomas went with Marion Scott to see Gurney in his Dartford asylum.

At first the patient seemed normal; then, still obsessed with sinister messages, he said, 'It was wireless that killed Edward.' Helen waited, and they spoke of the country near Gloucester before going into another room, where there were other patients and a piano, and Ivor Gurney played. Helen Thomas heard that Gurney avoided the asylum's garden, thinking it tame compared to the wilder land of his imagination. Attempting perhaps to evoke this wildness, on another visit she brought Edward Thomas's old maps so that they could trace where he'd walked near Dymock; and Gurney, who'd known the landscape, seemed happy as this, or his version of it, came back.

She thought that he should be released, but it was believed that he would kill himself if he were.

Ivor Gurney died in December 1937 of pleurisy and tuberculosis. He'd just seen the proofs of the number of *Music and Letters*, put together by Marion Scott and Gerald Finzi, that was entirely about his work. Unable to take it in, Gurney murmured 'It is too late ...' He was buried at Twigworth, near Gloucester. A later attempt at a memorial came in 1954 when Edmund Blunden edited and introduced a selection of seventy-eight of Gurney's poems. The book received little attention. The great War Poets boom had not yet begun.

Ivor Gurney had been helped by Eddie Marsh; Edward Thomas too had known Marsh and had been at the Poetry Bookshop in January 1913 for the launch of the first Georgian anthology. The Georgians then had seemed fresh, even shocking. It was Marsh's hour. By 1918, that was passing.

A Georgian volume, the fourth, came out in November 1919, also published by Harold Monro at the Poetry Bookshop, with a very short introduction by Marsh, still the editor, that included the facetious comment, 'I hope it may be thought to show that what for want of a better word is called Peace has not interfered with the writing of good poetry.' The sense of a dying movement was intensified when the critic Middleton Murry, among others, declared that most of the poems were limp.

Marsh had another try in November 1922, with a final volume that, for the first time, included Blunden. Now sales crashed: 8,000, in contrast to the 19,000 of November 1915. Marsh himself was caricatured in H. G. Wells's 1925 novel *Men Like Gods* as the civil servant Freddie Mush, renowned for his 'Taste. Good taste ... He's dreadfully critical and sarcastic. Mr Mush with his preposterous eyeglass and love of good food ... spoke in a kind of impotent falsetto ...'

In 1926, Robert Graves, who'd been in the later volumes, claimed that the Georgians had become too 'concerned with Nature and love and leisure and old age and childhood and animals and sleep and other uncontroversial subjects'. By then Graves was in thrall to the American modernist writer Laura Riding; and 1922, the year of the last Georgian collection, was also the year of Eliot's *The Waste Land*, of Joyce's *Ulysses*, of Virginia Woolf's *Jacob's Room*.

Virginia Woolf thought at the end of 1918 how quickly the war had faded, perhaps not surprising since few of her friends had had any part in it. Six years later, when describing a farewell dinner given for Edmund Blunden who was going to teach at Tokyo University, she made no mention of the poet's time in the trenches – so vital to his writing – even though he was clearly still suffering from it. Instead she wondered loftily, 'Did we believe in Blunden's genius? Had we read his poems? How much sincerity was there in the whole thing?' Sincerity there would have been, for many people loved Blunden, even if some, notably Siegfried Sassoon, looked on him with condescension.

Woolf was thinking of the limitations of Blunden's work. Memories of such strong and terrifying experiences did impose a limit, through their power. The poets couldn't leave the war, even if, like Robert Graves, they wanted to move on. When Graves lived in a village near Oxford, many of the locals called him Captain Graves (a title which Thomas Hardy said he envied). As a veteran, he was asked by the vicar to speak at a church service commemorating the war dead and rebelled by choosing as his text poems by Sassoon and Owen instead of the patriotic theme of dying for your country. Graves's affair with Laura Riding took him into new territory; and his autobiography *Goodbye to All That*, a best-seller in 1929, showed a resolve to leave England. After 1918, as if determined to forget, to avoid dreams of a lost pre-1914 paradise, he often seemed didactic and brisk, even when his subject was love. 'The Rock Below', from the 1923 collection *Whipperginny*, displays hope of rebirth, of escape. Graves stayed apart from Eliot and Pound and is closer to another kind of poetry: a realism, even nostalgia, that stretches from Hardy, Masefield, through the Georgians, through parts of Auden and MacNeice, to Larkin and to Hughes. Edward Thomas is there, as are post-war Sassoon and Blunden.

Isaac Rosenberg is harder to place. The first peacetime edition of his poems (published in 1922) had a long introduction by the Georgian poet Laurence Binyon, to whom Rosenberg had sent his work. This starts patronizingly with 'Of the many young poets who gave their lives in the war, Isaac Rosenberg was not the least gifted,' noting also that 'whatever criticism can be made of his poetry, its faults are plainly those of excess rather than deficiency'. Binyon goes on to quote from the poet's letters and say how the 'straining and tormenting of the language', the immaturity, didn't reflect enough the hard work and rigorous 'self criticism' of their author. He left Rosenberg out of his 1924 anthology *Golden Treasury of Modern Lyrics*.

The next Rosenberg collection came in 1937. T. S. Eliot refused to write a foreword because (he said) of the conflict with his position at Faber & Faber (a rival publisher), and W. B. Yeats declared he couldn't stand the 'windy' poetry, so it was left to Siegfried Sassoon, who felt flattered to be asked. The trouble was that Sassoon, although admiring the poems, couldn't think of what to say about them; they were so different from his own writing, particularly from what it had become after the war. One of the editors offered a phrase about Rosenberg being 'a fruitful fusion between English and Hebrew culture'; probably Sassoon himself came up with the idea that the verses were 'scriptural and sculptural'. The leading critic F. R. Leavis wrote an article in praise of Rosenberg; Marsh continued rather dutifully to try to help 'poor little Isaac Rosenberg's' reputation as an artist and a poet. In the next war, the poet Keith Douglas, remembering 'Break of Day in the Trenches', wrote in 'Desert Flowers':

> Living in a wide landscape are the flowers –
> Rosenberg, I only repeat what you were saying ...

A new *Collected Poems* (with the same Sassoon foreword) came out in 1949. By then Rupert Brooke's war had been eclipsed; fading also was the idea of a lost generation of brave young British aristocrats who might have saved the world. Between the wars, partly because of their mother's memoir of them, the Grenfell boys – Julian and Billy – were seen in some conservative circles as magnificent examples of English manhood and chivalry. There were admirers whom they and their family would probably not have wanted, like the best-selling historian Arthur Bryant, an apologist for Hitler, who compared Julian to 'a trumpet call in men's hearts to remind them how valiant, how beautiful, how generous man at his best could be'. But as the war became thought of as inexcusable rather than glorious, 'Into Battle' could seem offensive, if beautiful, even typical of an absurd euphoria that had led to slaughter. The socialist critic and poet Jon Silkin wanted to exclude Julian Grenfell's poem from his 1978 *Penguin Book of First War Poetry*, putting it in only because of its fame. To Silkin, Rosenberg seemed the greatest poet of the war.

By the 1960s, Wilfred Owen was the modern master. The preface to his poetry ('This book is not about heroes. English poetry is not yet fit to speak of them …') said that his poems were about the transformation of war from the Edwardian view of military glory formed by Newbolt, Kipling and W. E. Henley or by G. A. Henty's popular historical novels – and maintained by Brooke and Grenfell – to one of horrific suffering.

Owen's ascent had been slow. In 1919, the Sitwells printed seven of his poems in their journal *Wheels*, dedicating the edition 'To the Memory of Wilfred Owen M.C.' It was ironic; Owen had been proud to be thought a Georgian whereas *Wheels*, more modernist, had been set up in opposition to Marsh's anthologies, although it had far fewer sales. Some critics paid attention; the traditionalist J. C. Squire dismissed Owen, but Middleton Murry told Katherine Mansfield, 'It's what Sassoon might have done, if he were any real good.'

In 1920, Chatto and Windus published *The Poems of Wilfred*

Owen, edited by Edith Sitwell and introduced by Siegfried Sassoon, who had wanted to leave out the famous preface, thinking that it took attention away from the poems. Sassoon's introduction avoided analysis, saying that the book showed 'profound humanity' and 'absolute integrity of mind', and that he agreed with Owen's view of the war. Mrs Owen, Wilfred's adoring mother, was pleased. Edmund Blunden, in the *Athenaeum*, under the headline 'The Real War', declared that these poems were by 'one of the few spokesmen of the ordinary fighting man' who had articulated rebellion, in spite of his pride in enduring the pain and his wish to do his duty as an officer. For Blunden, after reading Owen, 'it is almost impossible to conceive of any other point of view ... There is no other philosophy in modern war.'

The small edition sold out. Edith Sitwell was an inaccurate editor and corrected several errors in a quick, and small, reprint. Scott Moncrieff, Robert Nichols and Middleton Murry reviewed the book, all, to Sassoon's fury, mentioning the rumour of Owen's 1917 cowardice.

In 1931 came the most complete and accurate edition yet of Wilfred Owen's work, edited, at Sassoon's request, by Edmund Blunden. This stayed within a quite small readership. But the poet's fame was growing. By 1933, W. H. Auden was writing of Owen and Katherine Mansfield in 'The Malverns':

> 'The poetry is in the pity,' Wilfred said,
> And Kathy in her journal, 'To be rooted in life,
> That's what I want.'
> These moods give no permission to be idle;
> For men are changed by what they do;
> And through loss and anger the hands of the unlucky
> Love one another.

Wilfred Owen was enlisted by the 1930s left when Stephen Spender claimed that among Owen's post-war themes would have been 'the industrial towns and distressed areas' of Britain. The public school-educated, publicity-conscious and boyishly handsome Spender was sometimes mocked as 'the Rupert Brooke of the depression', an indication of the fall in Brooke's standing. By 1936, Owen's manuscripts were on show in the British Museum, alongside classics of English literature. But there were still no entries for him in the 1953 edition of *The Oxford Dictionary of Quotations*.

Another poet of genius tried to stop this gradual sanctification. W. B. Yeats thought that war should be written about in the style of Homer, as an epic of courage, even glory. He left Owen out of his 1937 anthology *The Oxford Book of Modern Verse*, writing to a friend that the poet was 'unworthy of the poets' corner of a country-newspaper ... He is all blood, dirt & sucked sugar stick ... he calls poets "bards", a girl a "maid" and talks about "Titanic Wars" ... There is every excuse for him, but none for those who like him.'

Owen's exclusion from Yeats's eccentric book was criticized, especially as some war poems were selected; Sassoon made it with his 'On Passing the New Menin Gate', Blunden had 'In Festubert' and 'Report on Experience', Grenfell got in with 'Into Battle' (much more Yeats's style) and Herbert Read with the long 'The End of a War'. Others like Robert Nichols (who, Yeats said, had submitted a number of 'unreadable, vague, rhetorical and empty' poems) and Rupert Brooke were represented by peacetime work. Yeats disliked poems about individual suffering, preferring robustness. He wrote in the introduction of how a friend of his had heard some soldiers back from the Boer War describe repeatedly 'and always with loud laughter' how an unpopular sergeant hit by a shell had 'turned round and round like dancer wound in his own entrails'. To Yeats 'that too may be a right way of seeing war'.

A very influential anthology published in 1936, *The Faber Book of Modern Verse*, edited by Michael Roberts, adopted a view similar to Auden's. Roberts, a poet himself (and much more on the left than Yeats), excluded all poets whom he thought hadn't contributed to an advance in poetic 'technique', even if – as with Blunden, de la

Mare and Charles Sorley – he admired them. This gave the book a modernist flavour, with several American poets and Eliot and Pound well represented; there were also the young, often political 1930s writers like Auden, Spender, MacNeice and Day Lewis. Sassoon was out completely, as was Gurney, but Owen had seven poems and Rosenberg five, with Herbert Read – an Eliot admirer who had written war poetry – in with eight and Graves with thirteen (but no war poems).

By the mid-thirties, the war did seem horrible to most people. But with this came a fascination among those who'd been too young to fight. Young people began to feel shocked at what an older generation had brought on the world, yet also guilty at having missed the great test. Christopher Isherwood's father had been killed in the trenches; Isherwood, influenced (as he said) by Owen and Sassoon, turned against flag-waving patriotism and 'the old men who had made the war', yet admitted to being 'secretly attracted to it'. Philip Toynbee, a rebellious public schoolboy, murmured the name Passchendaele 'in an ecstasy of excitement and regret'.

In 1927, Siegfried Sassoon went back to Flanders. He drove across the battlefields with Glen Byam Shaw, the young actor whom he loved, weeping at the memories. He wrote 'On Passing the New Menin Gate' about the pompous memorial designed by the imperial architect Sir Reginald Blomfield for Ypres and inscribed with the names of the dead.

Sassoon had tried politics and lecture tours; he discovered sex, fooling himself that he could reform his decadent lovers, all the time feeling a bit lost. Thomas Hardy became an idol and Edmund Blunden an essential friend; to see the two together at Max Gate, Hardy's home in Dorset, allowed Sassoon to imagine a world that might respond to his increasingly traditionalist style. When, in 1924, Blunden went to teach in Japan, Sassoon missed him badly; and nostalgia became more intense as he became less inspired by the present. 'On Passing the New Menin Gate' evoked the bitterness and anger of his war.

The anger prompted a yearning for a better place, a once happy land. Towards the end of the 1920s, Siegfried Sassoon began his prose trilogy about innocence ending in the tragedy of the trenches. In *Memoirs of a Fox-hunting Man*, *Memoirs of an Infantry Officer* and *Sherston's Progress*, he chose the format of partly fictionalized memoirs, where the narrator George Sherston resembles the author, with a childhood of tranquillity, horses and cricket, before the western front. But there's none of Sassoon's own pre-war turmoil; sex appears only obliquely, as in Sherston's crush on another young horseman.

It wasn't only Sassoon who looked back. Blunden's war memoir, *Undertones of War*, published in the same year, 1928, starts with two quotations: one from the articles of the Church of England; the other from John Bunyan. Both infer, through beautiful but archaic language, how the modern world and its weapons had destroyed the idea of a noble war. The inclusion of certain poems – 'The Zonnebeke Road', 'The Watchers' (recalling comradeship and kindness), 'Vlamertinghe: Passing the Chateau', 'Gouzeaucourt: The Deceitful Calm' and others, many written since 1918 – revealed yet more covering of old ground. Edmund Blunden couldn't get the war out of his mind, saying that the rabbit holes in a calm Wiltshire garden were like the rutted aftermath of the Somme. He revisited the Flanders battlefields and, not believing that the war veteran Hitler could want another war, stayed naively sympathetic to German intentions. The rich Sassoon could afford the time to remember; Blunden worked obsessively, teaching in Japan, Oxford and Hong Kong, producing a stream of poems, articles, reviews, books and letters; Graves's widow said that her husband had kept himself far too busy to be melancholy.

These were part of the war's literary resurrection at the end of the 1920s. In 1927 came T. E. Lawrence's *Revolt in the Desert* and Max Plowman's *A Subaltern on the Somme*; a year later *Memoirs of a Fox-hunting Man* and *Undertones of War* and the last volume of Ford Madox Ford's quartet of novels, *Parade's End*; in 1929, Robert

Graves published *Goodbye to All That*, its brisk tone different from Sassoon's and Blunden's artful prose. 'If I can be said to have a prose-style,' Graves explained, 'I learned it at Wrexham when a young officer. Captain "Shots" Jones taught me to compose field-messages to the formula of: "Time, place, date – from whom, to whom – who, how, when, where, why – how dispatched", cutting out everything not pertinent to the message.' This was fine but the book's inaccuracy and indiscretion caused offence. Sassoon was furious when Graves revealed Mrs Sassoon's attempts to reach Siegfried's dead brother through spiritualism and quoted an un-published Sassoon poem that showed the poet on the edge of a breakdown.

Graves believed that an artist could tell 'the truth by a con-densation and dramatisation'. In *But It Still Goes On*, published in 1930, he did a parody of an English officer (repressed, homosexual, vain) possibly based on Siegfried Sassoon – whom he felt should have lent him more money – and with echoes of Owen. To this character, called David, the war came as a kind of relief. 'Do you know how a platoon of men will absolutely worship a good-looking gallant young officer?' he declares. 'If he's a bit shy of them and decent to them they get a crush on him. He's a being apart – an officer's uniform is most attractive compared with the rough shape-less private's uniform ... a very very strong romantic link. That's why I had the best platoon and then the best company in the battalion. My men adored me and were showing off all the time before the other companies. They didn't bring me flowers. They killed Germans for me instead and drilled like angels ...' He goes on to say, 'I like to boss people I'm in love with, to have them look up to me ...' Graves's poetry went back also, as in his 1938 'Recalling War' and, in 1947, 'The Last Day of Leave (1916)'.

Some war veterans thought these books too depressed, too bitter and despairing, or, in *Goodbye to All That*, too keen on paying off old scores. It's true that they imply victimhood and pessimism, the sacrifice of innocents against a relentless enemy. Much British writing about the First World War makes it hard to recall that the Allies had won, that despair wasn't universal. Hadn't Owen boasted to his mother that he had 'fought like an angel'? Hadn't he said on the western front that there was no other place that he would rather be?

Charles Carrington, whose *A Subaltern's War* came out in 1929, said that he wanted to 'strike a responsive chord in the hearts of some old soldiers who are tired of the uniform disillusion of most war books. For it is time the world remembered that among the fifteen million there were other types as well as the conventional "Prussian militarists", and the equally conventional "disillusioned" pessimists.' But it wasn't only the poets who were critical. By the 1930s, the war's commanders were under attack from politicians and strategists, in the writings of the influential military thinker Basil Liddell Hart or in Lloyd George's memoirs which criticized Haig for the losses of the Somme and Passchendaele. The view that this had been a grotesquely mishandled, even unnecessary, war began to take hold.

When Robert Graves went to Max Gate in 1920, Thomas Hardy advised him against free verse, thinking it would never mean much in England: 'all we can do is to write on the old themes in the old styles, but try to do a little better than those who went before us'. A poet who ignored this was David Jones, a former private in the Royal Welsh Fusiliers, the regiment of Sassoon and Graves.

Jones's *In Parenthesis*, published in 1937, is a modernist war epic – part poetry, part prose – and also a startlingly vivid account of what it felt like to be in the trenches. Set on the western front from December 1915 to July 1916, during the build-up to the Somme, using soldiers' slang and jokes, the poem sees beauty in a 'Waste Land', a mysterious world of 'sudden violences and long stillnesses'. Mechanical power, the war of shells and machines, comes into this 'place of enchantment' and wrecks it. Jones sees the experience as the climax of what soldiers had known for centuries, at Agincourt, Waterloo and Hastings. Myth and allusion – to ancient Welsh verses, to the Bible, to chivalry and *The Song of Roland*, to Shakespeare, to *Alice in Wonderland* – crowd into the narrative as when the Queen of the Wood gives garlands to those killed in a battle at Mametz. David Jones denied that *In Parenthesis* was a war book; it was, he said, about life and virtues made clear in war. To T. S. Eliot and W. H. Auden it had genius. *In Parenthesis* should be read as a whole; extracts seem discordant and pointless. After the war Jones wrote poetry and drew and painted – which brought admiration but little money. A quiet man, he tried to live up to the qualities he'd seen in the infantrymen on the Somme.

Robert Nichols lived at a perpetual shout, his best-selling poems and post-war lecture tour of the United States boosting his Byronic side. Graves, once an admirer, saw instability inherited from a mother who'd been treated in a mental hospital, perhaps why Nichols had lasted such a short time in the line. What came after those three weeks with the artillery was, Graves said, 'a terrific comet of success in poetry in 1917', the American lectures when Nichols 'told frightful lies about his war service', then 'passionate terrible love affairs'. One of these was with the bohemian heiress Nancy Cunard, who wrote in her diary of a 'mad' young man who 'thinks he is a genius instead of which he is really a shocking poet ...'. Nichols once threw a revolver at her feet, begging her to stop him from shooting himself.

To escape, Robert Nichols went to Japan, to teach at Tokyo University, preceding Edmund Blunden as a professor there. He married (it didn't last), tried screenwriting in Hollywood, wrote plays that included a vast unfinished version of *Don Juan* and, by 1939, was in debt and living in the south of France. Hoping to revive his fame, he worked on an anthology of First War poetry; by January 1940 the introduction had reached eighty-two pages, with only fifty-one pages of poems. When the Germans invaded France, Nichols crossed the Channel and settled in Cambridge, where he met a new mistress – 'the great love of my life'. In 1942, his selected poems, *Such Was my Singing*, was published. The reviews were lukewarm.

Nichols once told Marsh that his favourite music was 'the sound of my own voice'. His introduction to the anthology of First War poetry, eventually published in 1943, was almost a hundred pages long, taking the form of an imaginary conversation between himself as a First War veteran and Julian Tennyson, the great-great-grandson of the Victorian poet laureate. Tennyson is about to go off to fight in the Second World War and, over tea ('you'll find a tea cake under the lid to your left'), Nichols recalls his noble aspirations of 1914, learned from Alfred de Vigny and Tolstoy; how there'd been amateurism and chivalry among the British, quite different to German cold-blooded professionalism. In the book were Brooke's five sonnets, four poems by Owen, thirteen by Sassoon, Sorley in with only 'All the Hills and Vales Along', nine by Blunden and eight by Graves, including 'Recalling War'. Nichols gave himself two: 'Battery Moving Up' and the post-war 'Epic Wind' as an epilogue. The book had nothing by Edward Thomas or Ivor Gurney or Isaac Rosenberg. The sequence, as in his own earlier *Ardours and Experiences*, showed a fall into disillusion, perhaps increased after its publication when young Tennyson was killed fighting the Japanese in Burma in 1945. Nichols died of heart failure in 1944 – bitter, self-pitying, angry that he'd been forgotten.

For Siegfried Sassoon the 1930s were hard as his marriage – a strange leap after his affair with the androgynous young aristocrat Stephen Tennant – failed. New life in a country house bought with a legacy from a rich aunt failed to inspire his poetry, a disappointment for him; his memoirs may have sold well, but to be a great lyric poet was what Sassoon wanted, not a poet of war, a satirist or a writer of prose. One consolation was a son George, born in 1936, but the brilliant boy soon became caught up in his father's possessiveness and collapsing marriage.

Sassoon needed another country. So he made further idylls of the pre-1914 world, in books like *The Old Century* and *The Weald of Youth* – autobiographies that no longer sheltered behind the fictional character of George Sherston yet still left sex out, partly because his adored, prim mother was alive and homosexuality remained (until 1967) a criminal offence in Britain. Anger became sweet, soft or stale poetry, even if he detested modern life. His poems about the Second World War are like Rupert Brooke's patriotic sonnets of 1914.

Sassoon thought that, if 'little Wilfred' had lived, they could together have made an alternative to modernism, to Eliot's fragmented world; yet he also felt jealous of his former disciple's fame. Might it have been better if he, not Owen, had been killed? Other figures from the past came back, shaped by nostalgia. In the poem 'A Fallodon Memory', Edward Grey, the Foreign Secretary in August 1914, whom Sassoon had met with Grey's stepson Stephen Tennant, becomes 'human-simple yet profound', a countryman and ornithologist, tragically deprived by blindness of his beloved birds and Northumbrian landscape – with no mention of the failure of Grey's diplomacy or his part in taking Britain to war. With nostalgia came confusion. As Sassoon absorbed new revelations of German war aims and territorial ambitions, he began to doubt his own protest of 1917. Had he been wrong to call for peace? The turbulence and loneliness, the waste, haunted him. He longed for a more purposeful and ordered life, for spiritual rest. In 1957, Siegfried Sassoon converted to Roman Catholicism, welcoming its clear answers and its discipline.

By then, there'd been another war. The Second World War felt different; earlier poets had already written about the shock of mass warfare: also there was no doubt that Nazi Germany had to be beaten. Alan Ross, a young poet who joined the navy, wrote that 'acceptance rather than protest on the Sassoon and Owen level was the only valid response', and this made for a less emotional or angry poetry. One British poet who wrote about the fighting was Keith Douglas. Douglas relished battle, like Julian Grenfell, but saw the hopelessness of the brave amateurism of young Grenfell-like officers. His poem 'Aristocrats' expresses pity, not anger, at their innocence and faith.

British poets of the Second World War wrote mostly in a traditional way, like their First War predecessors. In the 1950s, the hold of modernism weakened further when new writers like Philip Larkin and Kingsley Amis rebelled against obscurity, metropolitan sophistication, Pound, Eliot and foreign influence. But the inspiration now was more likely to be not a lost pastoral England (although there were glimpses of it) but northern provincial towns. Philip Larkin, however, pleased Sassoon by telling him in a letter of his dislike of 'symbolic poetry, or poetry full of quotations from other writers and other languages. I think sometimes it was an evil day when English poetry fell into the hands of the Americans and the Irish. From which you may gather that Pound and Eliot and Joyce are not my favourite authors.' Larkin's 'MCMXIV', about England on the eve of the First World War, shows a country about to lose that innocence to which Sassoon looked longingly back. In his 1973 *Oxford Book of Twentieth Century Verse* Larkin went against Yeats's earlier judgement by including seven poems by Owen (but not 'Strange Meeting', perhaps because it was thought by some to be unfinished). Also in were Brooke's 'The Soldier', Edward Thomas's 'As the Team's Head-Brass' and 'In Memoriam (Easter, 1915)'.

Robert Graves returned to England when the Second World War began. He lived in the west country and joined the Home Guard, going back to Majorca when peace came. England was (he said) always his poetic inspiration, and the welterweight boxing cup from Charterhouse stayed on his desk. Graves didn't write much about Spain or Majorca, except in the olive groves of his love poetry. In 1969, he said of his war poems, 'I destroyed them. They were journalistic.' He passed judgement on Sassoon and Owen, the characteristically plain speaking becoming even plainer. 'Owen and Sassoon were homosexuals, though Sassoon tried to think he wasn't. To them, seeing men killed was as horrible as if you or I had to see fields of corpses of women.' That year he told the comedian Spike Milligan that 'Sassoon's idealism, like Wilfred Owen's, was mixed up with homosexuality. They killed to prove their manhood, wept because of their womanhood for the corpses they left in their trail.' Sassoon's view of Graves in 1962 was 'How right dear Robbie Ross was when he said that "Robert is half school-boy and half school-master."'

Robert Graves remained proud that he'd fought. In 1968, he wrote that a compromise peace had been impossible because of German atrocities. The war's worst horror had been Haig's 1917 offensive – the third battle of Ypres or Passchendaele – 'the most unspeakably horrible, pointless, and costly campaign ever fought by British troops'. For Graves, however, the war had 'given me not only an unsurpassable standard of danger, discomfort, and horror by which to judge more recent troubles, but a confidence in the golden-heartedness and iron endurance of my fellow countrymen (proved again in Hitler's war), which even the laxity of this new plastic age cannot disturb'. Like Blunden, he remembered the virtues of that terrifying time.

Siegfried Sassoon wanted people to read the devotional poems inspired by his conversion to Catholicism rather than his writings about the First World War. The others show how hard it was to leave such an ordeal. Nichols never recovered from shell shock and Gurney's and Blunden's post-war poetry shows the strength of memory. Graves tried harder to move on. He set up a court in exile, explored myth and feminine power, believing that poetry was magical, that reality and literal truth were not poetic. Avoiding the political themes of the 1930s or social comment, he became dismissive of *Goodbye to All That*, declaring that it had been written for money: that was why he put in what he thought were commercial subjects – kings, mothers, food, ghosts and poets ('People like reading about poets. I put in a lot of poets'). The book isn't an anti-war book, its author said, but a history of what had happened to him during the war.

Edmund Blunden went back most years to Flanders. On one of his last visits, he sat on a hill above Ancre with his young wife

Claire, sensing old terrors behind the now peaceful scene. That year, Blunden represented tradition in an election for Oxford's professorship of poetry, standing against the American (and favourite of the 1960s) Robert Lowell. It was Blunden who won, Lowell graciously declaring admiration for his opponent's work. But the new professor was already ill, suffering from the aftermath of wartime gas attacks, and found the lecturing a dreadful burden, so he gave up the post. A year later, he was back on the western front, again with Claire, writing to Sassoon that there had been 'many thoughts and mentions of you'. He knew that Siegfried Sassoon, one of the few left who understood what the war had been like, was dying.

In September 1967, after a Roman Catholic funeral, Sassoon was buried at Mells, in an Anglican churchyard, near the medieval manor house, as if to assert the England that pervades much of his later work. Blunden followed seven years later; his grave is at Long Melford, in the cemetery of the church there. In December 1985, Robert Graves died, on Majorca, where he is buried. At his memorial service in London later that month, the last post was played by a bugler from the Royal Welsh Fusiliers.

By then, the poets' war was seen as the truth, judging by the flood of novels and films about it. This infuriated historians such as John Terraine or Correlli Barnett. Why, they asked, should what had ended in victory for the Allies be shown so often as a series of failed attacks from water-filled trenches across lunar landscapes threaded with barbed wire, in an atmosphere of dread, under the command of stupid, moustachioed, out-of-touch generals sheltering in châteaux miles to the rear? This, they claimed, was the real myth. They protested against vilification of Haig, saying that his task – of satisfying political pressure, of training the flood of volunteers and conscripts, of dislodging an enemy who had the huge advantages given to defenders by modern technology and weapons – was almost impossible.

Haig was not a great general, although his supporters have

worked hard to try to make him one. Not until the last months of the war did British tactics have overwhelming success, demonstrating an exceptionally long time of learning. The war poets saw the earlier failed offensives. Only Owen was at the front for the final surge. And the historians faced a growing wave, of art and emotion. The pacifist Benjamin Britten, a conscientious objector in the Second World War, put Owen's poems into his *War Requiem*, first performed (and hailed as a masterpiece) in the new Coventry Cathedral in May 1962. A year later came a new edition of Owen's poems, edited by Cecil Day Lewis, now a best-seller. Joan Littlewood's theatrical production *Oh, What a Lovely War!* followed in 1963, using music and words, including songs from the war, to ridicule the generals and politicians, reaching large audiences six years later as a film.

Anthologies of war poetry carried the message of early illusion crumbling into the despair. In 1964, *Up the Line to Death*, the first substantial post-Second War collection, edited by Brian Gardner, took pride in digging out lesser-known poets but was dominated by Owen, Sassoon, Nichols and Rosenberg – with not much by Blunden, Thomas or Brooke and nothing by Gurney. *Men Who March Away*, published the following year and edited by Ian Parsons, followed this arc as well; again Owen, Sassoon, Rosenberg, more this time by Thomas, but Gurney in with only three poems. The BBC *Great War* series – one of the longest-ever television documentaries – came out in 1964. Historians were called in to advise, the commentary was objective and not mocking, the survivors interviewed were dignified, but the solemn music, grainy photographs and flickering film conveyed disaster and doom.

Class-baiting intensified the row. *Oh, What a Lovely War!* portrayed Haig and the generals as privileged, remote and stupid, and the war itself as a colossal error thrust on a guileless Europe by defunct *anciens régimes*. To others, however, it was the poets, especially those who had been to public schools, who were out of touch. Their nostalgia, their contrasting of idyllic pre-war innocence with the hellish western front, showed glib emotion, particularly when it came from rich *rentiers* like Siegfried Sassoon who'd learned unreal romantic idealism at their public schools. This was individual suffering rather than general truth, as Yeats had said. The England of Sassoon's *Memoirs of a Fox-hunting Man* may have looked beautiful, but it was reeling from a long agricultural depression that drove the young into the slums of the industrial cities where life was not that much better than in the trenches.

The barrage thudded on. Defenders of Haig and the High Command said that the war should be seen from October 1918, not from 1 July 1916, the first day of the Somme. The Somme was terrible for the Germans as well; even the third battle of Ypres had seen British success in the hot dry spell in September and early October 1917 under General Plumer (who looked like a caricature First War commander). The British were unique in having no pre-war conscription, in having to recruit, equip and train a massive volunteer force after the early high casualty rate suffered by the small regular army. Britain was not prepared for a large continental land war – again not the fault of the generals. It had been thought that the Royal Navy, an economic blockade and generous trans-fusions of cash could be Britain's contribution, with the fighting on land left mostly to her allies.

There were mistakes, not least in Haig's obstinacy and determination to go on, at the Somme and at Ypres in the autumns of 1916 and 1917. But the British army rallied after Loos in September 1915, then after the Somme's first day, then after what Blunden thought had been the worst of all, the fighting round Ypres in October and November 1917. The last months of the war, from July until November 1918, saw British victories.

What the poets wrote was seductive, often spellbindingly good, so much so that it was claimed they contributed to the climate of appeasement in the 1930s: the wish to avoid war at almost any price. It's hard to prove this; certainly they show sympathy for enemy soldiers – although never for German war aims – and Sassoon and

Blunden were drawn to pre–Second World War pacifist movements like the Peace Pledge Union. War memoirs and novels were influential because of their sales, greater than poetry. More effective still was Keynes's brilliant polemic, *The Economic Consequences of the Peace*, published in December 1919 and a best-seller all over the world. The book's argument – that the victorious powers had been much too harsh on Germany – prepared the way for a revulsion against the Treaty of Versailles (and sympathy for the German sense of injustice) a decade later.

There's the claim that Britain should never have fought at all: that by sticking to a treaty with Belgium the British prolonged the fighting (and led later to Hitler) instead of accepting as inevitable what might have been a benign German domination of continental Europe, an early version of the modern European Union. German demands on defeated Russia, and the nature of the Kaiser's neurotic and feverish regime, show this to be too optimistic.

So was the war like the 1989 television comedy *Blackadder*, with the idiotic Haig, dim generals and tragic doomed soldiers? Or was it a question of hanging on against the most powerfully militarized European power that had long prepared for a great European war? James Jack's view seems sound. Jack, who began the war as a captain and ended it commanding an infantry brigade, was a realist, certainly not a poet. The war, he knew, had been hell; he'd been in all the major battles on the western front and there should be no glorifying of it. But Jack took pride in the 'complete' defeat of the German army. 'The entire manhood of Germany and all her resources' had been behind the troops whose leaders had been trained to handle vast formations. Allied forces had risen above the lamentable preparations for war. It was the politicians who had put the nation in danger by 'neglecting its armaments and the training of personnel wanted to handle them'.

Surely it's necessary to separate politics, even history, from the poetry. The work of the British First World War poets can be seen as one of the most powerful collective statements not just against what happened on the western front but against all war. But it reflects individual experience rather than objective judgement. How could it do otherwise? Every work of art is restricted by what has inspired it, and war is a more powerful restriction than most. War poetry can't be isolated from its circumstances – a limitation perhaps and also one that acts against broader historical truth.

By 1914, in Britain, poetry had become more suited to what it would need to express. The new realism of the Georgians, alongside their romance with rural life, let poets treat war and its pain realistically, without bombast, after the early burst of patriotic feeling, with the added emotional power of nostalgia. Among the downland, fields and woods of the Somme, Flanders and Picardy, the soldiers thought of the gentle rolling lands of southern England, although Graves hankered after north Wales. Dreams of pastoral calm could lessen the shock of industrial war and make its poetry stronger through contrast and emotion.

It was not only what the poets saw that raised them above the Georgians. Their pre-war and post-war lives show them as extraordinary: often tormented casualties of their age, not typical of it. But they were strong enough to make a world that stands alone, bound by the feelings and vision of eleven fragile young men who were unlikely warriors.

AFTERMATH POEMS

Everyone Sang

Everyone suddenly burst out singing;
And I was filled with such delight
As prisoned birds must find in freedom,
Winging wildly across the white
Orchards and dark-green fields; on – on – and out of sight.

Everyone's voice was suddenly lifted;
And beauty came like the setting sun:
My heart was shaken with tears; and horror
Drifted away ... O, but Everyone
Was a bird; and the song was wordless; the singing will never be done.

SIEGFRIED SASSOON

Laventie

One would remember still
Meadows and low hill
Laventie was, as to the line and elm row
Growing through green strength wounded, as home elms grow.
Shimmer of summer there and blue autumn mists
Seen from trench-ditch winding in mazy twists.
The Australian gunners in close flowery hiding
Cunning found out at last, and smashed in the unspeakable lists.
And the guns in the smashed wood thumping and griding.

The letters written there, and received there,
Books, cakes, cigarettes in a parish of famine,
And leaks in rainy times with general all-damning.
The crater, and carrying of gas cylinders on two sticks
(Pain past comparison and far past right agony gone)
Strained hopelessly of heart and frame at first fix.

Café-au-lait in dug-outs on Tommies' cookers,
Cursed minniewerfs, thirst in eighteen-hour summer.
The Australian miners clayed, and the being afraid
Before strafes, sultry August dusk time than death dumber –
And the cooler hush after the strafe, and the long night wait –
The relief of first dawn, the crawling out to look at it,
Wonder divine of Dawn, man hesitating before Heaven's gate.
(Though not on Coopers where music fire took at it.
Though not as at Framilode beauty where body did shake at it)
Yet the dawn with aeroplanes crawling high at Heaven gate
Lovely aerial beetles of wonderful scintillate
Strangest interest, and puffs of soft purest white –
Soaking light, dispersing colouring for fancy's delight.

Of Maconachie, Paxton, Tickler, and Gloucester's Stephens;
Fray Bentos, Spiller and Baker, odds and evens
Of trench food, but the everlasting clean craving
For bread, the pure thing, blessed beyond saving.
Canteen disappointments, and the keen boy braving
Bullets or such for grouse roused surprisingly through
(Halfway) Stand-to.
And the shell nearly blunted my razor at shaving;
Tilleloy, Fauquissart, Neuve Chapelle, and mud like glue.

But Laventie, most of all, I think is to soldiers
The town itself with plane trees, and small-spa air;
And vin, rouge-blanc, chocolat, citron, grenadine:
One might buy in small delectable cafés there.
The broken church, and vegetable fields bare;
Neat French market town look so clean,
And the clarity, amiability of North French air.

Like water flowing beneath the dark plough and high Heaven,
Music's delight to please the poet pack-marching there.

IVOR GURNEY

1916 Seen from 1921

Tired with dull grief, grown old before my day,
I sit in solitude and only hear
Long silent laughters, murmurings of dismay,
The lost intensities of hope and fear;
In those old marshes yet the rifles lie,
On the thin breastwork flutter the grey rags,
The very books I read are there – and I
Dead as the men I loved, wait while life drags

Its wounded length from those sad streets of war
Into green places here, that were my own;
But now what once was mine is mine no more,
I seek such neighbours here and I find none.
With such strong gentleness and tireless will
Those ruined houses seared themselves in me,
Passionate I look for their dumb story still,
And the charred stub outspeaks the living tree.

I rise up at the singing of a bird
And scarcely knowing slink along the lane,
I dare not give a soul a look or word
Where all have homes and none's at home in vain:
Deep red the rose burned in the grim redoubt,
The self-sown wheat around was like a flood,
In the hot path the lizard lolled time out,
The saints in broken shrines were bright as blood.

Sweet Mary's shrine between the sycamores!
There we would go, my friend of friends and I,
And snatch long moments from the grudging wars,
Whose dark made light intense to see them by.

Shrewd bit the morning fog, the whining shots
Spun from the wrangling wire; then in warm swoon
The sun hushed all but the cool orchard plots,
We crept in the tall grass and slept till noon.

EDMUND BLUNDEN

The Mangel-Bury

It was after war; Edward Thomas had fallen at Arras –
I was walking by Gloucester musing on such things
As fill his verse with goodness; it was February; the long house
Straw-thatched of the mangels stretched two wide wings;
And looked as part of the earth heaped up by dead soldiers
In the most fitting place – along the hedge's yet-bare lines.
West spring breathed there early, that none foreign divines.
Across the flat country the rattling of the cart sounded:
Heavy of wood, jingling of iron; as he neared me I waited
For the chance perhaps of heaving at those great rounded
Ruddy or orange things – and right to be rolled and hefted
By a body like mine, soldier still, and clean from water.
Silent he assented; till the cart was drifted
High with those creatures, so right in size and matter.
We threw with our bodies swinging; blood in my ears singing;
His was the thick-set sort of farmer, but well-built –
Perhaps long before his blood's name ruled all:
Watched all things for his own. If my luck had so willed
Many questions of lordship I had heard him tell – old
Names, rumours. But my pain to more moving called
And him to some barn business far in the fifteen acre field.

IVOR GURNEY

It is Near Toussaints

It is near Toussaints, the living and dead will say:
'Have they ended it? What has happened to Gurney?'
And along the leaf-strewed roads of France many brown shades
Will go, recalling singing, and a comrade for whom also they
Had hoped well. His honour them had happier made.
Curse all that hates good. When I spoke of my breaking
(Not understood) in London, they imagined of the taking
Vengeance, and seeing things were different in future.
(A musician was a cheap, honourable and nice creature.)
Kept sympathetic silence; heard their packs creaking
And burst into song – Hilaire Belloc was all our Master.
On the night of all the dead, they will remember me,
Pray Michael, Nicholas, Maries lost in Novembery
River-mist in the old City of our dear love, and batter
At doors about the farms crying 'Our war poet is lost',
'Madame – no bon!' – and cry his two names, warningly, sombrely.

IVOR GURNEY

The Rock Below

Comes a muttering from the earth
    Where speedwell grows and daisies grow,
'Pluck these weeds up, root and all,
    Search what hides below.'

Root and all I pluck them out;
    There, close under, I have found
Stumps of thorn with ancient crooks
    Grappled in the ground.

I wrench the thorn-stocks from their hold
    To set a rose-bush in that place;
Love has pleasure in my roses
    For a summer space.

Yet the bush cries out in grief:
    'Our lowest rootlets turn on rock,
We live in terror of the drought
    Withering crown and stock.'

I grow angry with my creature,
    Tear it out and see it die;
Far beneath I strike the stone,
    Jarring hatefully.

Impotently must I mourn
    Roses never to flower again?
Are heart and back too slightly built
    For a heaving strain?

Heave shall break my proud back never,
    Strain shall never burst my heart:
Steely fingers hook in the crack,
    Up the rock shall start.

Now from the deep and frightful pit
    Shoots forth the spiring phoenix-tree
Long despaired in this bleak land,
    Holds the air with boughs, with bland
Fragrance welcome to the bee,
    With fruits of immortality.

ROBERT GRAVES

The Zonnebeke Road

Morning, if this late withered light can claim
Some kindred with that merry flame
Which the young day was wont to fling through space!
Agony stares from each grey face.
And yet the day is come; stand down! stand down!
Your hands unclasp from rifles while you can,
The frost has pierced them to the bended bone?
Why see old Stevens there, that iron man,
Melting the ice to shave his grotesque chin:
Go ask him, shall we win?
I never liked this bay, some foolish fear
Caught me the first time that I came in here;
That dugout fallen in awakes, perhaps,
Some formless haunting of some corpse's chaps.
True, and wherever we have held the line,
There were such corners, seeming-saturnine
For no good cause.

              Now where Haymarket starts,
There is no place for soldiers with weak hearts;
The minenwerfers have it to the inch.
Look, how the snow-dust whisks along the road
Piteous and silly; the stones themselves must flinch
In this east wind; the low sky like a load
Hangs over – a dead-weight. But what a pain
Must gnaw where its clay cheek
Crushes the shell-chopped trees that fang the plain –
The ice-bound throat gulps out a gargoyle shriek.
That wretched wire before the village line
Rattles like rusty brambles or dead bine,
And there the daylight oozes into dun;

Black pillars, those are trees where roadways run.
Even Ypres now would warm our souls; fond fool,
Our tour's but one night old, seven more to cool!
O screaming dumbness, O dull clashing death,
Shreds of dead grass and willows, homes and men,
Watch as you will, men clench their chattering teeth
And freeze you back with that one hope, disdain.

EDMUND BLUNDEN

First Time In

After the dread tales and red yarns of the Line
Anything might have come to us; but the divine
Afterglow brought us up to a Welsh colony
Hiding in sandbag ditches, whispering consolatory
Soft foreign things. Then we were taken in
To low huts candle-lit, shaded close by slitten
Oilsheets, and there but boys gave us kind welcome,
So that we looked out as from the edge of home.
Sang us Welsh things, and changed all former notions
To human hopeful things. And the next day's guns
Nor any line-pangs ever quite could blot out
That strangely beautiful entry to War's rout;
Candles they gave us, precious and shared over-rations –
Ulysses found little more in his wanderings without doubt.
'David of the White Rock', the 'Slumber Song' so soft, and that
Beautiful tune to which roguish words by Welsh pit boys
Are sung – but never more beautiful than here under the guns' noise.

IVOR GURNEY

Poem for End

So the last poem is laid flat in its place,
And Crickley with Crucifix Corner leaves from my face
Elizabethans and night-working thoughts – of such grace.

And all the dawns that set my thoughts new to making;
Or Crickley dusk that the beech leaves stirred to shaking
Are put aside – there is a book ended; heart aching.

Joy and sorrow, and all thoughts a poet thinks,
Walking or turning to music; the wrought-out links
Of fancy to fancy – by Severn or by Artois brinks.

Only what's false in this, blood itself would not save,
Sweat would not heighten – the dead Master in his grave
Would my true following of him, my care approve.

And more than he, I paid the prices of life
Standing where Rome immortal heard October's strife,
A war poet whose right of honour cuts falsehood like a knife.

War poet – his right is of nobler steel – the careful sword –
And night walker will not suffer of praise the word
From the sleepers, the custom-followers, the dead lives unstirred.

Only, who thought of England as two thousand years
Must keep of today's life the proper anger and fears:
England that was paid for by building and ploughing and tears.

IVOR GURNEY

278

On Passing the New Menin Gate

Who will remember, passing through this Gate,
The unheroic Dead who fed the guns?
Who shall absolve the foulness of their fate, –
Those doomed, conscripted, unvictorious ones?
    Crudely renewed, the Salient holds its own.
    Paid are its dim defenders by this pomp;
    Paid, with a pile of peace-complacent stone,
    The armies who endured that sullen swamp.

Here was the world's worst wound. And here with pride
'Their name liveth for ever,' the Gateway claims.
Was ever an immolation so belied
As these intolerably nameless names?
Well might the Dead who struggled in the slime
Rise and deride this sepulchre of crime.

SIEGFRIED SASSOON

The Bohemians

Certain people would not clean their buttons,
Nor polish buckles after latest fashions,
Preferred their hair long, putties comfortable,
Barely escaping hanging, indeed hardly able;
In Bridge and smoking without army cautions
Spending hours that sped like evil for quickness,
(While others burnished brasses, earned promotions).
These were those ones who jested in the trench,
While others argued of army ways, and wrenched
What little soul they had still further from shape,
And died off one by one, or became officers.
Without the first of dream, the ghost of notions
Of ever becoming soldiers, or smart and neat,
Surprised as ever to find the army capable
Of sounding 'Lights out' to break a game of Bridge,
As to fear candles would set a barn alight:
In Artois or Picardy they lie – free of useless fashions.

IVOR GURNEY

The Watchers

I heard the challenge 'Who goes there?'
Close-kept but mine through midnight air;
I answered and was recognized
And passed, and kindly thus advised:
'There's someone crawlin' through the grass
By the red ruin, or there was,
And them machine guns been a firin'
All the time the chaps was wirin',
So Sir if you're goin' out
You'll keep your 'ead well down no doubt.'

When will the stern fine 'Who goes there?'
Meet me again in midnight air?
And the gruff sentry's kindness, when
Will kindness have such power again?
It seems as, now I wake and brood,
And know my hour's decrepitude,
That on some dewy parapet
The sentry's spirit gazes yet,
Who will not speak with altered tone
When I at last am seen and known.

EDMUND BLUNDEN

The Silent One

Who died on the wires, and hung there, one of two –
Who for his hours of life had chattered through
Infinite lovely chatter of Bucks accent;
Yet faced unbroken wires; stepped over, and went,
A noble fool, faithful to his stripes – and ended.
But I weak, hungry, and willing only for the chance
Of line – to fight in the line, lay down under unbroken
Wires, and saw the flashes, and kept unshaken.
Till the politest voice – a finicking accent, said:
'Do you think you might crawl through there: there's a hole?'
   In the afraid
Darkness shot at; I smiled, as politely replied –
'I'm afraid not, Sir.' There was no hole, no way to be seen.
Nothing but chance of death, after tearing of clothes.
Kept flat, and watched the darkness, hearing bullets whizzing –
And thought of music – and swore deep heart's oaths
(Polite to God) – and retreated and came on again.
Again retreated – and a second time faced the screen.

IVOR GURNEY

I Saw England – July Night

She was a village
Of lovely knowledge
The high roads left her aside, she was forlorn, a maid –
Water ran there, dusk hid her, she climbed four-wayed.
Brown-golden windows showed last folk not yet asleep;
Water ran, was a centre of silence deep,
Fathomless deeps of pricked sky, almost fathomless
Hallowed an upward gaze in pale satin of blue.
And I was happy indeed, of mind, soul, body even
Having got given
A sign undoubtful of dear England few
Doubt, not many have seen,
That Will Squele he knew and so was shriven.
Home of Twelfth Night – Edward Thomas by Arras fallen,
Borrow and Hardy, Sussex tales out of Roman heights callen.
No madrigals or field-songs to my all reverent whim;
Till I got back I was dumb.

IVOR GURNEY

The Interview

Death I have often faced
In the damp trench – or poisoned waste:
Shell or shot, gas or flying steel, bayonet –
But only once by one bullet my arm was wet
With blood. Death faced me there, Death it was that I faced.
But now by no means may it come to me.
Mercy of Death noways vouchsafed to pain.
Were but those times of battle to come again!
Or even boat-sailing, danger on a mimic inland sea!
Death moaning, Death flying, shrieking in air.
Desiring its mark sufficient everywhere – everywhere.
Interview enough. But now I can not get near
Such challenge or dear enmity; pain more than fear
Oppresses me – Would that might come again!
Death in the narrow trench … or wide in the fields.
Death in the Reserve, where the earth wild beautiful flowers yields.
Death met – outfaced – but here: not to be got.
Prayed for, truly desired, obtained not –
A lot past dreadfulness, an unhuman lot.
For never Man was meant to be denied Chance
Of Ending pain past strength – O for France! For France!
Death walked freely – one might be sought of him
Or seek, in twilight or first light of morning dim.
Death dreadful that scared the cheeks of blood,
Took friends, spoilt any happy true-human mood,
Shrieked in the near air – threatened from up on high.
Dreadful, dreadful. But not to be come by
Now, confined – no Interview is ever here.
And worse than Death is known in the spirit of fear.
Death is a thing desired, never to be had at all –
Spirit for Death cries, nothing hears; nothing granted here. O

If Mercy would but hear the cry of the spirit grow
From waking – till Death seems far beyond a right,
And dark is the spirit has all right to be bright.
Death is not here – save mercy grant it. When
Was cruelty such known last among like-and-like men?
An Interview? It is cried for – and not known –
Not found. Death absent what thing is truly Man's own?
Beaten down continually, continually beaten clean down.

IVOR GURNEY

Two Voices

'There's something in the air,' he said
  In the farm parlour cool and bare;
The plain words in his hearers bred
  A tumult, yet in silence there
All waited; wryly gay, he left the phrase,
Ordered the march and bade us go our ways.

'We're going South, man'; as he spoke
  The howitzer with huge ping-bang
Racked the light hut; as thus he broke
  The death-news, bright the skylarks sang;
He took his riding-crop and humming went
Among the apple-trees all bloom and scent.

Now far withdraws the roaring night
  Which wrecked our flower after the first
Of those two voices; misty light
  Shrouds Thiepval Wood and all its worst:
But still 'There's something in the air' I hear,
And still 'We're going South, man,' deadly near.

EDMUND BLUNDEN

Gouzeaucourt: The Deceitful Calm

How unpurposed, how inconsequential
Seemed those southern lines when in the pallor
    Of the dying winter
    First we went there!

Grass thin-waving in the wind approached them,
Red roofs in the near view feigned survival,
    Lovely mockers, when we
    There took over.

There war's holiday seemed, nor though at known times
Gusts of flame and jingling steel descended
    On the bare tracks, would you
    Picture death there.

Snow or rime-frost made a solemn silence,
Bluish darkness wrapped in dangerous safety;
    Old hands thought of tidy
    Living-trenches!

There it was, my dears, that I departed,
Scarce a greater traitor ever! There too
    Many of you soon paid for
    That false mildness.

EDMUND BLUNDEN

War Books

What did they expect of our toil and extreme
Hunger – the perfect drawing of a heart's dream?
Did they look for a book of wrought art's perfection,
Who promised no reading, nor praise, nor publication?
Out of the heart's sickness the spirit wrote.
For delight, or to escape hunger, or of war's worst anger,
When the guns died to silence and men would gather sense
Somehow together, and find this was life indeed.
And praise another's nobleness, or to Cotswold get hence.
There we wrote – Corbie Ridge, or in Gonnehem at rest.
Or Fauquissart or world's death songs, ever the best.
One made sorrows' praise passing the church where silence
Opened for the long quivering strokes of the bell –
Another wrote all soldiers' praise, and of France and night's stars –

Served his guns, got immortality, and died well.
But Ypres played another trick with its danger on me,
Kept still the needing and loving-of-action body;
Gave no candles, and nearly killed me twice as well.
And no souvenirs, though I risked my life in the stuck Tanks.
Yet there was praise of Ypres, love came sweet in hospital –
And old Flanders went under to long ages of plough thought in my pages.

IVOR GURNEY

A Fallodon Memory

One afternoon I watched him as he stood
In the twilight of his wood.
Among the firs he'd planted, forty years away,
Tall, and quite still, and almost blind,
World patience in his face, stood Edward Grey;
Not listening,
For it was at the end of summer, when no birds sing:
Only the bough's faint dirge accompanied his mind
Absorbed in some Wordsworthian slow self-communing.

In lichen-coloured homespun clothes he seemed
So merged with stem and branch and twinkling leaves
That almost I expected, looking away, to find
When glancing there again, that I had daylight dreamed
His figure, as when some trick of sun and shadow deceives.

But there he was, haunting heart-known ancestral ground;
Near to all Nature; and in that nearness somehow strange;
Whose native humour, human-simple yet profound,
And strength of spirit no calamity could change.
To whom, designed for countrified contentments, came
Honours unsought and unrewarding foreign fame:
And, at the last, that darkened world wherein he moved
In memoried deprivation of life once learnt and loved.

SIEGFRIED SASSOON

The Last Day of Leave (1916)

We five looked out over the moor
At rough hills blurred with haze, and a still sea:
Our tragic day, bountiful from the first.

We would spend it by the lily lake
(High in a fold beyond the farthest ridge),
Following the cart-track till it faded out.

The time of berries and bell-heather;
Yet all that morning nobody went by
But shepherds and one old man carting turfs.

We were in love: he with her, she with him,
And I, the youngest one, the odd man out,
As deep in love with a yet nameless muse.

No cloud; larks and heath-butterflies,
And herons undisturbed fishing the streams;
A slow cool breeze that hardly stirred the grass.

When we hurried down the rocky slope,
A flock of ewes galloping off in terror,
There shone the waterlilies, yellow and white.

Deep water and a shelving bank.
Off went our clothes and in we went, all five,
Diving like trout between the lily groves.

The basket had been nobly filled:
Wine and fresh rolls, chicken and pineapple –
Our braggadocio under threat of war.

The fire on which we boiled our kettle
We fed with ling and rotten blackthorn root;
And the coffee tasted memorably of peat.

Two of us might stray off together
But never less than three kept by the fire,
Focus of our uncertain destinies.

We spoke little, our minds in tune –
A sigh or laugh would settle any theme;
The sun so hot it made the rocks quiver.

But when it rolled down level with us,
Four pairs of eyes sought mine as if appealing
For a blind-fate-aversive afterword: –

'Do you remember the lily lake?
We were all there, all five of us in love,
Not one yet killed, widowed or broken-hearted.'

ROBERT GRAVES

Report on Experience

I have been young, and now am not too old;
And I have seen the righteous forsaken,
His health, his honour and his quality taken.
This is not what we were formerly told.

I have seen a green country, useful to the race,
Knocked silly with guns and mines, its villages vanished,
Even the last rat and the last kestrel banished –
God bless us all, this was peculiar grace.

I knew Seraphina; Nature gave her hue,
Glance, sympathy, note, like one from Eden.
I saw her smile warp, heard her lyric deaden;
She turned to harlotry; – this I took to be new.

Say what you will, our God sees how they run.
These disillusions are His curious proving
That He loves humanity and will go on loving;
Over there are faith, life, virtue in the sun.

EDMUND BLUNDEN

Recalling War

Entrance and exit wounds are silvered clean,
The track aches only when the rain reminds.
The one-legged man forgets his leg of wood,
The one-armed man his jointed wooden arm.
The blinded man sees with his ears and hands
As much or more than once with both his eyes.
Their war was fought these twenty years ago
And now assumes the nature-look of time,
As when the morning traveller turns and views
His wild night-stumbling carved into a hill.

What, then, was war? No mere discord of flags
But an infection of the common sky
That sagged ominously upon the earth
Even when the season was the airiest May.
Down pressed the sky, and we, oppressed, thrust out
Boastful tongue, clenched fist and valiant yard.
Natural infirmities were out of mode,
For Death was young again: patron alone
Of healthy dying, premature fate-spasm.

Fear made fine bed-fellows. Sick with delight
At life's discovered transitoriness,
Our youth became all-flesh and waived the mind.
Never was such antiqueness of romance,
Such tasty honey oozing from the heart.
And old importances came swimming back –
Wine, meat, log-fires, a roof over the head,
A weapon at the thigh, surgeons at call.
Even there was a use again for God –
A word of rage in lack of meat, wine, fire,
In ache of wounds beyond all surgeoning.

War was return of earth to ugly earth,
War was foundering of sublimities,
Extinction of each happy art and faith
By which the world had still kept head in air,
Protesting logic or protesting love,
Until the unendurable moment struck –
The inward scream, the duty to run mad.

And we recall the merry ways of guns –
Nibbling the walls of factory and church
Like a child, piecrust; felling groves of trees
Like a child, dandelions with a switch.
Machine-guns rattle toy-like from a hill,
Down in a row the brave tin-soldiers fall:
A sight to be recalled in elder days
When learnedly the future we devote
To yet more boastful visions of despair.

ROBERT GRAVES

ACKNOWLEDGEMENTS

NOTES

BIBLIOGRAPHY

INDEX OF POEMS

INDEX

Acknowledgements

I am very grateful to the following and to their representatives for allowing me to use material that is still in copyright: the Blunden family and David Higham Associates (Edmund Blunden); the Graves family, the Carcanet Press and United Artists (Robert Graves); Mrs Anne Charlton (Robert Nichols); the executors of the late George Sassoon and the Barbara Levy Literary Agency (Siegfried Sassoon). This book's existence owes a huge amount to Kate Harvey and Kris Doyle of Picador in London and to Jonathan Galassi of Farrar, Straus and Giroux in New York; my thanks to them, and to Peter James, its brilliant copy editor. My agent, Gill Coleridge, has been most supportive throughout. My wife, Caroline, has, as always, given me a calm and loving atmosphere in which to write.

Notes

PRELUDE

2 'hated' the army: Nicholas Mosley, *Julian Grenfell* (London 1976), p. 213.

2 'Nobody ever told me': Isaac Rosenberg, *Collected Works*, ed. Ian Parsons (London 1979), p. 181.

2 'the fiendish persistence': Rosenberg, *Selected Poems and Letters*, ed. Jean Liddiard (London 2003), p. 122.

2 'it is the same': *ibid.*

3 'that yearning exotic music': Max Egremont, *Siegfried Sassoon* (London 2005), p. 61.

4 'It may hold off': H. G. Wells, *Mr Britling Sees It Through* (London 1985 edn), pp. 75–6.

6 'Were we so totally unfit?': E. M. Forster, *The Longest Journey* (London 1907), p. 98.

7 'the peace of Europe': *Manchester Guardian*, 30 July 1914.

8 'the gospel of joy': Richard Davenport-Hines, *Ettie: The Intimate Life and Dauntless Spirit of Lady Desborough* (London 2008), pp. 6–7.

8 'this utterly abominable': Mosley, *Julian Grenfell*, p. 206.

8 'the utter beastliness': *ibid.*

8 'ugly cataracts of brick': Forster, *The Longest Journey*, p. 336.

9 'indolent days leaving': Wells, *Mr Britling*, p. 116.

9 'intimations of the future': *ibid.*, p. 47.

9 'everlasting children': *ibid.*

10 'Nine-tenths of the Tradition': Christopher Hassall, *Edward Marsh* (London 1959), p. 17.

11 'I HATE the upper classes': Rupert Brooke and James Strachey, *Friends and Apostles: The Correspondence of Rupert Brooke and James Strachey 1905–1914*, ed. Keith Hale (New Haven and London 1998), p. 49.

11 'great, easy-going, tolerant': Ford Madox Ford, *Return to Yesterday* (Manchester 1999 edn), p. 312.

12 'Patriotism for ... Great, noble ... Thank God I'm English': Forster, *The Longest Journey*, pp. 55–6.

13 'a civilized out-of-door life': A. G. Bradley *et al.*, *A History of Marlborough College* (London 1923), pp. 169–70.

13 'a tale of Harrow': Wilfred Owen, *Collected Letters*, ed. Harold Owen and John Bell (Oxford 1967), p. 535.

14 'the best piece of Nation': *ibid.*, p. 570.

14 'an embarrassment': see Peter Parker, *The Old Lie: The Great War and the Public School Ethos* (London 1987), p. 193.

14 'the lower classes': C. H. Sorley, *The Letters of Charles Sorley*, ed. W. R. Sorley (Cambridge 1916), p. 38.

15 'five years': *ibid.*, p. 129.

15 'England is seen': *ibid.*, p. 209.

15 'the poet of the tramp': *ibid.*, p. 45.

15 'undoubtedly a poet': *ibid.*, p. 46.

15 'all through the closing': *ibid.*, p. 52.

16 'Even the weeks': Owen, *Collected Letters*, p. 352.

16 'the roar could be': Sorley, *Letters*, p. 93.

16 'I felt that perhaps': *ibid.*, p. 97.

16 'it is chiefly': *ibid.*, p. 102.

16 'simple day system': *ibid.*, p. 103.

16 'there is something': *ibid.*

16 'in the midst': *ibid.*, p. 198.

17 'a bigot and a braggart': *ibid.*, p. 192.

17 'spent his life': *ibid.*, p. 93.

17 'inconceivable that the army': *ibid.*, p. 132.

17 'Down with the Serbs': *ibid.*, p. 213.

18 'wayside crucifixes': Robert Graves, *Goodbye to All That* (London 1995 edn), p. 32.

18 'hellish': Anne and William Charlton, *Putting Poetry First: A Life of Robert Nichols 1893–1944* (Norwich 2003), p. 16.

19 'all she stood for': *ibid.*, p. 39.

19 'I have read the whole': Christopher Hassall, *Rupert Brooke* (London 1964), p. 78.

20 'That is exactly what': Leonard Woolf, *Beginning Again* (London 1964), pp. 18–19.

20 'with a hysterical despair': Hassall, *Rupert Brooke*, p. 128.

21 'a Shelleyan eagerness': *ibid.*, p. 240.

21 'a kind people': Rupert Brooke, *Collected Poems, with a Memoir*, ed. Edward Marsh (London 1918), p. lix.

21 'German culture': *ibid.*, p. lxiii.

21 'I renounce England': *ibid.*, p. lxiv.

22 'by the organ pealing': Hermione Lee, *Virginia Woolf* (London 1996), p. 296.

22 'under that irresponsible': Hassall, *Rupert Brooke*, p. 438.

22 Brooke on Dymock: Matthew Hollis, *Now All Roads Lead to France* (London 2011), p. 117.

22 'all was foretold': Edward Thomas, *The Annotated Collected Poems*, ed. Edna Longley (Tarset 2008), p. 203.

23 'I was born to be a ghost': *ibid.*, p. 202.

24 'I sat thinking about ways': Hollis, *Now All Roads*, p. 21.

24 'the simple and the primitive': *ibid.*, p. 39.

25 'I believe he has taken': *ibid.*, p. 97.

25 'a mild fellow': *ibid.*, p. 62.

26 'absolutely delightful': Egremont, *Sassoon*, p. 62.

28 'the look of latent force': Michael Hurd, *The Ordeal of Ivor Gurney* (Oxford 1978), p. 33.

28 'London is worse': *ibid.*, p. 45.

29 'Your best poems': Siegfried Sassoon and Edmund Blunden, *Selected Letters of Siegfried Sassoon and Edmund Blunden*

1919–1967, ed. Carol Z. Rothkopf, 3 vols (London 2012), vol. I, p. 87.

29 'golden security': Simon Nowell-Smith (ed.), *Edwardian England 1901–1914* (Oxford 1964), pp. 572–3.

29 'C.H. was never out': Barry Webb, *Edmund Blunden* (New Haven and London 1990), p. 42.

30 'no sort of feeling': *ibid.*, p. 27.

30 'deep gentleness': *ibid.*, p. 44.

30 'it looks as though': *ibid.*

30 'I feel my own life': Owen, *Collected Letters*, p. 282.

32 'I love music': *ibid.*, p. 255.

33 'a chamber of horrors': *ibid.*, p. 285.

33 'glowed with a strange': Hassall, *Edward Marsh*, p. 281.

33 'I dislike London': Rosenberg, *Selected Poems*, p. 131.

34 'clogged up with gold dust': *ibid.*, p. 133.

34 'Think of me': *ibid.*, p. 134.

35 'how I love': Julian Grenfell, *Julian Grenfell, Soldier & Poet: Letters and Diaries 1910–1915*, ed. Kate Thompson (Hertford 2004), p. 93.

35 'must be a raving lunatic': *ibid.*, p. 94.

35 'Isn't it an exciting': *ibid.*, p. 211.

35 'wonderful speech': *ibid.*, p. 213.

1914

39 'that I should be blown': Hassall, *Brooke*, p. 457.

39 'Rupert, you': *ibid.*

39 'the general idea': Charlton and Charlton, *Putting Poetry First*, p. 39.

39 'the only thing': Egremont, *Sassoon*, p. 63.

39 'since getting the commission': Sorley, *Letters*, p. 225.

40 'fine fettle': Brigadier General J. L. Jack, *General Jack's Diary 1914–1918*, ed. John Terraine (London 1964), p. 22.

41 'War is the great scavenger': Samuel Hynes, *War Imagined: The First War and English Culture* (London 1990), pp. 12–14.

41 'Heaven knows how long': Egremont, *Sassoon*, p. 65.

42 'For the joke of seeing': Sorley, *Letters*, p. 227.

43 'a grand place': Richard Perceval Graves, *Robert Graves: The Assault Heroic* (London paperback edn 1995), p. 117.

44 'all these days': Brooke, *Collected Poems*, p. cxxv.

44 'guarding a footbridge': Hassall, *Brooke*, p. 458.

44 'if Armageddon is on': *ibid.*, p. 459.

44 'I wanted to use': *ibid.*

44 'for us a national duty': Martin Gilbert, *Winston Churchill*, vol. III (London 1971), p. 110.

45 'last letters': Brooke, *Collected Poems*, p. cxxviii.

45 'My dear, it did bring home': *ibid.*

45 'the rotten ones': *ibid.*, p. cxxx.

46 'a witness to one': Hassall, *Brooke*, p. 466.

46 'half the youth': *ibid.*

46 'the wicked folly': Gilbert, *Churchill*, vol. III, p. 130.

46 'in a swaggering way': *ibid.*, p. 132.

47 'the sight of Belgium': Hassall, *Brooke*, p. 471.

47 'the central purpose': *ibid.*

47 'England is remarkable': Brooke, *Collected Poems*, p. cxxxii.

48 'It's all the best fun': Grenfell, *Letters and Diaries*, p. 223.

48 'it is all the most wonderful fun': Mosley, *Julian Grenfell*, p. 237.

49 'One's nerves are really': *ibid.*, p. 241.

49 'I've never seen': *ibid.*

49 'laughing and talking': *ibid.*, p. 242.

49 '105 partridges': *ibid.*, p. 243.

50 'Isn't it luck': *ibid.*, p. 245.

50 'the happiest I have': Charlton and Charlton, *Putting Poetry First*, p. 39.

51 'Honestly & bar all rotting': G. Harbord to Sassoon, 15 December 1914, Imperial War Museum.

1915

65 'We don't seem': Sorley, *Letters*, p. 225.

65 'rough ... good': Brooke, *Collected Poems*, p. cxxxvi.

65 'I've never been quite': *ibid.*, p. cxxxviii.

66 'I am thinking': Rosenberg, *Collected Works*, p. 216.

66 'I do now most intensely': Owen, *Collected Letters*, p. 341.

67 'a little ugliness': *ibid.*

67 'Do you know': *ibid.*, p. 367.

67 'I seem without a footing': *ibid.*, p. 320.

68 'A young writer': Hassall, *Brooke*, p. 502.

68 'Mind you take care': *ibid.*, p. 496.

68 'knightly presence': Sir Ian Hamilton, *Gallipoli Diary*, vol. I (London 1920), p. 71.

68 'unperceptive': Hassall, *Brooke*, p. 501.

68 'happy force': *ibid.*, p. 503.

69 'very incomparable': Brooke, *Collected Poems*, p. clviii.

69 'like madness': Hassall, *Brooke*, p. 516.

69 'far too obsessed': Sorley, *Letters*, p. 263.

70 'romanticism he so hated': Hassall, *Brooke*, p. 520.

70 'inspired by romantic thoughts': P. N. Furbank, *E. M. Forster: A Life*, vol. II: *Polycrates' Ring* (London 1978), p. 19.

70 'I got Brooke's poems'; Grenfell, *Letters and Diaries*, p. 267.

70 'to disguise the Cavalry Corps': *ibid.*, p. 270.

70 'You should have seen': Mosley, *Julian Grenfell*, p. 247.

71 'I wish they'd let me': *ibid.*

71 'a very hot day': *ibid.*, p. 252.

71 'although I like': *ibid.*

71 'petrified': *ibid.*

71 'divine': *ibid.*, p. 253.

72 'wonderful sunny': *ibid.*, p. 256.

72 'Wrote poem': *ibid.*

72 'You once gave me': *ibid.*, p. 260.

72 'practically wiped out': *ibid.*

72 'the most radiant smile': *ibid.*, p. 265.

72 'extraordinarily living': *ibid.*, p. 266.

73 'did not look': *ibid.*, p. 214.

73 'it is like a picnic': Sorley, *Letters*, p. 268.

73 'in England never': *ibid.*, p. 275.

73 'we have seen': *ibid.*, p. 281.

73 'The thought, the aspiration': Hollis, *Now All Roads*, p. 227.

74 'enlisted or fought': *ibid.*

74 'curious': Egremont, *Sassoon*, p. 71.

75 'Walked into Bethune': Siegfried Sassoon, *Diary 1915–1918*, ed. Rupert Hart-Davis (London 1983), p. 21.

76 'I was not anxious': Edmund Blunden, *Undertones of War* (London 1983 edn), p. 3.

76 'the vital spot': J. C. Dunn, *The War the Infantry Knew* (London 1994 edn), p. 161.

76 'raw enthusiasts': *ibid.*

77 'mismanagement at the top': *ibid.*, p. 163.

77 'on the eve': Sorley, *Letters*, p. 311.

78 'exaltation': Robert Nichols (ed.), *Anthology of War Poetry 1914–1918* (London 1943), p. 34.

78 'sheer foolery': Charlton and Charlton, *Putting Poetry First*, p. 46.

78 'very hard fighting': *ibid.*, p. 51.

78 'your heart was': *ibid.*

79 'I cannot remember': Ivor Gurney, *War Letters*, ed. R. K. R. Thornton (London 1984), pp. 45–6.

79 'Rupert Brooke soaked': Hurd, *The Ordeal*, p. 56.

79 'Have you read': Gurney, *War Letters*, p. 27.

80 'so well': Hollis, *Now All Roads*, p. 251.

80 'a criminal thing': Rosenberg, *Collected Works*, p. 216.

80 'I thought if I'd join': *ibid.*, p. 227.

1916

111 'a stupid rightness': Wells, *Mr Britling*, p. 296.

112 'very fine country': Cambridge University Library Add 9454/3/583.

112 'It seems ridiculous': Egremont, *Sassoon*, p. 80.

112 'since they shot Tommy': Sassoon, *Diary 1915–1918*, p. 52.

112 'These six months': Egremont, *Sassoon*, p. 91.

113 'I think S.S.'s verses': *ibid.*, p. 85.

113 'hate': Sassoon, *Diary 1915–1918*, p. 52.

113 'O yes, this is': Egremont, *Sassoon*, pp. 88–9.

114 'it gave me': Hurd, *The Ordeal*, p. 54.

114 'nowhere could I': *ibid.*

115 'I am not greatly': *ibid.*, p. 60.

115 'We go tomorrow': *ibid.*, p. 63.

115 'curious names': *ibid.*, p. 64.

115 'This kind of life': Rosenberg, *Selected Poems and Letters*, p. 146.

115 'Believe me the army': Rosenberg, *Collected Works*, p. 230.

116 'my being a Jew': Rosenberg, *Selected Poems and Letters*, p. 141.

116 'not quite certain': Jean Moorcroft Wilson, *Isaac Rosenberg: The Making of a Great War Poet* (London 2008), p. 281.

117 'some weeks before': Graves, *Complete Poems*, vol. I (Manchester 1995), pp. 39–40.

119 'a pointless feat': Graves, *Goodbye to All That*, p. 188.

119 'Won't they leave us': Egremont, *Sassoon*, p. 106.

120 'never had shells': Blunden, *Undertones of War*, p. 104.

120 'as Lazarus was': *ibid.*, p. 95.

121 'feat of arms': *ibid.*, p. 103.

121 'the Somme raised': Charles Edmonds (Charles Carrington), *A Subaltern's War* (London 1929), pp. 35 and 19.

122 'Phoebus Apollo': Lady Desborough, *Pages from a Family Journal 1888–1915* (Eton 1916), p. 556.

122 'It's a toss up': Moorcroft Wilson, *Rosenberg*, p. 325.

123 'Now began three months': F. E. Whitton, *The History of the 40th Division* (Aldershot 1926), p. 42.

123 'budding genius': Moorcroft Wilson, *Rosenberg*, p. 331.

123 'we have pups': Rosenberg, *Selected Poems and Letters*, p. 146.

123 'the happiest for years': Gurney, *War Letters*, p. 75.

124 'Floreat Gloucestriensis': *ibid.*

124 'my dear lady': *ibid.*

124 'the Army is an awful life': *ibid.*, p. 70.

124 'a delight of rolling country': *ibid.*, p. 82.

124 'We suffer pain': *ibid.*, p. 113.

125 'how physically unsophisticated': Harold Owen, *Journey from Obscurity*, vol. III (Oxford 1965), p. 134.

125 'animal sports': Owen, *Collected Letters*, pp. 392–3.

125 'always humorous': Thomas, *The Annotated Collected Poems*, p. 282.

126 'the most depressed man': *ibid.*

126 'I don't believe': Hollis, *Now All Roads*, p. 294.

126 'run risks': *ibid.*, p. 295.

1917

151 'the wholesale slaughter': David Jones, *In Parenthesis* (London 2010 edn), p. ix.

152 'There is a fine': Owen, *Collected Letters*, p. 421.

152 'Have no anxiety': *ibid.*, p. 427.

152 'I suppose I can': *ibid.*, pp. 431–2.

153 'remember that': Helen Thomas, *Under Storm's Wing* (Manchester 1988), p. 172.

153 'Am I to stay': Edward Thomas, *The Childhood of Edward Thomas* (London 1983 edn), p. 164.

154 'It was just another': Hollis, *Now All Roads*, p. 327.

154 'I haven't met': Egremont, *Sassoon*, p. 123.

154 'I never understood': Thomas, *The Childhood of Edward Thomas*, p. 176.

155 'capable of the most suicidal exploits': Egremont, *Sassoon*, p. 131.

155 'and give my afternoons': Owen, *Collected Letters*, p. 446.

155 'going over the top': *ibid.*, p. 458.

156 'for twelve days': *ibid.*, p. 452.

156 'shaky and tremulous': Dominic Hibberd, *Wilfred Owen* (London 2002), p. 242.

157 'completely hopeless': Moorcroft Wilson, *Rosenberg*, p. 281.

157 'the severance of all': *ibid.*, p. 360.

158 'elemental': Rosenberg, *Selected Poems and Letters*, p. 35.

158 'more boisterously happy': Moorcroft Wilson, *Rosenberg*, p. 369.

158 'I cannot keep out': Hurd, *The Ordeal*, p. 97.

158 'a garden to dig in': *ibid.*, p. 98.

159 'precious little of value': Gurney, *War Letters*, p. 159.

159 'a great loss': *ibid.*, p. 158.

159 'very interesting': *ibid.*, p. 178.

159 'hardly any': *ibid.*

159 'It is good news': *ibid.*, p. 180.

160 'a darling land': *ibid.*, p. 186.

160 'I hope you will send': *ibid.*, p. 187.

161 'aggression and conquest': for the statement see Sassoon, *Diaries 1915–1918*, p. 173.

161 'completely mad': Egremont, *Sassoon*, p. 152.

162 'we should all die': Blunden, *Undertones*, p. 165.

163 'aim in war': Owen, *Collected Letters*, p. 467.

163 'a great child': *ibid.*, p. 482.

163 'I have just been': *ibid.*, pp. 484–5.

163 'modest and ingratiating': Siegfried Sassoon, *Siegfried's Journey* (London 1945), p. 58.

164 'talks as badly': Owen, *Collected Letters*, p. 487.

164 'cut capers': *ibid.*, p. 489.

164 'I hate washy pacifists': *ibid.*, p. 498.

165 'damn fine': Jon Stallworthy, *Wilfred Owen* (London 1974), p. 229.

165 'Captain Graves': Owen, *Collected Letters*, p. 499.

165 'I go out of': *ibid.*, p. 521.

165 'almost a laughing matter': Blunden, *Undertones*, p. 165.

165 'the general grossness': *ibid.*

167 'mournful passion': Ann Thwaite, *Edmund Gosse* (London 1984), p. 471.

167 'Nichols, Graves and Sassoon': Robert Graves, *In Broken Images: Selected Letters 1914–1946*, ed. Paul O'Prey (London 1982), p. 74.

168 'When Rupert Brooke': Gurney, *War Letters*, p. 232.

168 'I don't think R.G.': Sassoon, *Diaries 1915–1918*, p. 195.

168 'an incomprehensible look': Owen, *Collected Letters*, p. 521.

169 'an attempt to show': Egremont, *Sassoon*, p. 175.

169 the new Rupert Brooke: Harry Ricketts, *Strange Meetings: The Poets of the Great War* (London 2010), p. 129.

169 'offensive to come back': Cynthia Asquith, *Diaries 1915–1918* (London 1968), p. 381.

170 'raved and screamed': Charlton and Charlton, *Putting Poetry First*, p. 71.

170 'Sassoon has power': Rosenberg, *Collected Works*, p. 267.

171 'I am back in the trenches': *ibid.*

1918

199 'quiet little person': Hibberd, *Owen*, p. 298.

200 'the immense desire': Ernst Jünger, *Storm of Steel* (London 2003 edn), p. 232.

200 'We will become': Rosenberg, *Selected Poems and Letters*, p. 175.

200 'How small a thing': Rosenberg, *Collected Works*, p. 298.

202 'With our backs': for this see Duff Cooper, *Haig*, vol. II (London 1936), p. 275.

202 'I knew I should': Vera Brittain, *Testament of Youth* (London 1933), p. 420.

203 'my little friend': Notes for *Siegfried's Journey*, Sassoon collection, Cambridge University Library.

203 'have done just': *ibid.*

203 'the best poet': Egremont, *Sassoon*, p. 196.

204 'damned hankering': *ibid.*, p. 205.

204 'a portrait of war': *ibid.*, p. 204.

204 'safe smugness': *ibid.*, p. 206.

205 'what would he': *Times Literary Supplement*, 8 August 1918.

205 'a disgraceful sloppy': Virginia Woolf, *Diary*, vol. I: *1915–1919*, ed. Anne Olivier Bell (London 1977), p. 171.

206 'piece' of England: Owen, *Collected Letters*, p. 570.

206 'When I go': *ibid.*, p. 430.

206 'I lost all': *ibid.*, p. 580.

206 'every word, every figure': *Collected Letters*, p. 510.

206 'I came out': *ibid.*, p. 580.

207 'It is a great': *ibid.*, p. 591.

207 'a loathsome ending': Sassoon, *Diaries 1915–1918*, p. 282.

207 'the tall Shelley-like': Webb, *Blunden*, p. 56.

208 'I am glad': Gurney, *War Letters*, p. 261.

208 'you'll have to': Graves, *The Assault Heroic*, p. 198.

209 'cursing and sobbing': Graves, *Goodbye to All That*, p. 248.

209 'icebergs': Charlton and Charlton, *Putting Poetry First*, p. 86.

209 'very much I think': *ibid.*, p. 87.

Aftermath

239 'youth, charm, genius': manuscript at Rugby School.

239 'ablest of men': Virginia Woolf, *Letters*, vol. III, ed. Nigel Nicolson (London 1977), p. 178.

240 'A great pamphlet': *Nation*, 6 December 1919.

240 'mere journalism': *London Mercury*, December 1919.

241 'every word, every figure': Owen, *Collected Letters*, p. 510.

241 'I don't want': see Wilfred Owen, *The Complete Poems and*

Fragments, ed. Jon Stallworthy, 2 vols (London 2013 edn), vol. I, p. 193.

241 'wonderfully normal': Hurd, *The Ordeal*, p. 132.

243 'detested mere cleverness': Edward Thomas, *Collected Poems* (London 1920), p. v.

243 'It was wireless': Hurd, *The Ordeal*, p. 168.

244 'It is too late': *ibid.*, p. 169.

244 'I hope it may': Edward Marsh (ed.), *Georgian Poetry 1918–19* (London 1919), prefatory note.

244 'Taste. Good taste': H. G. Wells, *Men Like Gods* (London 1923), p. 29.

244 'concerned with Nature': Richard Perceval Graves, *Robert Graves: The Years with Laura Riding 1926–40* (London paperback edn 1995), p. 44.

245 'Did we believe': Virginia Woolf, *Diary*, vol. II: *1920–1924*, ed. Anne Olivier Bell (London 1978), p. 297.

246 'Of the many young poets': Isaac Rosenberg, *Poems*, ed. Gordon Bottomley (London 1922), p. 1.

246 'windy': Moorcroft Wilson, *Rosenberg*, p. 378.

246 'a fruitful fusion': Rosenberg, *Poems*, p. ix.

246 'poor little Isaac': Edward Marsh and Christopher Hassall, *Ambrosia and Small Beer: The Record of a Correspondence between Edward Marsh and Christopher Hassall*, arranged by Christopher Hassall (London 1964), p. 53.

247 'a trumpet call': the Earl of Lytton, *Antony (Viscount Knebworth): A Record of Youth* (London 1935), p. 568.

247 'It's what Sassoon': John Middleton Murry, *Letters of John Middleton Murry to Katherine Mansfield*, ed. C. A. Hankin (London 1983), p. 234.

248 'profound humanity': Egremont, *Sassoon*, p. 257.

248 'one of the few': 'The Real War', *Athenaeum*, 10 December 1920.

248 'the industrial towns': Stephen Spender, *The Destructive Element* (London 1935), pp. 220–1.

249 'the Rupert Brooke': Stephen Spender, *The Thirties and After* (London 1978), p. 17.

249 'unworthy of the poets' corner': Jon Stallworthy, 'Yeats as Anthologist', in A. Norman Jeffares and K. G. W. Cross (eds), *In Excited Reverie: A Centenary Tribute to W. B. Yeats* (London 1965), p. 190.

249 'unreadable, vague': *ibid.*, p. 183.

249 'and always with loud': W. B. Yeats (ed.), *The Oxford Book of Modern Verse* (Oxford 1936), p. xxxv.

250 'the old men': Christopher Isherwood, *Diaries*, vol. I: *1939–60*, ed. Katherine Bucknell (London 1996), p. 5.

250 'in an ecstasy': Samuel Hynes, *The Auden Generation* (London 1976), p. 21.

252 'If I can be': Robert Graves, *But It Still Goes On* (London 1930), p. 155.

252 'the truth by a condensation': Graves, *The Assault Heroic*, p. 288.

252 'Do you know how': Graves, *But It Still Goes On*, p. 245.

253 'strike a responsive chord': Edmonds, *A Subaltern's War*, pp. 8–9.

253 'all we can do': Graves, *Goodbye to All That*, p. 275.

254 'a terrific comet': Ritchie, *Strange Meetings*, p. 212.

254 'mad': Charlton and Charlton, *Putting Poetry First*, pp. 95–6.

254 'the great love': *ibid.*, p. 214.

255 'the sound of my': Marsh and Hassall, *Ambrosia and Small Beer*, p. 213.

255 'you'll find a tea cake': Nichols (ed.), *Anthology of War Poetry*, p. 17.

256 'acceptance rather than': Alan Ross, *Blindfold Games* (London 1986), p. 239.

257 'symbolic poetry': Egremont, *Sassoon*, p. 483.

257 'I destroyed them': Robert Graves, *Conversations with Robert Graves*, ed. Frank L. Kersnowski (Jackson, Miss., and London 1989), p. 96.

257 'Sassoon's idealism': Robert Graves and Spike Milligan, *Dear*

Robert, Dear Spike: The Graves–Milligan Correspondence, ed. Pauline Scudamore (Stroud 1991), p. 94.

258 'How right dear Robbie': Egremont, *Sassoon*, p. 478.

258 'the most unspeakably horrible': George A. Panichas (ed.), *Promise of Greatness* (London 1968), p. 8.

258 'given me not only': *ibid.*, p. 11.

258 'People like reading': Graves, *But It Still Goes On*, p. 15.

259 'many thoughts and mentions': Sassoon and Blunden, *Selected Letters*, vol. III, p. 315.

262 'complete': Jack, *General Jack's Diary*, pp. 306–7.

Bibliography

Editions of Poets Used

Blunden, Edmund. *Poems of Many Years* (London 1957).
——— *Overtones of War: Poems of the First World War*, ed. Martin Taylor (London 1996).
Brooke, Rupert. *Collected Poems, with a Memoir*, ed. Edward Marsh (London 1918).
Graves, Robert. *Complete Poems*, 3 vols, ed. Beryl Graves and Dunstan Ward (Manchester 1995–9 edn).
Grenfell, Julian. Manuscripts in the Cowper/Grenfell papers in the Hertfordshire Archives, ref. DE/X789/F23.
Gurney, Ivor. *Collected Poems*, ed. P. J. Kavanagh (Manchester 2004 edn).
Nichols, Robert. *Ardours and Endurances* (London 1917).
——— *Aurelia and Other Poems* (London 1920).
Owen, Wilfred. *The Complete Poems and Fragments*, ed. Jon Stallworthy, 2 vols (London 2013 edn).
Rosenberg, Isaac. *The Poems and Plays of Isaac Rosenberg*, ed. Vivian Noakes (Oxford 2004).
Sassoon, Siegfried. *Collected Poems 1908–1956* (London 1961).
——— *The War Poems* ed. Rupert Hart-Davis (London 1983).
Sorley, Charles. *Marlborough and Other Poems* (Cambridge 1916).
Thomas, Edward. *The Annotated Collected Poems*, ed. Edna Longley (Tarset 2008).

OTHER WORKS

Asquith, Cynthia. *Diaries 1915–1918* (London 1968).

Barnett, Correlli. *The Collapse of British Power* (London 1972).

Beckett, Ian F. W. *The First World War 1914–1918* (Harlow 2001).

—— *The Making of the First World War* (London and New Haven 2012).

Bergonzi, Bernard. *Wartime and Aftermath* (Oxford 1993).

—— *Heroes' Twilight* (Manchester 1996 edn).

Blunden, Edmund. *Cricket Country* (London 1945).

—— *Undertones of War* (London Penguin edn 2000).

Boden, Anthony (ed.). *Stars on a Dark Night: Letters of Ivor Gurney to the Chapman Family* (Stroud 2004 edn).

Bond, Brian. *A Victory Worse than Defeat? British Interpretations of the First World War* (London 1997).

—— *The Unquiet Western Front* (Cambridge 2002).

—— *Survivors of a Kind: Memoirs of the Western Front* (London 2008).

Bradley, A. G. et al. *A History of Marlborough College* (London 1923).

Brittain, Vera. *Testament of Youth* (London 1933).

Brooke, Rupert. *Letters*, ed. Geoffrey Keynes (London 1968).

—— *The Poetical Works*, ed. Geoffrey Keynes (London 1974 edn).

—— and James Strachey. *Friends and Apostles: The Correspondence of Rupert Brooke and James Strachey 1905–1914*, ed. Keith Hale (New Haven and London 1998).

Caesar, Adrian. *Taking It Like a Man: Suffering, Sexuality and the War Poets* (Manchester 1993).

Cecil, Hugh. *The Flower of Battle: British Writers and the First World War* (London 1995).

Charlton, Anne and William. *Putting Poetry First: A Life of Robert Nichols 1893–1944* (Norwich 2003).

Cohen, Joseph. *Journey to the Trenches: The Life of Isaac Rosenberg* (London 1975).

Cooper, Duff. *Haig*, vol. II (London 1936).

Cuthbertson, Guy, and Lucy Newlyn. *Branch-Lines: Edward Thomas and Contemporary Poetry* (London 2007).

Dakers, Caroline. *The Countryside at War* (London 1987).

Davenport-Hines, Richard. *Ettie: The Intimate Life and Dauntless Spirit of Lady Desborough* (London 2008).

Desborough, Lady. *Pages from a Family Journal 1888–1915* (Eton 1916).

Douglas, Keith. *The Complete Poems* (London 2011 edn).

Dunn, J. C. *The War the Infantry Knew* (London 1994 edn).

Edmonds, Charles (Charles Carrington). *A Subaltern's War* (London 1929).

Egremont, Max. *Under Two Flags: The Life of Major General Sir Edward Spears* (London 1997).

———— *Siegfried Sassoon* (London 2005).

Ferguson, Niall. *The Pity of War* (London 1998).

Ford, Ford Madox. *Return to Yesterday* (Manchester 1999 edn).

Forster, E. M. *The Longest Journey* (London 1907).

———— *Howards End* (London 1910).

Furbank, P. N. *E. M. Forster: A Life*, vol. I: *The Growth of the Novelist*, vol. II: *Polycrates' Ring* (London 1977–8).

Fussell, Paul. *The Great War and Modern Memory* (Oxford 1975).

Gardner, Brian (ed.). *Up the Line to Death: The War Poets 1914–1918* (London 2007 edn).

Gilbert, Martin. *Winston Churchill*, vol. III (London 1971).

Graham, Desmond. *Keith Douglas* (Oxford 1974).

———— *The Truth of War: Owen, Blunden, Rosenberg* (Manchester 1984).

Graves, Richard Perceval. *Robert Graves: The Assault Heroic* (London paperback edn 1995).

———— *Robert Graves: The Years with Laura Riding* (London paperback edn 1995).

———— *Robert Graves and the White Goddess* (London paperback edn 1998).

Graves, Robert. *Goodbye to All That* (London 1995 edn).

Graves, Robert. *But It Still Goes On* (London 1930).

—— *In Broken Images: Selected Letters 1914–1946*, ed. Paul O'Prey (London 1982).

—— *Between Moon and Moon: Selected Letters 1946–1972*, ed. Paul O'Prey (London 1984).

—— *Poems about War*, ed. William Graves (London 1988).

—— *Conversations with Robert Graves*, ed. Frank L. Kersnowski (Jackson, Miss., and London 1989).

—— and Spike Milligan. *Dear Robert, Dear Spike: The Graves–Milligan Correspondence*, ed. Pauline Scudamore (Stroud 1991).

Grenfell, Julian. *Julian Grenfell, Soldier & Poet: Letters and Diaries 1910–1915*, ed. Kate Thompson (Hertford 2004).

Gurney, Ivor. *War Letters*, ed. R. K. R. Thornton (London 1984).

—— *Collected Letters*, ed. R. K. R. Thornton (Manchester 1991).

Hamilton, Sir Ian. *Gallipoli Diary*, vol. I (London 1920).

Hassall, Christopher. *Edward Marsh* (London 1959).

—— *Rupert Brooke* (London 1964).

Hibberd, Dominic. *Owen the Poet* (London 1986).

—— *Wilfred Owen: The Last Year* (London 1992).

—— *Harold Monro* (Basingstoke 2001).

—— *Wilfred Owen* (London 2002).

—— and John Onions (eds). *Poetry of the Great War* (London 1986).

—— and —— (eds). *The Winter of the World: Poems of the First World War* (London 2007).

Hollis, Matthew. *Now All Roads Lead to France: The Last Years of Edward Thomas* (London 2011).

Hurd, Michael. *The Ordeal of Ivor Gurney* (Oxford 1978).

Hynes, Samuel. *The Auden Generation* (London 1976).

—— *War Imagined: The First War and English Culture* (London 1990).

—— *The Soldiers' Tale* (London 1998).

Isherwood, Christopher. *Diaries*, vol. I: *1939–60*, ed. Katherine Bucknell (London 1996).

Jack, Brigadier General J. L. *General Jack's Diary 1914–1918*, ed. John Terraine (London 1964).

Jones, David. *In Parenthesis* (London 2010 edn).

Jones, Nigel. *Rupert Brooke* (London 1999).

Jünger, Ernst. *Storm of Steel* (London 2003 edn).

Kendall, Tim. *Modern British War Poetry* (Oxford 2006).

—— (ed.). *The Oxford Handbook of British and Irish War Poetry* (Oxford 2007).

Keynes, Geoffrey. *The Gates of Memory* (Oxford 1981).

Larkin, Philip (ed.). *The Oxford Book of Twentieth-Century English Verse* (Oxford 1973).

—— *Required Writing* (London 1983).

—— *Further Requirements* (London 2001).

Leavis, F. R. *New Bearings in English Poetry* (London 1932).

Lee, Hermione. *Virginia Woolf* (London 1996).

Lytton, the Earl of. *Antony (Viscount Knebworth): A Record of Youth* (London 1935).

Macaulay, Rose. *Non-Combatants and Others* (London 1916).

McPhail, Helen, and Philip Guest. *Wilfred Owen* (Barnsley 1998).

—— *Edmund Blunden* (Barnsley 1999).

—— *Graves and Sassoon* (Barnsley 2001).

Marsh, Edward (ed.). *Georgian Poetry 1918–19* (London 1919).

—— *A Number of People* (London 1939).

—— and Christopher Hassall. *Ambrosia and Small Beer: The Record of a Correspondence between Edward Marsh and Christopher Hassall*, arranged by Christopher Hassall (London 1964).

Mosley, Nicholas. *Julian Grenfell* (London 1976).

Motion, Andrew. *The Poetry of Edward Thomas* (London 1980).

—— (ed.). *First World War Poems* (London 2003).

Murry, John Middleton. *Letters of John Middleton Murry to Katherine Mansfield*, ed. C. A. Hankin (London 1983).

Nichols, Robert (ed.). *Anthology of War Poetry 1914–1918* (London 1943).

Nowell-Smith, Simon (ed.). *Edwardian England 1901–1914* (Oxford 1964).

Osborne, E. B. (ed.). *The Muse in Arms* (London 1917).

Owen, Harold. *Journey from Obscurity*, 3 vols (London 1963–5).

——— *Aftermath* (Oxford 1970).

Owen, Wilfred. *Collected Letters*, ed. Harold Owen and John Bell (Oxford 1967).

Panichas, George A. (ed.). *Promise of Greatness* (London 1969).

Parker, Peter. *The Old Lie: The Great War and the Public School Ethos* (London 1987).

Parsons, Ian (ed.). *Men Who March Away: Poems of the First World War* (London 1965).

Ricketts, Harry. *Strange Meetings: The Poets of the Great War* (London 2010).

Robbins, Keith. *Sir Edward Grey* (London 1971).

Rosenberg, Isaac. *Poems*, ed. Gordon Bottomley (London 1922).

——— *Collected Works*, ed. Ian Parsons (London 1979).

——— *Selected Poems and Letters*, ed. Jean Liddiard (London 2003).

——— *The Poems and Plays of Isaac Rosenberg*, ed. Vivian Noakes (Oxford 2004).

——— *Whitechapel at War: Isaac Rosenberg and his Circle* (London 2008).

Ross, Alan. *Blindfold Games* (London 1986).

Sassoon, Siegfried. *Memoirs of a Fox-hunting Man* (London 1928).

——— *Memoirs of an Infantry Officer* (London 1930).

——— *Sherston's Progress* (London 1936).

——— *The Old Century and Seven More Years* (London 1938).

——— *The Weald of Youth* (London 1942).

——— *Siegfried's Journey* (London 1945).

——— *Diaries 1920–1922*, ed. Rupert Hart-Davis (London 1981).

——— *Diaries 1915–1918*, ed. Rupert Hart-Davis (London 1983).

——— *Diaries 1923–1925*, ed. Rupert Hart-Davis (London 1985).

——— and Edmund Blunden, *Selected Letters of Siegfried Sassoon and*

Edmund Blunden 1919–1967, ed. Carol Z. Rothkopf, 3 vols (London 2012).

Seymour, Miranda. *Ottoline Morrell: Life on a Grand Scale* (London 1992).

—— *Robert Graves: Life on the Edge* (London 1995).

Seymour-Smith, Martin. *Robert Graves* (London 1982).

Sheffield, Gary. *Forgotten Victory: The First World War: Myths and Realities* (London 2001).

Silkin, Jon. *Out of Battle: The Poetry of the Great War* (Oxford 1972).

—— (ed.). *The Penguin Book of First World War Poetry* (London 1979).

Sorley, C. H. *The Letters of Charles Sorley*, ed. W. R. Sorley (Cambridge 1916).

—— *The Poems and Selected Letters of Charles Hamilton Sorley*, ed. Hilda D. Spear (Dundee 1978).

—— *Collected Poems*, ed. Jean Moorcroft Wilson (London 1985).

—— *Collected Letters of Charles Hamilton Sorley*, ed. Jean Moorcroft Wilson (London 1991).

Spender, Stephen. *The Destructive Element* (London 1935).

—— *The Thirties and After* (London 1978).

Stallworthy, Jon. 'Yeats as Anthologist', in A. Norman Jeffares and K. G. W. Cross (eds), *In Excited Reverie: A Centenary Tribute to W. B. Yeats* (London 1965).

—— *Wilfred Owen* (London 1974).

—— (ed.). *The Oxford Book of War Poetry* (Oxford 1988 edn).

—— *Survivors' Songs: From Maldon to the Somme* (Cambridge 2008).

—— (ed.). *Three Poets of the First World War: Ivor Gurney, Isaac Rosenberg, Wilfred Owen* (London 2011).

Steiner, Zara, and Keith Neilson. *Britain and the Origins of the First World War* (Basingstoke 2003 edn).

Stephens, Martin. *The Price of Pity* (London 1996).

Strachan, Hew. *The First World War*, vol. I: *To Arms* (Oxford 2001).

Thomas, Edward. *Richard Jefferies* (London 1909).

—— *The South Country* (London 1909).

Thomas, Edward. *In Pursuit of Spring* (London 1914).
––––– *Collected Poems* (London 1920).
––––– *The Childhood of Edward Thomas* (London 1983 edn).
––––– *Collected Poems and War Diary*, ed. R. George Thomas (London 2004).
Thomas, Helen. *Under Storm's Wing* (Manchester 1988).
Thwaite, Ann. *Edmund Gosse* (London 1984).
Trevelyan, G. M. *Grey of Fallodon* (London 1937).
Walter, George (ed.). *The Penguin Book of First World War Poetry* (London 2006 edn).
Webb, Barry. *Edmund Blunden* (London and New Haven 1990).
Welland, Dennis. 'Sassoon on Owen', *Times Literary Supplement*, 31 May 1974.
Wells, H. G. *Mr Britling Sees It Through* (London 1985 edn).
––––– *Men Like Gods* (London 1923).
Whitton, F. E. *The History of the 40th Division* (Aldershot 1926).
Wilson, Jean Moorcroft. *Charles Hamilton Sorley* (London 1985).
––––– *Siegfried Sassoon: The Making of a Poet* (London 1998).
––––– *Siegfried Sassoon: The Journey from the Trenches* (London 2003).
––––– *Isaac Rosenberg: The Making of a Great War Poet* (London 2008).
Woolf, Leonard, *Beginning Again* (London 1964).
Woolf, Virginia, *Letters*, vols 1–5, ed. Nigel Nicolson and Joanne Trautmann (London 1977–84).
––––– *Diaries*, vols 1–5, ed. Anne Olivier Bell and Andrew McNeillie (London 1977–84).
Yeats, W. B. (ed.). *The Oxford Book of Modern Verse* (Oxford 1936).

Index of Poems

Index

Page numbers in *italic* indicate the texts of poems. Ranks and titles are generally the highest mentioned in the text.

Index

Blunden, Edward (*cont.*)
 revisits Flanders, 258; elected Oxford
 Professor of Poetry, 259; death, 259;
 drawn to pacificism before Second
 World War, 262; 'Almswomen', 240;
 'The Festubert Shrine', *135–6*;
 'Gouzeaucourt: The Deceitful Calm',
 251, *287*; 'In Festubert', 249; *1916 Seen
 from 1921*, 269–70; 'The Midnight
 Skaters', 29; 'Report on Experience', 249,
 292; 'The Silver Bird of Herndyke Mill',
 114; 'Two Voices', 120, *286*; *Undertones
 of War*, 251; 'Vlameringhe: Passing the
 Chateau', 166, *189*, 251; 'The Watchers',
 251, *281*; 'The Zonnebeke Road', 251,
 275–6
Boer War (1899–1902), 1, 3, 7
Bomberg, David, 2, 10, 33
Bottomley, Gordon, 116, 122, 157
Brest Litovsk, treaty of (1918), 199
Brewer, Herbert, 27
Britain: avoids conscription, 4, 31, 261; effect
 of war on, 4; and impending war, 5–8, 27;
 pre-war unrest and change in, 7–9;
 empire, 8; public school system, 12, 29,
 76; and outbreak of war, 40; introduces
 conscription, 111; strategy after Somme,
 152; retreat before German spring
 offensive (1918), 200; justification for
 entering war, 262
British Expeditionary Force: casualties, 76,
 111
Brittain, Vera, 202
Britten, Benjamin: *War Requiem*, 260
Brooke, Rupert: joins Fabians, 3, 11; and
 Isaac Rosenberg, 10; published in
 Georgian Poetry, 11, 25, 169; romantic
 life-style, 15, 20; background, 19–22; and
 outbreak of war, 19, 39; reputation, 19;
 appearance, 20; affair with Ka Cox, 21,
 39; moodiness, 21; nervous collapse, 21;
 visits Germany, 21; travels to USA and
 South Seas, 22; on English peace, 25;
 Sassoon meets, 26; Grenfell praises, 35;
 Marsh helps to enlist, 41; on 'foreign
 field', 42, 60; sees action at Antwerp,

44–7; returns to England, 47–8; sent to
 Dardanelles, 65–6; death and obituary,
 67–9; poetry criticized, 69–70;
 inexperience, 77; spirit of poetry, 81;
 Gurney on, 115, 159; Gurney dedicates
 book to, 167–8; Virginia Woolf on, 205,
 239; memorialized, 239; post-war
 reputation, 239–40, 249; in Yeats's
 Oxford Book of Modern Verse, 249; in
 Larkin's Oxford anthology, 257;
 Collected Poems, 205, 239; 'The Dead',
 58, 65; 'Fragment', 90; 'Heaven', 48; *1914
 and Other Poems* (ed. Marsh), 69; 'The
 Old Vicarage at Grantchester', 21–2;
 'Peace', *57*; 'The Soldier', 47, 60, 65, 67,
 69, 240, 257; 'Tiare Tahiti', 22, 48
Browne, Denis, 44, 46
Browning, Robert, 15, 166
Brunswick manifesto, 291
Buchan, John, 122
Burne-Jones, Sir Edward, 13
Byron, George Gordon, 6th Baron, 15

Cambrai, battle of (1917), 166, 200
Cambridge Magazine, 113
Carpenter, Edward, 3
Carrington, Charles, 121
Chaliapin, Feodor Ivanovich, 41
Chambrin, 119
Charterhouse school, 12, 17, 43
Chatto and Windus (publishers), 247
Chemin des Dames, 152, 156, 162
Chesterton, G. K., 15
Christ's Hospital school, 29–30, 75
Churchill (Sir) Winston: Marsh serves as
 private secretary, 11; forms Royal Naval
 Division, 44; defends action at Antwerp,
 46–7; plans Dardanelles campaign, 65
Cohen, Mrs (Rosenberg's benefactor), 33
Cohen, Reuben ('Crazy'), 116
Colefax, Sibyl, Lady, 169
Cornford, Frances, 39
Cox, Ka, 21, 39
Craiglockart Sanatorium, Scotland: Owen
 and Sassoon at, 13, 156, 162–3, 168
Crécy, 203

Index

Cuinchy (village), 114
Cunard, Nancy, 254

Daily Herald, 240
Dardanelles Straits, 65, 69, 76
Davies, W. H., 26
Day Lewis, Cecil, 250, 260
de la Mare, Walter, 15, 154, 168, 243, 249–50
Delville Wood, 120
Dent, Edward Joseph, 47, 70, 75, 121, 204, 240
Desborough, Ethel, Lady (Grenfells' mother), 1, 72; *Pages from a Family Journal*, 121
Desborough, William Henry Grenfell, Baron (Grenfells' father), 73
Domvast, 203
Donne, John, 20
Douglas, Lord Alfred, 203
Douglas, Keith, 256; 'Aristocrats', 256; 'Desert Flowers', 246
Drinkwater, John, 22, 25
Dunkerley, William *see* Oxenham, John
Dymock, Gloucestershire, 22–3, 25, 28, 42, 51

Edward VII, King, 17
Eliot, T. S., 169, 241, 246, 250, 254, 256–7; *The Waste Land*, 245

Farjeon, Eleanor, 23, 26
Festubert, 114
Finzi, Gerald, 242, 244
First World War: poets, ix–xi, 108, 261–3; casualties, 3, 121, 202; western front, 3; outbreak, 4, 17, 39–40; ends, 207; evaluated, 259–61
Flanders: Allied retreat (1914), 43
Flecker, James Elroy, 169
Foch, Marshal Ferdinand, 202
Ford, Ford Madox, 11; *Parade's End*, 251
Forster, E. M.: on Brooke's sonnets, 70; in Alexandria, 201, 203; *Howards End*, 8–9; *The Longest Journey*, 6, 8, 12
France: and outbreak of war, 5, 32–3; famines and poor harvests, 8, 12;

impoverished nobility, 8; social ambitions, 24; relations with Austria, 32–3; German advance through (1914), 43; in American War of Independence, 45; financial state, 45; role of monarchy, 77–8; and defence of Verdun, 118; casualties, 121; army mutinies, 162; part-occupied by Germany, 162; counter-attack (1918), 202; censorship, 230; public opinion in, 230
Franz Ferdinand, Archduke of Austria, 6, 17, 26
Fraser, Claude Lovat, 117
French, Field Marshal Sir John, 30, 78
Freyberg, Bernard, VC, 169
Fricourt, 113, 188
Frost, Robert, 22, 24–6, 51, 52, 74, 126, 153, 243; *North of Boston*, 26
Fry, Roger, 33

Gallipoli, 76, 151
Gardner, Brian: (ed.) *Up the Line to Death*, 260
gas (poison), 71, 76–7
Georgian Poetry (ed. Marsh), 11, 20–1, 24, 26, 157, 167, 169, 244
Germany: and outbreak of war, 4–5; unification, 5; Sorley in, 15–17, 42; student fraternities, 15; supports Austria-Hungary, 17; Robert Graves in, 18; Brooke visits, 21; early advance in France (1914), 43; war aims, 44, 262; attack on Verdun, 118; casualties, 121, 202; territorial occupation, 162; negotiates peace with Soviet Russia, 170, 199; strength in 1917–18, 170, 199–200; spring offensive (1918), 200–1; control of Romanian oilfields, 201; internal unrest, 202; repelled, 202; sense of injustice over Treaty of Versailles, 262
Gertler, Mark, 10–11
Gibson, Wilfred, xi, 15, 21–2, 25, 65, 69. 168
Gosse, Edmund, 26, 40, 167; 'War and Literature' (essay), 41
Goya, Francisco, 166
Grantchester, 20–1

Lords, House of: constitutional crisis (1911), 12

Lowell, Robert, 259

Ludendorff, General Erich von, 170, 200

Lusitania, RMS, 66, 156

Macaulay, Rose: *Non-Combatants and Others*, 111

McCrae, John: 'In Flanders Fields', 111–12, 166

MacNeice, Louis, 246, 250

Mallory, George, 18

Mametz Wood, 118

Manchester Guardian, 7

Mansfield, Katherine, 247–8

Marlborough, John Churchill, 1st Duke of, 74

Marlborough school, 13–16, 26–7

Marne: battle of the (1914), 44, 49; French counter-attack (1918), 202, 205

Marsh, Sir Edward: Gertler introduces Rosenberg to, 10; Georgian anthologies, 11, 15, 157, 167, 169, 244; falls for Rupert Brooke, 20, 22; and Edward Thomas, 26; praises and mentors Sassoon, 26, 240; helps Gurney, 28; helps Rosenberg, 33–4, 66, 123, 156–7, 246; helps Brooke's army career, 41, 44, 46; sends Inge's remarks to Brooke, 68; obituary of Brooke, 69; letter from Graves and Sassoon, 75; Sassoon confesses being changed by trenches, 113; sends Rosenberg poems to Abercrombie, 116; and Sassoon's statement opposing war, 161; Nichols meets, 167; Owen meets, 199; edits Brooke's *Collected Poems*, 205, 239; caricatured by Wells, 244

Masefield, John, 11, 14, 124, 167; 'August 1914', 41

Masterman, C. F. G., 41

Menin Road, 71

Messines, 162

Milligan, Spike, 257

modernism, 241, 243

Monro, Harold, 47, 52, 117, 244

Monroe, Harriet, 153

Morrell, Lady Ottoline, 122, 154, 160, 168, 204

Morrell, Philip, 154, 160

Morris, William, 13

Murry, John Middleton, 160, 204, 244, 247, 248

Music and Letters (magazine), 244

Nash, Paul, 125

Nation (magazine), 204, 240

Nesbitt, Cathleen, 44–5, 47

Neuve Chapelle, 114–15, 119

Nevinson, Christopher, 2

New Numbers (magazine), 65, 68

Newbolt, Sir Henry, 247; 'The Vigil', 40

Nichols, Robert: background, 18–19; enlists, 19, 39; commissioned, 42, 50; held in England, 50; elegy to Brooke, 69; in France, 78; health and mental problems, 79, 258; Gurney admires, 159; success and reputation, 166–7, 169–70, 203; Graves's regard for, 168; not pacifist, 170; Sassoon hopes for elegy by, 203; claims Sassoon deliberately shot, 204; lecture tour of USA, 209, 240, 254; admires Brooke, 239; reviews Owen's *Poems*, 248; in Yeats's *Oxford Book of Modern Verse*, 249; post-war activities, 254–5; writes introduction to anthology of First War poetry, 254–5; death, 255; *Ardours and Endurances* (collection), 79, 166–7, 255; 'Battery Moving Up to a New Position from Rest Camp: Dawn', 78, *98–100*; 'Dawn on the Somme', *222*; 'The Day's March', 78; 'Five Sonnets upon Imminent Departure', 78; *Invocation* (collection), 78, 79; 'The Secret', *218*; 'Thanksgiving', 78, *91*

Nicholson, Nancy: marriage to Graves, 199, 208, 240

Nivelle, General Robert, 152, 154

Novello, Ivor, 169

Oh, What a Lovely War (stage musical and film), 260

Orpen, William, 35

Illustration Credits